DON McNEILL
and His

Breakfast Club

Don McNeill
and His

Brea

John
Doolittle

kfast
Club

UNIVERSITY OF NOTRE DAME PRESS • NOTRE DAME, INDIANA

Copyright © 2001
University of Notre Dame
Notre Dame, Indiana 46556
All Rights Reserved
http://www.undpress.nd.edu

Manufactured in the United States of America

Photos courtesy of the McNeill family archives
CD engineered by John Holt

Library of Congress Cataloging-in-Publication Data
Doolittle, John, 1941–
Don McNeill and his Breakfast Club / John Doolittle.
p.   cm.
Includes bibliographical references and index
ISBN 0-268-00898-1 (alk. paper)
1. McNeill, Don (Donald Thomas), 1907–1996   2. Radio broadcasters—
United States—Biography.   3. Breakfast Club (Radio program)   I. Title.
PN1991.4.M39 D66   2001
791.44'028'092—dc21

00-012457

∞ *This book is printed on acid-free paper.*

To those who offer inspiration
to begin a new day.

Thank you Ellen

Contents

Acknowledgments

This book reflects the generous support and interest of many people who were associated with Don McNeill and his career as a broadcaster. Foremost among them are his sons, Tom, Don, and Bob, who are not only part of the story, but enabled it to be told more completely. Their willingness to share family history and documents provided a rich source of material for this story. Tom, in particular, was enthusiastic about the project from its inception and a source of inspiration to see it through to its completion. Agnes Donohue provided a delightful perspective on her brother's life. In addition, the McNeill grandchildren shared their recollections about their famous relative.

The archives of several libraries fortunately had assembled materials that were immensely valuable to the chronicling of the thirty-five plus years of the *Breakfast Club*'s life. The McNeill Collection at Marquette University is a treasure trove of McNeill history. Charles Elston and Philip Runkel provided sanity for my hours and days spent searching through the hundreds of boxes and tapes in the library's Special Collection rooms. Chicago's Museum of Broadcast Communications and its Radio Hall of Fame provided more valuable research material. Bruce DuMont and his staff were generous in making their tapes and facilities available. American University's Library shared its extensive audiotape collection of old radio as did the Recorded Sound Division of the Library of Congress in Washington, D.C., and the Museum of Television and Radio in New York City.

Thanks to those whose insights enabled the telling of a richer story—Byron Baxter, Matilda Bobula, Ray Barnes, Del Cowling, Don Dowd, Jr., Terry (Petersen) Dowd, Pat Ferrari, Tom Fouts, John Grams, Betty Johnson, Lynwood King, Irv Kupcinet, Patsy Lee, Ed McLaughlin, Mary Anne Luckett, Bob Morton, Dorothy Mulroy, Pat Murphy, Bob Newkirk, Dick Noel, Sterling "Red" Quinlan, Chuck Shaden, and Gloria Vann.

Grateful acknowledgment goes to Jim Langford for the interest and expertise he and the University of Notre Dame Press staff provided in making this book a reality.

A final appreciation goes to the many people who recalled their fond memories of the *Breakfast Club* and, in doing so, provided encouragement for the writing of this book.

Introduction

One cannot really understand America during its crucial decades from the 1920s to the 1960s without paying close attention to the growth, development, and pervasive power of radio. During the decades before television came to dominate the media, radio was a primary source of news, sports, and entertainment. Every living room gave a place of honor to the family radio; the airwaves brought the world into every home.

It was by radio that FDR buoyed the spirits and hopes of Americans in the depths of the Great Depression and, years later, that his voice rallied the country after the devastation of Pearl Harbor. It was radio that brought home the voices and sounds of World War II: voices like those of Edward R. Murrow, Robert Trout, and Lowell Thomas; sounds of airplanes and bombs, canons and machine guns; and finally, after the most devastating bombing in history, news of the longed-for surrender.

Radio was how America attended the great spectacles of sport: Don Dunphy described the feats of Joe Louis, Jersey Joe Wolcott, Sugar Ray Robinson, Tony Zale, Rocky Marciano, and many more who quickly became household names. Graham McNamee, Red Barber, Ted Huising, and Mel Allen were just some of the voices that helped make baseball America's pastime. College football, bowl games, and the NFL relied on radio to carry their narratives to fans across the nation.

On the lighter side, radio entertained housewives with mid-morning soap operas, and children came home from school eager to tune in to *Terry and the Pirates*, *Sky King*, the *Lone Ranger*, or *Sergeant Preston of the Royal Mounted Police*.

In the evenings, families gathered to hear Jack Benny, *Fibber McGee and Molly*, *Amos 'n' Andy*, or one of a seemingly endless number of quiz shows.

It is in this context that Don McNeill's *Breakfast Club* stands out as a true phenomenon. No daily network radio show had as long a continuous life or as dedicated a following as did the *Breakfast Club* starring Don McNeill. It quickly climbed to the top of the ratings charts and stayed there for over three decades. Celebrities clamored to be on the show, but most of McNeill's interviews were with people from the studio audience. It was McNeill who set the precedent of literally taking his show on the road—to cities across the United States and even to Europe—always to be welcomed by huge crowds of Breakfast Clubbers. When one of the show's sponsors offered membership cards in the *Breakfast Club* to listeners who wrote in, the promotion had such an overwhelming response that it was called off after the first million requests arrived.

For more than thirty years, this warm, unassuming, and entertaining show was a weekday staple across America. Children grew up and had children who grew up starting their day by tuning in at 8:00 A.M. and hearing the sound of laughter mixed with drum rolls, musical fanfare with the announcement that

> It's time for your family to join the millions of families from coast to coast and listen to America's favorite, the *Breakfast Club* with Don McNeill.

The music continued as a friendly sounding voice sang a greeting:

> Good morning Breakfast Clubbers, good morning to ya, we woke up bright and early just to howdy-do ya.

Toastmaster Don McNeill led the cast and his listeners through a spirited hour that became a reminder to America that it was time to start another day. In addition to the Four Calls to Breakfast at the beginning of each quarter-hour, regular listeners knew to expect the March around the Breakfast Table at 8:30 A.M. Other regular features, including the Silent Prayer, Hymn Time, Memory Time poems, and visits by the friendly spinster, Aunt Fanny, gave the show a warm aura. Between songs and commercials, McNeill's upbeat and cheerful manner shone through during his daily walk into the studio audience to invite anyone with a funny or interesting story to come up to the

microphone. His manner was both sincere and casual, which made
him seem more like a friendly neighbor rather than a radio star. Listeners liked the McNeill style and the *Breakfast Club* became one of
the most popular daytime programs on network radio. Year after year
McNeill and his crew continued to make mornings fun for their listeners, relying on the same structure that framed the show when it
began in 1933. When the final *Breakfast Club* was aired in 1968, the
show had set a record for longevity by continuing on network radio
for thirty-five and a half years. For that entire time, the show was
based in Chicago. McNeill enjoyed the audiences he attracted in the
Windy City. His audiences were often from small towns and rural
areas and his success in making his guests' stories come alive on radio
rightly enhanced his reputation as an interviewer.

Don McNeill was only twenty-five years old when he took on the
task of hosting a national program. Broadcasting was and is a rough
place even for experienced performers, let alone young newcomers. In
the early 1930s, the radio industry was building itself into a national
entertainment and advertising medium, and it was hungry for people
with ideas and talent. McNeill demonstrated that he had both.

Don McNeill was born and raised in the midwest where he attended college and, in 1929, began his career in radio and newspapers. That was not a great year to graduate from college and begin
looking for a job, especially since his father had just faced a major set-
back in business. How McNeill became one of the most well-known
personalities in the country can be partially explained by the fact he
had talent—he could write, draw, and speak effectively—but more
importantly, he had resolve and enthusiasm, which carried him
through many of the challenges that he faced while trying to establish himself as a radio performer. He also had the good fortune to be
in Chicago where radio was developing its roots for national network
distribution.

Drawing from his first experiences in front of a microphone,
McNeill had discovered some concepts that worked on radio and put
them on his *Breakfast Club*. The show's early hour made it a less
desirable venue for aspiring entertainers, but it offered McNeill a
chance to demonstrate his ability. A remarkable communication
occurred between McNeill and his listeners—both discovered how
important they were to each other, and this stimulated McNeill to
create a lively, informative, entertaining, and inspired show.

In 1933 when the *Breakfast Club* was first heard, Americans were
in the midst of an economic depression. The culture was continuing

to make a shift from being a predominantly rural to an urban society. At the same time, threats of war were rumbling across Europe. The influence of these changes was captured in magazines, movies, popular music, and radio. Those media provide a snapshot of the lifestyles, tastes, and sentiment of a nation undergoing dramatic economic, political, and social change.

Radio is a fascinating medium for examining cultural history because it permeated the culture and allowed for a wide variety of expressive forms. It communicated fiction by taking it to a dramatic form much like motion pictures but without the expense. Radio could instantly transmit news events as well as longer pieces, often borrowing content from newspapers but with the ability to infuse the story with dramatic reality.

In addition to offering immediacy, radio was ubiquitous. By 1939 over three-quarters of the homes in the country had a radio, making it a powerful communication system. Unlike newspapers which were tied to regional areas, national radio networks created a community that overcame geographic and economic differences, and in doing so brought Americans together in a daily forum where they could hear about life beyond their own experience. The key to the incredible growth of the radio as a dynamic form of communication was the programming of shows that attracted larger and larger audiences.

The *Breakfast Club* was the kind of program that capitalized on radio's community-building potential. In time, the networks and sponsors saw that they could count on McNeill and his show to deliver a sizable audience year after year. That, in turn, gave McNeill independence from network interference and ensured the longevity of his show.

The *Breakfast Club* had polish, fluidity, and sparkle; listening to it was a pleasant way to start the day. Music was a big part of the show and provided an emotional uplift for the entire hour. Signature themes for each segment and the daily hymn plus popular songs gave the program both variety and richness. McNeill's role was crucial because it was he who infused the program with an on-air style that was friendly, humorous, and chatty. Because of his ease with himself and the folks he talked with, McNeill came across as a friend, and that is the way his regular listeners experienced him. He was both whimsical and serious; he was often jovial and corny, and he never shied from communicating his values—civility to all, respect for the family and marriage, compassion for others, and a spirituality that was the source of his inner strength. Beginning in October 1944 and on every broadcast thereafter, he made time available for a silent prayer by inviting everyone in the studio and radio audience to join him: "Each in his own words, each in his own way, for a world united in peace—bow your heads and let us pray."

The program appealed to people in all segments of society. When the *Breakfast Club* went on the road for special broadcasts originating from auditoriums in cities across America, it typically played to a capacity audience. But it never lost its midwestern roots; it had a flavor of down-to-earth friendliness that remained throughout its long tenure. McNeill clearly reached into the homes and hearts of the people and their loyalty to him made sponsors and network affiliate stations anxious to carry the show. Although radio was the primary medium for the program, television also played a role in the life of the *Breakfast Club*. Attempts to simulcast this successful radio show on television in the 1950s served as an illustration of some crucial differences between the two media.

This book tells the story of Don McNeill and his *Breakfast Club*. People who remember McNeill's rousing greeting every weekday morning, the lively theme songs, and the daily march around the breakfast table will enjoy revisiting the show. But this story is not simply an exercise in nostalgia. There are a number of lessons to be learned from McNeill's life and career. One has to do with the willingness to work hard in one's chosen field, but without ever losing sight of the real priorities in life, especially that of family. Another is a message of personal integrity—that it is possible to be a celebrity and reach millions of people in a meaningful way without becoming aloof on the one hand or pandering to base instincts or titillating subject matter on the other. McNeill enjoyed his celebrity, but he never fell victim to it or let it misguide him. He always treated his audiences and guests with respect and kindness. In return, he received the trust and affection of millions of Americans.

There are other things this book hopes to offer. It is a narrative told against the backdrop of some of the most harrowing and fascinating decades in American history. The very nature of the story makes it a kind of introduction to the history of radio, its growth, zenith, and decline as it ceded the priority of place to television.

Those who are uninitiated into the ritual of the *Breakfast Club* will find here an opportunity to experience the unabashed energy of the show and its emphasis on being entertaining rather than informative. Historically important events and celebrities often were part of the show, but they were subsumed under the larger purpose which was for the cast and audience to enjoy each other's company every morning.

The *Breakfast Club* worked because McNeill injected it with his sense of humor, good character, and unwavering respect for the listener. Commentator Paul Harvey, upon learning that McNeill was planning to retire after a run for three and a half decades, summed it up this way:

> Don McNeill came to the top during the depths of a depression and helped Americans keep faith. Through the Lindbergh kidnapping and the Dillinger escapades, from the charleston through the frug, from earliest radio's crackly headphones through living color TV, the Breakfast Club gave continuity and credulity to a sometimes incredible industry. . . . One can never truly see the size of a tree until it is felled; until it lies there stretched out on the ground leaving such a vast, empty place against the sky. He was a big one.[1]

This is his story.

Accompanying the book is a CD containing some highlights from the *Breakfast Club*'s history. The selections include significant broadcasts such as Germany's surrender during World War II, Don McNeill's mock presidential campaign, and the *Breakfast Club*'s twentieth anniversary show as well as such regular features as March Time, the Silent Prayer, a visit from Aunt Fanny, and Sam's Almanac. McNeill's sons, Tom, Don, and Bob, narrate the recording.

1

McNeill Takes the Long Way from Milwaukee to Chicago

In the early 1930s radio networks were discovering how to produce programs that would attract larger audiences and, therefore, more sponsors. People would tune in nightly to learn about the doings of their favorite radio characters who might resemble their neighbors. Programs such as *Vic and Sade*, *Lum 'n' Abner*, *Amos 'n' Andy*, and *Fibber McGee and Molly* were first heard nationwide from studios in Chicago and each reflected values associated with the central part of the nation.

Actors on *Vic and Sade* did not come across to listeners as performers, but rather as real inhabitants of a world they could understand. The show's creator and writer, Paul Rhymer, was from Bloomington, Illinois, and he drew from his background to create a small-town setting with off-beat characters. Rhymer's scripts were crafted with a subtle lightness that allowed serious issues to waft around the unadorned, low-key humor. Although *Lum 'n' Abner* was created by two Arkansas natives, Chet Lauck and Norris Goff, their network radio premiere in 1931 was also in Chicago on NBC. The program centered on the daily activities in the Jot 'Em Down Store in the mythical Pine Ridge. Jim and Marian Jordan were from small towns near Peoria, Illinois. After ten years of radio experience in Chicago, including a stint on the *Breakfast Club*, in 1935 they began performing in a series *Fibber McGee and Molly*. Jim played Fibber, a braggart who was forever starting something he couldn't complete. Marian, as Molly, was kind and served as a stabilizer to Fibber. *Amos 'n' Andy* was initially heard on a local Chicago station, WGN, as *Sam and Henry* before being picked up by NBC. The black-face comedy created by two white performers, Charles Corell and Freeman Gosden, soon became one of the most listened-to shows in the nation and its popularity provided networks with an incentive to replicate such success.

Many of the daytime soap operas like *Helen Trent* and *Ma Perkins* and numerous dramatic shows such as *First Nighter* and *Lights Out* also started in Chicago. It made sense to originate network programs from Chicago for several reasons. A number of the nation's leading advertising agencies were headquartered in the city, which made it easier to attract sponsors for new program ideas. Geographically, it worked because the city served as a major switching point for radio programs. In the early 1930s, network feeds from New York went to affiliate stations as far west as Chicago. Then the same program was produced again hours later for a feed to west coast stations and was sent over lines from Chicago. In 1931, Chicago's status as a creative center for network radio was enhanced by NBC when it opened new studios on the top two floors of the Merchandise Mart, which, when completed, was the largest commercial building in the country and one of Chicago's most impressive structures. Shortly after the facility was opened, the network moved some 50 programs from New York to Chicago, bringing to 120 the number of programs that originated in the midwest.[1]

The programs emanating every day from NBC Chicago were a hit with listeners and sponsors. The unadorned slices-of-life reflected a reality that many listeners found both comforting and amusing. Vestiges of this style continue to the present with the low-key humor of Bob Newhart, Stan Freberg, and Garrison Keillor. Keillor's *Tales from Lake Wobegon* can be traced to the foibles of the Gook family on *Vic and Sade* or the daily activities of *Lum 'n' Abner* at their Jot 'Em Down Store.

In Louisville, two young radio performers were experimenting with their version of slice-of-life humor on a weekly evening program over WHAS, billing themselves as *The Two Professors of Coo Coo College*. Van Fleming sang and played guitar while Don McNeill played clarinet. They both acted out inanities in their make-believe classroom such as the monthly student fire drills. In the skit, listeners heard the shuffling of students marching outside. Once the classroom was emptied of students, the professors decided to actually start a fire with a cigarette lighter. They marveled at the sight while the listeners heard the crackle of flames engulfing the building. When they were not burning down the school, the professors regularly featured their pet students, Joie the seal and a parrot named Chloe. Joie was often paired with Willie the Walrus in a parody of the Jack Sharkey–Max Schmeling fight of 1930. Typically, Joie would end up flat on his back at the end of a round but was saved each time by the bell on the count of nine.

The boys had spunk and were continuously polishing their act. Feeling a bit cocky, they risked their future with the Louisville station by auditioning in Chicago for a network time slot. Their boss agreed to their taking a day off from their duties, but when they needed an extra day to complete the audition, the boss wired the pair to "get on back here." They returned to a tense situation at the station, but the gamble paid off because their audition was good enough to entice a sponsor, Quaker Oats, to give them a contract to perform their antics on NBC's west coast network out of San Francisco.

Van and Don became the early morning performers over NBC's nine stations along the west coast. Their showmanship was improving with practice. McNeill began taking dancing and music lessons so the pair could begin making personal appearances. Their first booking was a small mining town in northern California where they were scheduled to perform four shows, but when only fifteen people turned out for the first one, the others were canceled.

Radio was still a novelty and needed time to develop as an entertainment and marketing medium, but success stories were being made. In 1932, NBC was paying Freeman Gosden and Charles Correll $5,000 a week to be *Amos 'n' Andy* and the network considered the deal a bargain.[2] After only two years on the network, *Amos 'n' Andy* captured the bulk of the radio audience every night and in doing so showed sponsors how effective radio advertising could be. It was the lure of having a successful program that prompted networks to reward performers with higher pay.

Quaker Oats was paying McNeill $1,000 a month in 1931 and he felt pretty flush. It was a lot better than the $15 a week he earned on his first radio job at WISN in Milwaukee. McNeill had taken that job in order to help pay for school expenses while pursuing his degree in journalism at Marquette University after his father's furniture factory in Sheboygan, Wisconsin, failed. The job entailed his being an announcer, sports commentator, radio column editor, and clean-up man around the office. When McNeill found the courage to ask the manager for a three-dollar raise it was gruffly refused with the suggestion that "there's no future [for you] in radio. You'd better get into something else." That advice challenged McNeill to look for work at a rival Milwaukee station, WTMJ, which paid him $30 a week to do essentially the same work plus write and illustrate (McNeill could draw) a radio column for the *Milwaukee Journal*. He had to arrange his classes to accommodate the demanding work that required him to be at the station seven days a week, often working from six in the morning until two the next morning. Within a year's time he was earning $50 a week plus commission payments for commercials. One of McNeill's programs, *Dinner Table of the Air*, brought him some recognition after a poll of *Milwaukee Journal* readers selected it as one of their favorite radio features. He also showed his promise at selling, since he was now earning a commission on all sales he brought to the station and he was good enough to be getting a paycheck that was uncomfortably close to that of his manager.[3]

The fact that *Coo Coo College* had a sponsor and was heard on nine stations rather than one had given the Two Professors a taste of the good life. McNeill rented a comfortable apartment and bought a sporty Chrysler Phaeton. In his spare time he thought about the woman who had swept him off his feet when they met at Marquette University. McNeill first noticed Kay Bennett at a fraternity dance which both had attended with different dates, but they caught one another's eye after he brazenly mentioned that her slip was showing. He was taken with her exuberance and ease with people. In his words, she simply "melted my reserve" and she was everything the introverted McNeill wanted to be. She liked his dash (McNeill wore a raccoon coat) and thought he danced "divinely." She worked as secretary for the dean of Marquette's journalism program, Jerry O'Sullivan, so they had plenty of opportunity to see one another. That fraternity party marked the beginning of the couple's dating relationship which continued after McNeill left Milwaukee for Louisville.

In San Francisco one night, McNeill climbed atop Telegraph Hill and thought about Kay and how a year earlier when she was visiting him in Louisville they took a drive and ended up at Cherokee Park where he gave her an engagement ring. Sitting alone in San Francisco, McNeill made up his mind to bring Kay out to California so they could be married. He went back to his apartment and wrote her with a plan for their wedding. He told her about the perfect place he had found for the ceremony, a Spanish mission–style Catholic church, St. Brendan's, on Russian Hill. Among the arguments he made in the letter was the fact that his radio contract had just been renewed for another thirteen weeks. Kay agreed and they set a date for that September. An entourage from the midwest, including both sets of parents and McNeill's sister Agnes, went to San Francisco for the wedding.

In 1932 the United States was feeling the increasing effects of the worldwide economic depression. Therefore, it was not surprising when Quaker Oats dropped its sponsorship of all radio programs, including *Lum 'n' Abner* and the *Two Professors*. Thinking they had a good act and would find new sponsors, the pair went back east to sell their show first in Chicago and then in New York. In spite of their experience, no one wanted to hire them, so they split up, hoping to find better luck alone. Looking for work, McNeill began calling on agencies, stations, and networks while he and Kay were forced to make do in the cheapest apartment they could find in Queens. Running the Chrysler became too costly and it was put in storage. Kay meagerly apportioned the couple's food supply in order to make it through the weeks with enough to eat, but after several months McNeill admitted defeat. He withdrew what little money they had left and the couple headed back to Milwaukee. The New York banks closed the next day.

Kay took the hard times in stride with the view that living on five dollars a week gave them experience in setting values, reasoning that the struggle gave them a chance to get to know one another better and learn to face reverses without worry. Despite their hardships, they made two rules for themselves: strive to be happy and remember to give a little and take a little.[4]

Arriving in Milwaukee they saved money by moving in with Kay's parents, who were accustomed to having a full house. Kay was the youngest of the Bennett brood which consisted of three girls and five boys. Before becoming a city alderman, her father had worked for the Milwaukee Road Railroad. McNeill remembered many happy dinners at the Bennett house and was particularly fond of the home-baked bread served at every meal.

Milwaukee was friendlier to McNeill than New York had been and he found an announcing job at WTMJ where he demonstrated his comedic creativity on several shows such as *Around the Dinner Table*, *Homer Benchbottom* (a pre-game baseball interview program), and *Saturday Night Jamboree*, an audience participation show which sometimes featured Kay. The station was paying McNeill $85 a week, which was quite a bit less than he had made in San Francisco but was top dollar at WTMJ. In fact, it was ten dollars more than his immediate boss earned which didn't help their relationship. One day the manager told McNeill, "You've lost your radio personality. . . . I think you better look for something else." As an aside, the manager said he was interested in hiring Kay. Not surprisingly, she had no intention of taking her husband's former job.

Up to this point, radio had been a mixed blessing for McNeill. He enjoyed writing crazy skits and thinking up characters to act in them, but broadcasting offered little security. Although McNeill was active in dramatics at Marquette, his main interest had been in becoming an editorial cartoonist and a writer ever since he had shown real talent as editor of Marquette's yearbook, *The Hilltop*, his junior year. He wrote radio columns for the newspapers in Milwaukee and Louisville, but his primary work since graduating from college was performing in front of a microphone.

McNeill was not alone in his struggle to get a position. Finding and keeping jobs was a national concern as the Depression wreaked its havoc on the economy. In June 1933 McNeill once again was among the unemployed and determined to change that situation. President Roosevelt had yet to complete his first hundred days in office and most of the nation's banks were still taking a "holiday" which had begun the day after FDR's inauguration on March 4. Despite the grim national economy there were rays of hope. The new president reminded Americans that "the only thing we have to fear is fear itself." Congress had just passed several New Deal measures, such as the Reconstruction Finance Corporation, the Federal Emergency Relief Administration, and the Civilian Conservation Corps, to help people cope with a sagging economy.

Chicago was trying to shake off the Depression doldrums by hosting a world's fair, "The Century of Progress," which opened in June 1933 on the Lake Michigan waterfront. McNeill was optimistic when he learned that NBC was auditioning in Chicago for someone to emcee an early morning show called *Pepper Pot*. He asked the network for a chance to try out for the show, telling them about his background and enclosing sample scripts from his Milwaukee-based programs plus a photograph.

The NBC brass agreed to hear his ideas; after all the show needed a shot of fresh energy. The program was heard over stations on NBC's Blue Network,[5] which typically carried non-commercial and less popular shows. The network regarded the Monday through Saturday show as a public service which provided NBC with a morning presence on the air, and since the orchestra was already on staff, the cost of producing the program was modest.

On the day McNeill was scheduled to present himself to the network executives, Kay did the driving from Milwaukee. During the trip to Chicago, McNeill made notes about how the morning show might be produced. Scribbling all the way, he imagined a wake-up program divided into fifteen-minute segments which were to be announced as First, Second, Third, and Fourth Calls to Breakfast, much like one would hear while traveling on a passenger train. He had some ideas to make the hour both happy and inspiring by interspersing music with comical vignettes like he had done with success in his previous radio shows. He envisioned listeners having their breakfast during the show, and therefore decided to call it *Breakfast Club*.

McNeill's was one of three auditions NBC executives had scheduled to determine the next *Pepper Pot* host. When he arrived at the network offices, he was ushered into a studio that was bare except for a microphone. At six foot two, McNeill was an imposing young man in the empty room. He stepped up to the mike and began to tell the executives, who were listening in a nearby studio, about his plans for the show. In addition to the four wake-up calls, McNeill's Breakfast Club would feature his favorite poems mixed with a bit of philosophy, humor, a children's march around the house, and popular music featuring the orchestra and the show's male vocalist.

Seven of the eight executives who heard McNeill that day felt he made the poorest showing of the three auditions. Perhaps they found his somewhat nasal voice and colloquial style unsophisticated. However, one member of the panel, Sidney Strotz, liked what he heard and his vote counted more than the others. Strotz, the network's central division director, offered McNeill the job. Maybe someone better would come along but, for now, Strotz believed that McNeill's breezy and friendly manner would help the show. The pay was $50 a week and for this McNeill was required to write, direct, and emcee the morning show six days a week, be on hand for announcing duties, plus serve as emcee and writer for a weekly, nighttime show, *Jamboree*.

McNeill discovered his new job consumed about sixty hours a week and nearly all his energy. Preparing for the early morning show meant getting up before dawn. Then the rest of the day was occupied by his other announcing chores which kept him at the studio until mid-afternoon. After leaving work, he would concoct ideas and write them into scripts for the next day's program, a process that kept him busy late into the night and filled up his weekends. To be near the studio, McNeill took a room in an inexpensive hotel on North Clark Street. Years later he would recall cringing every time he drove by the hotel, remembering the rats which infested the place. The routine was wearing on McNeill, but fortunately that stress didn't come across on the air.

2

The Very
First Call to
Breakfast

When the *Breakfast Club* began, the cast and crew consisted of emcee Don McNeill, a twelve-piece staff orchestra directed by Walter Blaufuss, announcer Bill Kephart, singer Dick Teela, and engineer Charlie Butler. The orchestra members were selected from the roster of musicians on staff at NBC and frequently would change, but two assigned that first day would stay with the program, trumpeter Eddie Ballantine and pianist Bill Krenz. McNeill was responsible for filling the minutes when the orchestra wasn't playing and he did this virtually alone because the show had no producer or writers.

The first *Breakfast Club* program, June 23, 1933, included Walter Blaufuss conducting his own composition "Your Eyes Have Told Me So." Other songs on the maiden broadcast were "Nola" and "Too Much Mustard," which was used as the theme for the four calls to breakfast. McNeill read a poem and led a march around the table. His attempt to add humor came through on the maiden broadcast as a bit strained: "I was reading the paper this morning and I saw that chess has come into prominence again. They say that one chess factory is expanded and now employs twice as many men as before. I tell you it makes me feel good that you can double your chess expansion."[1]

The script for the show reveals reserve and formality, but with pockets of humor:

> Good morning. We invite you to join us around the breakfast table of the air as we share our breakfast club with us [sic]. Walter Blaufuss and the breakfasteers have a double order of cheer as your musical cocktail today—"Happy Days Are Here Again."
>
> [Musical interlude]
>
> Up at the head of our breakfast table of the air sits Dick Teela— toast of the breakfast club. Dick puts so much feeling into the singing of these romantic songs of his that he thought it affected his heart last week and he went to see a doctor about it. He asked the doc, "How's my heart?" and the doctor said, "I'll tell you in a minute—wait till I feel your purse." And after examining Dick's billfold the doctor decided that he seemed to be suffering from a bad case of shrinkage of the budget and a severe case of delegation of the pocketbook. So Dick continues to sing such songs as "Isn't It Romantic" from *Love Me Tonight*.

Later in the program McNeill imparted some of his philosophy along with an effort to show more personality to the audience.

> Around the breakfast table is a great place to philosophize— not for long though, because we're always in a hurry at breakfast nowadays. It seems it's become sort of a scramble to see who can finish his eggs first and then it's a scramble for the nearest exit. Sort of a case of scrambled eggs and scrambled exits. But we have a bit more leisure around our breakfast table of the air—time to talk a bit—and time to bring you the melodies you want to hear, and while you're served with a melodic waltz "Dreaming," digest this food for thought—"If you have nothing nice to say about a person isn't it better to hold your tongue until you have."[2]

McNeill began to put more of himself into the scripts.

> Breakfast Clubbers, this is the beginning of my second week as your toastmaster and I'm getting to like it more every day. Really, I think we Breakfast Clubbers are old friends by now. At least I feel that way about it and by your letters lots of you do,

too. So, let's go ahead together—smiling before breakfast and after breakfast . . . and I hope we can go on and on together.[3]

The *Breakfast Club* was beginning to become a routine for many listeners who enjoyed joining McNeill for breakfast. His remarks on the show often referred to everyone's getting up early for work.

It's the Breakfast Club for people who get up before breakfast and smile—not a toothpaste ad smile or a silly smirk—but one of those that comes naturally when you put up the shade in the morning and the sun's shining and even with mortgages and income tax and what not—everything isn't so bad after all—or a smile that was on when the boss of the house, that little two year old son or daughter of yours maybe, jumps on your bed and pokes you one on the jaw—that's what the Breakfast Club is for.

McNeill's effort to reach out to his listeners began to pay off when they wrote in to let him know how much they enjoyed the show. His reading portions of their letters on the air began to create a community of early-risers.

Let's take a one-minute peek at the mail sack again this morning. Ah here's one from Mrs. M. C. of Philadelphia: You are doing some real work to aid in the better homes movement—where women are concerned. Our monotonous dull routine work sends us all frequently to the depths of pitying ourselves and each morning I take myself to the dining room and tune in your exhilarating music and have many a laugh over the things you have to say—and when you order us back to the dishes I go cheerfully singing, glad to be alive.

McNeill's scripts from those first broadcasts provide evidence that he had a concept of what his audience might be up to during the show. The style is breezy, but the message leaves no doubt that he is aware of his listeners.

Well, breakfast clubbers, how are you feeling this morning? You all over labor day by now? That's swell. Is the house a mess today and you just sitting around hating to clean it? That's swell. Are you one of the hundreds of thousands who came to Chicago to see the world's fair and are your feet all swollen from

walking? That's swell. Did you sell all your hogs to the government? That's swell—then we won't have to sell the farm that's
sell or swell.[4]

The show was bright and up-beat. The NBC staff orchestra had a
sophisticated sound that blended well with McNeill's casual and
friendly style. After being on the air five months, McNeill wanted
some evidence as to how well the show was being received by its audience. On November 20, 1933, he began a week of broadcasts with a
request to his listeners:

> Breakfast Clubbers, it isn't often that your toastmaster is as seri-
> ous as he is right now. And here's the reason. I've never asked
> you to send in your letters before. Hundreds and hundreds of
> you have been kind enough to take upon yourself the little job
> of sitting down and writing us a line telling us how you like the
> breakfast club—and making little suggestions. And we appreci-
> ate those more than I can say—Walter Blaufuss, Dick Teela,
> and I read every letter. . . . Just drop us a line—a postcard will
> do—with any ideas—suggestions, gags or whatnot—that may
> occur to you and I'll be glad to use them on the breakfast club
> broadcasts. In other words this week we must make a sort of
> check of our membership. . . . There seem to be some people
> that don't believe you get up early enough to enjoy this break-
> fast club—I think you do—and if you write and let us know—if
> all of you write—that'll prove it.

The mail request worked. Listeners continued to send McNeill
their comments on the program and Kay McNeill helped by organizing and acknowledging the correspondence. Gradually the *Breakfast
Club* was establishing a small but loyal following.

Here is how one young member of the audience, Helen Tidwell,
recalls experiencing the program during its first years on the air.

> My father traded one of his pet "milk" cows for a console type
> radio. A beautiful piece of furniture, up on four legs, speakers
> covered with a fabric, dial, and four knobs, it was placed in our
> "parlor." The first morning after obtaining the "Squawk Box"
> (as [it was] sometimes referred to), my mother tuned in to a pro-
> gram called "Don McNeill's Breakfast Club." On that particular
> morning they had a cow mo-o-o-o-o-ing on the program. My

mother called to my father in another room and said, "Daddy, your cow is on the radio." Being only four or five years old, I wondered how Daddy's cow got in that radio and when it would come out. It never did.[5]

The morning show was a good place to begin a network radio career, but not where an ambitious performer like McNeill thought he would want to stay. Therefore, after doing the *Breakfast Club* for about a year, McNeill was offered a chance to return to New York for a weekly musical program for Pontiac with singer Jane Froman and Frank Black's thirty-five–piece orchestra plus an eighteen-member chorus. McNeill was to be the emcee and would blend those duties with some comedy sketches with Betty Winkler who would play his "dumb" stenographer. The Sunday broadcast required McNeill to leave Chicago on Thursday after his morning announcing duties. After about three weeks, he discovered that the opportunity was not turning out the way he envisioned when his portion of the show began getting smaller and no one was willing to give up any of their time on the air for the emcee's humor. Finally, McNeill complained to the producer, who said, "You can quit the show now and we'll pay you for the whole period."[6] Since there were twenty weeks in the contract, McNeill made out fairly well, but the experience was a painful reminder of previous jobs and it wasn't hard for Kay McNeill to make the case that his future was with the *Breakfast Club*. McNeill would continue to do other programs on the side, but he promised his wife that he would stick with the morning show. Leaving the *Pontiac Show* was embarrassing, but having the extra money came in handy because Kay was pregnant with the couple's first child.

The McNeills were eager to have children, especially Kay, who had pleasant memories of her large family, which included eight children. When they were living in San Francisco, she had a miscarriage and afterwards a doctor told McNeill his wife would never be able to have children. Therefore, the prospects of a baby were both exciting and challenging for McNeill who took his family responsibilities very seriously. In fact, he was very focused about everything he did as is evidenced by his record in college. When he was selected to be the valedictorian of Marquette's Class of 1929 he wrote his parents telling them of the honor in a letter that reveals McNeill's determination to move on with the next phase of his life. Yes, he was glad to be chosen the class speaker, but foremost on his mind was finding a job.

President Magee and Charlie Cobeen had picked me to give the valedictorian address for the entire senior class of the University. . . . This is the first time a Journalist has ever been picked . . . so I guess it's quite an honor.

Am working mighty hard at the Journal—put out both the Special Section today and Sunday's Radio Section all by myself. . . . Haven't heard any more as yet about the other jobs—have several on the string now but will know more in a week or two. I will try to get home a week from Saturday. This weekend I have to finish up my term papers. Have 3 more to write.

Nothing else new just jobs—jobs—jobs.[7]

McNeill had worked hard at many things in school during his years at Marquette. His grades kept him on the honor roll and entitled him to be elected to several honorary societies. He also found time to serve as president of his fraternity Beta Phi Theta, edit the school's yearbook, and even chair the homecoming dance. McNeill was a doer who was undoubtedly influenced by watching his father struggle with a business that eventually failed. He was determined to be a good provider for his family in spite of the faltering economy. While the nation was struggling with an economic depression it was clear to McNeill that in order to succeed he had to work hard and be the best at whatever he chose to do.

Struggles were not foreign to McNeill. He had been a sickly baby and his parents became alarmed when they discovered he had difficulty keeping food down. Their concern was so great that when McNeill was two years old they were persuaded to move from Galena, Illinois, to Sheboygan, Wisconsin, so as to have a ready supply of Jersey milk which they were told would be easier for McNeill to digest. Sheboygan was also where McNeill's paternal grandparents lived and where McNeill's father, Harry, was to take over management of a chair factory.

Grandfather Thomas McNeill made all the arrangements for his son's family to move to Wisconsin, including finding the position in the chair factory for his son and offering advice on the benefits of milk from Jersey cows. Thomas was a strong-willed individual who, despite being orphaned at age three, worked his way out of poverty to become one of the founders of the Sheboygan Chair Company. His parents were Irish immigrants who settled near Boston where Thomas was born. The youth had no schooling beyond the fourth grade, but was a

A McNeill cartoon
in Marquette's 1928
yearbook

voracious reader who loved learning and became the first president of the Sheboygan School Board. Thomas dissuaded his son from staying in high school beyond the first few months while instilling in him a passion for learning and appreciation of literature and music. Harry eventually earned his degree from the University of Wisconsin and set out on a career as a mining engineer, but he never was far from books and enjoyed quoting long memorized passages from Shakespeare and the Bible.

Thomas McNeill's strong will influenced his family and perhaps there was some truth to his notion that Jersey milk would strengthen his grandson, because McNeill started growing very fast, in fact, too fast, according to the family doctor. Later he developed rickets and, on doctor's orders, had to spend two hours a day lying on his back in the sun. The lanky lad must have yearned to play ball with friends or go fish and hunt with his dad and grandfather. Perhaps his experience of being alone in bed contributed to his sensitivity to the problems some people face. He survived these early illnesses, but his memory of himself as a boy was that of a gawky person.

> I was tall and stringy ever since I can remember, and the kids in Sheboygan used to tease me about my build. When I was playing in the school yard and Mother called me, the gang would jeer, "Daddy Long Legs, Mom's calling you!" This increased my self-disparagement until I acquired a complex and became unusually shy.[8]

It is a bit ironic that someone as shy as McNeill describes himself would consider a career as publicly demanding as broadcasting. Philip Zimbardo, a psychologist who directs Stanford University's Shyness Clinic, most likely would classify McNeill as being a "shy extrovert," described as being

> at their best when they can play well-rehearsed roles in clearly defined situations, and especially when they are in the driver's seat. Actors, politicians, college lecturers, reporters, TV talk-show hosts are more often of this breed than one would suspect. They create the illusion of "doing naturally" what takes a lot of practice and concentrated effort. . . . Their shyness expresses itself when they leave the stage, or the red recording light goes off and they, too, must deal with the spontaneity and unplanned give-and-take of everyday encounters with ordinary people.[9]

Zimbardo offers examples of shy extroverts from public life including Jimmy and Rosalyn Carter and Johnny Carson who told Mike Wallace during an interview about his two sides: one shy, the other a public performer. Carson said he could feel comfortable in front of an audience because he was in control but not so in social situations where he retreated. Whether he was covering up his shyness or not, by the time McNeill reached high school he behaved like someone who was socially at ease, if we can believe the account he wrote for his class's twenty-fifth reunion at Sheboygan's Central High School. McNeill could not attend the affair, as the *Breakfast Club* was originating from New York City that week, but he did draft a recollection of his teenage years to be read at the festivities.

> Many things stand out in my memories of Central High. . . . I was the lean, unbending butler in the class play, "Come Out Of The Kitchen." Funny that I should spend most of my radio and television commercial time now, selling kitchen products and kitchen appliances. Never quite got out of the kitchen, did I?
>
> Graduation exercises in my day were held in the school auditorium, while dances were staged in the school gym. Those were the days of the King Tut influence. We weren't guys and dolls, we were sheiks and shebas.
>
> Boys parted their well-oiled hair in the middle, wore sideburns and bell-bottom trousers. Pearl buttons decorated insert panels set in our trouser legs to accentuate the bell-bottom effect.

Girls wore dresses with disappearing waist-lines. That is, the
waist-lines practically blended in with the knee-line.

If someone could talk dad out of the Stanley Steamer, we
would spend hours driving up and down Eighth Street to see
what was doing. Then we would cool off with a double choco-
late soda at Gmach's Sweet Shop.

School mates on these excursions usually included Bob and
Edgar Jung, Tommy Gordon, Nick Hiltchen, Gertrude Bowler,
Mildred Olle, Mildred Robinson and Fred Hoppe. Wonder how
many of them recall the moaning saxophone I played?[10]

Watching McNeill work the audience during his show, one would
never guess he was introverted, but once the demands of the on-air role
were over he would beat a hasty retreat into himself. The control factor that Zimbardo mentions may have been at work, since McNeill was
definitely in charge of the *Breakfast Club*. McNeill faced a studio audience composed of "ordinary" people which he could control. McNeill
had a special ability to bring people out during interviews due, in part,
to his self-confessed liking for "people who aren't very likable." Throughout his many years on the air, McNeill initiated campaigns that were
directed toward helping people overcome personal handicaps.

McNeill let his jovial side show through and he brought his creativity to the mike each morning by doing skits with such cast members as Chickie and Toots (Jim and Marian Jordan) a year before
they became Fibber McGee and Molly and Bill Thompson who went
on to become "Mr. Wimple" on the Jordans' show. McNeill was
adept at creating ideas to enliven his show such as wacky characters
like Angelian Glutz. He wrote "One-Man; One-Act Plays," and
thought up a variety of musical gimmicks including: "Waltz Time,"
"Solo Time," "Musical Trips to Other Lands," "Famous Bits from
Famous Operas," and the "Rug Dance" when McNeill asked housewives across the nation to pick up their throw rugs and dance around
the house as the band played. The dance became one of the most
popular features on the show. Years after McNeill discontinued the
dance, a listener in St. Paul, Minnesota, Eve Tynan, sent him her
"Lament for the Rug Dance":

With tears in my eyes I stand and sigh
For the Rug Dance that used to be.
Oh, tell me not it is gone, kind sir—
Pray lend an ear to my plea.

I used to love to dip and glide,
To whirl across the floor,
To swing my arms from side to side
And bark my shins on the floor.

But now I sit in solemn mood,
No rug flies through the air,
For all is silent, as I brood
O'er the dance no longer on the air.[11]

The *Breakfast Club* was catching on with its audience, but Mc-
Neill was increasingly frustrated by the requirement to provide his
boss with a script of each program before it aired. Broadcasters, unlike
newspaper publishers, are licensed by the government in order to control who gets to operate one of the limited number of available frequencies of the broadcast spectrum. Another reason for government
regulation of broadcasting is the intrusive nature of the electronic
media. Books and newspapers can be more easily avoided, but broadcast signals permeate homes, cars, and lives. Sensitivity to the pervasive quality of broadcasting resulted in early radio programs sounding
stiff by today's standards. Announcers often wore tuxedos and scripts
sounded as starched as formal shirts. NBC wanted McNeill to write
out everything he planned to say on the *Breakfast Club* so it could be
reviewed and approved. Without a script anything might happen.

After months of pounding out scripts that contained jokes,
verses, and humorous incidents from the day's news, he was getting
tired. He finally built up the courage to tell his boss that "for 18
months I've written down every word used on my broadcast. From
here on you either let me extemporize or you find yourself another
boy." Whether it was a bluff or not is unclear, but shortly after that
the network decided to give McNeill the freedom to ad lib.[12] The decision was unusual in network radio, but McNeill had proven himself
to be reliably witty and clever without showing a hint of sarcasm or
double meaning that would hurt or embarrass anyone. NBC broke its
long-standing rule and agreed to let him go on the air without first
approving a script. Without the restraint of a script, the *Breakfast
Club* became more spontaneous and eventually earned the nickname
of the most "unrehearsed show in radio." Anything could happen and
often did, but always under the watchful eye of toastmaster McNeill
who determined the makeup and degree of humor that would be
allowed on the show.

The cast was willing to go along with McNeill's sense of whatever would make the show come alive. For example, one morning in 1936, just before the show, the network sent word it was taking forty minutes of the hour for a special program. Unperturbed by the abrupt change, McNeill decided to do a twenty-minute version of the *Breakfast Club* that contained all the elements of an hour-long show, except it went faster. Triple-time music included one or two lines of singing and McNeill rattled through his usual chatter. For occasional fun, McNeill created the McBreakfast Family (long before McDonald's offered its customers McMuffins for breakfast) consisting of Pa, Ma, and the seven little McBreakfasts. McNeill and Annette King played all the parts of this crazy family. These features and others were scripted in advance of the show, but pre-broadcast approval was no longer required and this contributed to the cast's sense of ease and flexibility on the air.

3

A Marine Makes
Way for
Studio Audiences

The conversation between McNeill and his team had an intimate quality that sounded like a few close friends sitting around a table enjoying themselves. The members of the cast and orchestra would be heard laughing at a joke or clapping after a musical number but, unlike nighttime radio, there was no audience. Then, in 1936, McNeill received a letter from a Marine being treated for tuberculosis at Ellis Island, New York. It was a sober story from Stanley McAllister who said he was not responding to the treatments and that his future was bleak. He told McNeill that for the past year he listened to the *Breakfast Club* nearly every morning in the hospital. Now, he had two requests, "First being that I want to go home to Seattle, Washington where I can be near my sister, and the second desire being to visit your studio and watch a Breakfast Club Broadcast."[1]

McNeill was deeply touched by the Marine's story and invited him to be a guest in Studio A in the Merchandise Mart during the show whenever he came to Chicago. Weeks later, the Marine got off the train on his way west and headed for the Merchandise Mart. By sitting in the studio during the broadcast that morning, Stanley McAllister changed the course of the *Breakfast Club* for other listeners who soon got the idea they, too, could watch the fun and even be interviewed by

McNeill as Stanley was. The change was gradual but noticeable until studio audiences became as much a part of the show as the orchestra and singers.

The studio audience provided McNeill with some built-in benefits. Not only did a live reaction make the show sound more exciting to listeners at home but, in addition, the audience provided McNeill with a constant supply of material to use each morning. Audience members handed in their cards containing clever poems and humorous stories in hopes of being called upon during the hour. It was like enlisting several hundred people every morning to help write the show.

McNeill was adroit at handling spontaneous interviews and liked nothing better than bantering with strangers in the audience. He had the ability to open people up so they felt comfortable telling him their unusual or humorous tale and then he would reply with a funny retort. The interviews usually took no more than about forty seconds. It was the kind of humor that doesn't produce huge laughs but rather empathetic chuckles. One morning McNeill began the show by talking with a woman named Maude, who wrote on her card how she hated soap operas because "nothing ever happened" and she didn't like talk shows. McNeill responded by reminding her she was at a talk show. Maude hit back saying, "You're okay, except when you get too silly." After each song or interview, McNeill would check in with Maude to see if the show was getting too silly. Just before the end of the program, Maude asked, "What in the world would you have done for material today, if I hadn't shown up?" The truth was that McNeill purposely didn't plan every minute of the show and instead relied on his own spontaneous response to the studio guests to build interest.

When McNeill strode into the audience he was imposing, to say the least, standing six foot two and weighing about two hundred pounds. Despite his size he engaged his guests with the bounciness of a younger and smaller man. His double chin and broad smile gave him the countenance of someone who was fun-loving and even comical. The majority of the *Breakfast Club* audience knew McNeill not by his looks, but by his voice with its noticeable midwestern twang, clear but not overly pronounced diction, and warmth. His size and conservative dress may have communicated that he was rather formal and stiff, but once McNeill began his gentle sparring during an interview, people could sense his warmth and friendly nature.

When schools were on break, it was common for the audience to be packed with youngsters who added a spark to March Time and, of course, the interview potential for McNeill. At times he would pose situations that the audience could think about and comment on, like a story he found in the news one day about a man who was driving along the Pennsylvania Turnpike while his wife slept in the back seat. The driver pulled into the rest stop to take a break and, while he was out of the car, his wife awoke and went to the women's room. The man returned and drove off without her. The response was immediate, with audience members offering opinions about who was right or wrong and telling about similar experiences.

The idea of watching a broadcast of the *Breakfast Club* caught on with listeners, many of whom included a visit to the program as part of their itinerary while in Chicago. Additional staff was required at NBC to handle the mounting requests for tickets. "They came by the hundreds—farmers, housewives, business men, secretaries, school children—from every walk of life."[2] The presence of a live audience had a noticeable impact on the sound of the program. When over a hundred people began filling the chairs set up in the studio the program sounded more energized and spontaneous. The audience's reaction to McNeill's quips or his ability to draw out a funny remark from a guest gave the routine a resonance that carried over to listeners at home. Singers and other cast members also benefited from the presence of the studio audience; it enhanced their ability to make songs and jokes more entertaining to listeners.

Seeing those smiling faces every morning in the studio audience convinced McNeill that he had made a success of what had been an early morning orphan. Another sign that the show had arrived was the attitude of the staff musicians who were assigned to play on the program. When McNeill first took over the show it was obvious that musicians saw the assignment as tantamount to punishment, since they were required to show up for 7:00 A.M. rehearsals. This attitude began to change, and soon orchestra members started requesting assignment to the *Breakfast Club* and several had become regulars on the show.

The *Breakfast Club* cast was getting larger, adding a female singer, Edna O'Dell, in 1935, plus several singing groups during the next few years. Some of these included the Cadets, Merry Macs, Songfellows, Three C's, Morin Sisters, Ranch Boys, King's Jesters, Hollywood Hi-Hatters, Doring Sisters, and Vagabonds. The last was an African-American group that was to be part of the Breakfast Club cast for a decade.

The male singers changed over the years, beginning in 1934 when Jack Owens took over for Dick Teela and held down the slot until he was lured by Hollywood to be the off-screen singer for stars like Jimmy Stewart. His replacements, Clark Dennis and later Johnny Johnston, stayed briefly before they too went to Hollywood. The next male singer, Jack Baker, joined the cast in 1936 and stayed eight years.

The female singers were also in flux, with Gale Page briefly replacing Edna O'Dell until she decided upon a career in the movies. Helen Jane Behlke sang on the show for a while as did Annette King. Helen and Annette each left the show when they married. Two singers replaced Annette, Evelyn Lynne and Nancy Martin.

These singers and the orchestra behind them provided a fresh and lively sound that captured the spirit of a new day. Conductor Walter Blaufuss wrote a theme that quickly became recognized as the musical signature for the show. Each call to breakfast had its own refrain of the song "Good Morning," a rousing tune with plenty of fanfare and a spirited cadence. This is the way it sounded in 1943:

> *First Theme*
> Good morning, Breakfast Clubbers, good morning to ya,
> We got up bright and early to howdy-do ya.
> The coffee's on, the table's set, the bacon's in the skillet,
> And Harry Kogen and his boys have tunes to fill it.
> So come on, gang, let's start this meeting,
> Just line up here—I'll call your name—and sing your greeting.
> Nancy Martin—
> [NANCY]: Well, how do you do.
> Jack Baker—
> [JACK]: Glad to see you.
> The Romeos, our guest today—
> [ROMEOS]: So Breakfast Clubbers, wake up and smile, a day
>   begun happy makes life worthwhile.
>
> *Second Theme*
> Good morning, Breakfast Clubbers, may we salute you,
> With second call to breakfast that's planned to suit you.
> [McNEILL]: We can't get them up, we can't get them, we can't
>   get 'em up in the morning.
> Second call to come to breakfast,
> Everybody come to breakfast.
> Eat your meal with Don McNeill,
> We serve a smile for you.

Third Theme
It's now third call to breakfast and marching time is near,
So why not march and listen, we'll play it for you here,
Good morning, good morning,
This comes right from the heart.
Good morning, good morning,
Let's go, it's time to start,
With our songs and laugh appeal,
Served to brighten up the meal,
Good morning, good morning,
Take a cue from Don McNeill.

Fourth Theme
Good morning, Breakfast Clubbers, it's time to sing ya
Another cheery greeting, so may we bring ya
Fourth call to breakfast.
We call forth to breakfast
Every Breakfast Clubber, young and old,
To come and join our happy, carefree fold.
So wake up Breakfast Clubbers, and smile awhile,
A day begun happy
Makes life worthwhile.

Closing
So long, you Breakfast Clubbers, this ends our meeting
But once again tomorrow you'll hear our greeting
[McNEILL]: America is up—The Breakfast Club now leaves
    the air.

The words to the theme would change over the years, but the melody became familiar to every American within earshot of a radio after June 1933. Orchestra leader Walter Blaufuss and McNeill teamed up to write several songs such as the hymn, "My Cathedral," which was first heard on the *Breakfast Club* the morning King George of England was buried in January 1936. Listeners wrote requesting that the tune be played again and the interest it created became a stimulus for the daily hymn, which became a regular feature on the show beginning that year. In 1939 Blaufuss and McNeill wrote a hymn that reflected the hopes for worldwide harmony of Pope Pius XI as he was near death. The selection, "Let Us Have Peace," was played regularly on the *Breakfast Club* throughout the years up to America's involvement in World War II.

The March around the Breakfast Table was a unique musical signature that McNeill created in the early years of the show. At the halfway point of the program, over a drum cadence, McNeill would invite everyone to get up and parade around the breakfast table while the orchestra played a rousing march. Children, like Ellen Truebenbach of Milwaukee, would listen in anticipation for the daily march.

> It was mostly a program to waken sleepy adults, but there was a part of the program that I looked forward to—the "March Around the Breakfast Table." I guess this was supposed to get one's blood circulating for the day ahead, and for me, it sure was fun. Our kitchen table was pushed up against the wall on one end, making it difficult to march around, but our dining room table was perfect. I can still see the sun shining on the lace tablecloth and the cut glass bowl in the center of the table. I marched till I was dizzy.[3]

Another veteran of the morning march, Ken Weigel, recalled that listening to the *Breakfast Club* had become a ritual in his South Dakota home when he was a boy. "Mom and I 'marched around the breakfast table' so many times we wore a run in the floor."[4]

One program feature McNeill wanted to make permanent on the *Breakfast Club* was a segment he called "Memory Time" during which he would read a poem or commentary about life's challenges. The feature was dismissed as being too sentimental by the manager of the Chicago station carrying the program, but McNeill persisted and Memory Time became a permanent feature on the show. McNeill confessed he wasn't particularly attracted to poetry himself, but years earlier in San Francisco he noticed the success one announcer had with his poetic readings. Memory Time gave McNeill an opportunity to express serious ideas, without editorializing, with themes that were in keeping with his philosophy for his family and the nation. Many of the poems were sent in by listeners and typically dealt with values not commonly heard on entertainment shows, "A Woman's Prayer (For the Child to Come)," "Mother Love," "The Little Boy Who Didn't Pass," "A Father's Confession to His Son," "A Creed for the Discouraged," "Recipe for a Happy Day," "Despondency," and "A Dog's Prayer for His Master." McNeill's matter-of-fact delivery of the poetry and

Sheet music from *My Cathedral*

homespun philosophy fit in with the rest of the broadcast in spite of the heavy sentiment. One listener wrote McNeill to say how one reading had changed her life.

> When you read a little poem on the radio, you really don't know whose ears it will reach, or what influence it will have on someone's life. About five years ago, you read a poem about an adopted child. That poem made up my mind for me, and so we adopted a baby, thirteen months old. We have had her now almost four years, and these years have been the happiest of our lives.[5]

One of the most requested features on Memory Time was read in 1946 and titled "A True Story," author unknown.

A battalion of soldier boys had been given copies of the Bible, the New Testament and the Old Testament. They were then given strict orders that each was to use the Bible at the services on Sunday.

The following Sunday, while the soldiers were at services, the officer of the day made an inspection and found that one soldier had not brought the new Bible so he was searched and the only thing that was found in his pocket was a deck of cards. He was told to report to the commanding officer on Monday morning.

The next day when he reported before his officer, he was reprimanded and then asked if he had anything to say in his own defense. This is the way he replied: "Sir, this pack of cards means a great deal in my life and tells me what is in the Bible, and even more, for—

> The One-spot tells me that there is but one God.
> The Two-spot tells me that the Bible is divided into two parts, the Old and the New Testaments.
> The Three-spot that there are three Persons in the Holy Trinity.
> The Four-spot that the New Testament was written by the four Evangelists, Matthew, Mark, Luke and John.
> The Five-spot that there are five Foolish and five Wise Virgins.
> The Six-spot that the world was created in six days.
> The Seven-spot that the seventh day of the week is the Sabbath, on which I must pay my respects to my Creator.
> The Eight-spot reminds me of the eight beatitudes, the greatest sermon preached by our Lord.
> The Nine-spot tells me of the nine lepers who did not return to the Savior to give thanks.
> The Ten-spot reminds me of the Ten Commandments which I must keep to save my soul.
> The Jack is the Knave, the Devil who goes about seeking the destruction of souls.
> The Queen is the Mother of Heaven, the Mother of God.
> The King is the Kingdom of Heaven which will be my reward of a good life.

Even more than that. This pack of cards is also an almanac for me.

> There are fifty-two cards in the deck, telling me there are fifty-two Sundays in the year. Add up all the spots and you will find 365 in all, telling me there are 365 days in the year.
>
> There are thirteen cards to the suite, which tells me there are thirteen lunar months in the year.
>
> In all there are twelve face cards to the suite, which tells me there are twelve calendar months in the year.
>
> There are four various suites: hearts, diamonds, spades and clubs, signifying the four seasons of the year: spring, summer, autumn and winter.
>
> There are light and dark cards, telling that each twenty-four hours is divided into day and night.

This is the meaning of the pack of cards to me, I have nothing more to say."

The soldier boy was forthwith honorably discharged.

Memory Time became a permanent fixture in the show and one which prompted hundreds of listeners to write in for copies of the day's poem or story. In order to lessen the burden of satisfying listener requests for some of the most popular stories and poems, McNeill published a booklet in 1938 titled *Memory Time* and made it available to listeners for a dollar. It became the model for future publications that were designed for listeners who wanted to learn more about the *Breakfast Club* cast and have copies of features heard during the broadcast. Every day's mail contained contributions of poems, essays, and stories listeners suggested be read on Memory Time. In order to make room for some of the better suggestions, McNeill began a new feature in 1937 called "Inspiration Time" which he slotted during the fourth quarter of the show and reserved for lighter or whimsical poems or messages.

Memory and Inspiration Times often reflected family values which, as any regular listener to the show soon discovered, meant a great deal to McNeill—and no family was as important to him as his own. When Tom McNeill was born October 28, 1934, McNeill didn't hesitate to share information about the baby's progress with his audience. At that time they were living in a small apartment on Chicago's north side in Rogers Park where mornings at 5:30 the entire family would be crowded into their tiny bathroom. McNeill would attempt shaving while Kay was bathing Tom. She had read that bright light was bad for a baby's eyes, so she covered the bathroom mirror's lamp with a towel on which McNeill would keep catching his razor while shaving. She would keep covering the light with the towel making it impossible for the shaving to progress.

Once when McNeill was ordered by his boss to prepare a special script for the next morning's show, he dutifully pulled out the typewriter and began writing after dinner. Tom had been crying earlier, but when McNeill started typing the crying suddenly stopped, in fact there was no noise coming from the baby's room. McNeill and Kay checked and found their son holding his breath. McNeill soothed Tom, put him back in bed, and returned to the typewriter, but each time the clicking of the keys resumed so would the breath-holding routine. The script never got written, but incidents like this gave McNeill plenty of ad libs—so much so that one day after the show he was called into the front office. The boss was upset with all the stories about the McNeill baby, and told him, "We presume that someone else has had a boy before, and perhaps it would be just as well for you to program a little music and something else, for a change, and shut up about your baby."[6]

News about the McNeill family would continue to be featured on the *Breakfast Club*, but not to the exclusion of other items of interest. McNeill didn't have to look farther than NBC's mail room to find material that would add interest to the hour.

Kay McNeill, in the early years of the show, read and answered most of the mail.[7] Many of the cards and letters were expressions of thanks from housewives and mothers who enjoyed the program. A Canadian newspaperman wrote McNeill about a loyal listener, a former jockey, who found listening to the *Breakfast Club* and particularly Memory Time had brought him inspiration while recovering in a Toronto hospital. Jimmie Darou had broken his back in a three-horse fall at a Montreal race track and his doctors had decreed he would never move again. McNeill was touched by the story and began talking about, and to, the jockey on the air. *Breakfast Club* listeners started writing to Darou, urging him to have faith. Later, McNeill got an encouraging letter from Darou: "I can move my fingers now," he wrote. "Our Breakfast Clubbers expect me to get better and I'm not going to let them down. Some day I'm going to surprise you."[8]

Eventually, Darou was well enough to leave the hospital and it was McNeill who offered a surprise when he helped the former jockey by staging a benefit in Montreal and using the proceeds to buy him his own business—a service station. Darou regained partial use of his legs but spent much of his time in a wheelchair. He succeeded in business and soon opened a second station and found time to publish a local newspaper, the *Montreal Gazette*, and marry the woman who had been his nurse in Toronto. The couple's honeymoon trip included a visit to Chicago and the *Breakfast Club*. The Darous kept McNeill and his listeners up to date on their activities, and when they adopted a son McNeill passed the news along to his listeners.

Darou's story became an example of the community and sense of family that the *Breakfast Club* was creating. The structure and personalities on the show contributed to the atmosphere of a family gathering, which every listener could join. Cast members chatted with McNeill about events in their lives that were interesting or humorous. For example, a musician on the show, Ralph Smith, was often featured playing the xylophone. Before beginning a solo, Smith would say, "Hello Mokey," to his dog who, he said, was listening at home. "Hello Mokey" soon became a regular expression on the *Breakfast Club*, and once, to Smith's surprise, the cast sneaked the dog into the studio so it could bark a hello back before the solo.

Everyone appearing on the *Breakfast Club*, including the toastmaster, was open to light-hearted ribbing. Despite his reserve off-mike, McNeill often became the object of gentle ridicule by none other than himself. Here is how McNeill spent a few moments on the *Breakfast Club* in 1937 interviewing McNeill:

Don: What's your name?
McN: Don McNeill.
Don: Your full name?
McN: (*Angrily*) Donald Thomas McNeill.
Don: Well, you don't need to get sore about it.
McN: I'm not.
Don: Okay.
McN: Where were you born, McNeill?
Don: Galena, Illinois, December 23, 1907.
McN: (*Thoughtfully*) Galena—that's known as the birthplace of glory, isn't it?
Don: Yes.
McN: Because *you* were born there?
Don: Well, General Grant was born there also—that might have had something to do with it.

McN: In fact, that's the reason for it?

Don: Yes.

McN: Okay. Why did you shorten your name to Don?

Don: My parents did that—they must have known I was going
to get up early every morning on the Breakfast Club.

McN: How's that?

Don: Well, they named me Dawn McNeill.

His family continued to provide McNeill with excellent material for the show. When Tom was fourteen months old, he made his first appearance on the program. A few months later, on April 14, 1936, the McNeill's second son, Don, was born and gave his papa even more to brag about. Telling his listeners about the boys' adventures and bringing them down to the show for special broadcasts made it clear to all that McNeill was a proud and happy father and husband. In the early days of the show, he would write sketches featuring a husband and wife as they navigated their way through a marriage. During interviews, one of the first questions McNeill would typically ask guests was, "Are you married?" Whenever members of the *Breakfast Club's* orchestra became new parents or grandparents, McNeill would mention it on the air. The McNeill family was important to him but so was the family of everyone who was part of the *Breakfast Club*—cast member or listener.

Bringing Sponsors
to the Table

With the responsibilities of a growing family, McNeill looked for ways to augment his income by moonlighting on other programs. In 1937 he emceed two afternoon shows, *Tea Time at Morrells* and Coca Cola's *Refreshment Club*. He also accepted an offer to announce a musical quiz show called *Tic Toc Time* for Hyde Park Beer that required his traveling to St. Louis for the Monday night broadcasts. The transportation back to Chicago in time for the next morning's *Breakfast Club* presented problems and McNeill's boss at the network was not happy.

> As we indicated to you this morning, we have been extremely concerned about your inability to make the "Breakfast Club" program on Tuesday mornings because of your Monday evening broadcast in St. Louis. This morning's lateness which resulted in your missing the entire program is the third time on which your St. Louis engagement has interfered with the "Breakfast Club" program. The last two consecutive programs, as you know, have been missed completely.
>
> In view of the fact that it has been definitely proved that due to current transportation conditions, you cannot perform in St. Louis on Monday night and give us any assurance of being in Chicago for the "Breakfast Club"

on Tuesday morning, we demand that you terminate your St. Louis appearances immediately unless the schedule there can be changed so as not to conflict with our program.[1]

McNeill's primary loyalty was with his morning show, but the lure of extra money from these sponsored programs was great. If the *Breakfast Club* were sponsored, McNeill's paycheck would grow. Radio networks had no problem selling sponsors on buying nighttime shows with stars since listening to the radio had become routine for Americans now that over three-quarters of the homes in the United States had radios.[2] More importantly, those radios were turned on in the typical home between three and four hours per day.[3] *Amos 'n' Andy* was sponsored by Pepsodent as early as 1929, Jack Benny helped introduce Jell-O to America, and *Fibber McGee and Molly* had a long association with Johnson's Wax.

Daytime soap operas and children's shows also had successfully attracted sponsors for CBS and NBC's Red Network. The *Breakfast Club* was carried over NBC's Blue Network which did not have a stable of soap operas and was less successful in attracting sponsors. Broadcasting industry data indicate that during the late 1930s the Blue Network attracted about one third as much advertising revenue as that of the Red Network.[4] Networks, advertising agencies, and sponsors were unfamiliar with selling an early-morning program like the *Breakfast Club*, which contributed to the inertia in not finding advertisers. No doubt the reason McNeill asked his listeners to write in their comments about the program was to use those cards and letters as evidence that the program was attracting a sizable audience.

In recalling the early years of the *Breakfast Club*, McNeill often reminisced about the show's negatives: no producer, no studio audience, and no sponsors. For six years McNeill worked on and off the air to find sponsors for a show that had built loyalty among its listeners. At every opportunity McNeill would talk with advertising executives in New York and Chicago about the growth of his audience and its potential value to clients. In correspondence with an account executive with the Rockwell-O'Keefe talent agency in New York, McNeill was not bashful about promoting both the *Breakfast Club* and himself:

the Breakfast Club finished fifth in a national poll conducted by Radio Guide Magazine, being the only morning show in the first 30, and the leading daytime and only sustaining feature in that category. Every year its popularity has increased, which must mean we wear well, and it is NBC's leading unsolicited mail puller.[5]

McNeill had a sense of the value and importance radio could play in selling products, which was evidenced years earlier in his senior thesis at Marquette University. In the paper, he explored radio as an advertising and promotion medium in general and specifically for a newspaper that also owned a radio station. In the thesis, he documented how the advertising manager of the *Oakland Tribune* believed that the paper's radio station, KLX, could reach women listeners.

> A request program of popular music is broadcast from 8 to 9 A.M. It is considered that classified advertising has a particular appeal to the woman reader. She makes up the list of vacant apartments, of houses for sale, of dining room sets, and alone, or in the company of her husband, investigates them. Prior to eight o'clock she is busy with the breakfast, subsequently to nine o'clock, if she is of the apartment house world, she is out. Later in the morning she is preparing lunch, and again in the afternoon we lose her. The program is rendered on two pianos and elicits from 35 to 55 requests an hour on a single telephone line and gives opportunity for the playing of about twenty popular choruses.[6]

The awareness of who is listening and what they are doing is more often associated with marketing than show business. McNeill's thesis demonstrated his understanding of radio as a powerful sales tool, which undoubtedly drove his determination to find sponsors for the *Breakfast Club*. Whenever McNeill mentioned the lack of sponsors for his show, listeners would write in to express their surprise that advertisers did not like the program as much as the listeners did. One fan in Wyoming even volunteered to be a sponsor when he wrote: "I have never done any sponsoring, but let me know about the duties and the pay!"

The first breakthrough in finding sponsors for the *Breakfast Club* was made by local stations that carried the show when a number of these outlets successfully attracted jewelry, bakery, and grocery stores to buy time adjacent to the program or during the breaks provided to local stations by the network. Finally, in 1940, the network began an aggressive effort to sell the show to sponsors by inviting over 120 radio station marketing and advertising executives to attend a broadcast of the *Breakfast Club*. The effort paid off, because by the next year the show had attracted its first national sponsors.

A Chicago meat packer, Swift & Company, had been using radio since 1927 when the firm bought time on WLS, Chicago, to air talks by its officials about the company and its history.[7] A few years later, Swift sponsored a number of network programs including a musical and comedy team *The Stebbins Boys*, a comedy show with vaudevillians *Olsen and Johnson*, and a program for girls *Junior Nurse Corps*. The girls' show was too successful, requiring so much follow-up response for the on-air premium offers that Swift pulled out.

Swift had determined that its primary advertising goal was to reach both young and older audiences, showcase the wide variety of products under the Swift name, and reach the greatest number of listeners. The Blue Network's midwest sales manager, Edwin R. Borroff, made a pitch to Swift executives that the *Breakfast Club* and its toastmaster were made to order for the food company. As Borroff put it, "Don McNeill will not only make folks run out and buy your ham and eggs, your shortening to fry them in, your butter to spread on the morning toast, he'll draw up a chair at the breakfast table, too. He's that kind of guy."[8] Swift's advertising director Vernon Beatty liked McNeill's casual and relaxed style and even the McNeill laugh, but he was reluctant to sign because that wasn't the way Swift did business. The founder of Swift & Company, Gustavus Franklin Swift, provided the firm with a motto that it used in making all major moves. Simply stated, it was a bottom-up philosophy where the company takes its orders from "our employees, the people from whom we buy, the people to whom we sell, and our shareholders." So, after hearing Ed Borroff's sales effort, Vernon Beatty sent feelers about the value of sponsoring the morning show to a sampling of Swift's employees and other people involved with the processing and marketing of its products, including retailers and farmers. The decision was made easier by the fact that many respondents said they were already listening to the *Breakfast Club* every day and enjoyed McNeill. Swift signed a contract in January 1941 to sponsor the third quarter hour of the show every Thursday, Friday, and Saturday. Their commercials were to be heard over seventy-five of the stations along the network. Other sponsors began to show their interest in becoming part of the morning show. In November, Cream O'Wheat signed up for the final quarter hour on Fridays and Saturdays over seventy stations. When the cereal firm took a hiatus after twenty weeks, their time was replaced by Acme Paint Company for thirteen weeks, until Cream O'Wheat returned later in 1942.

Other early *Breakfast Club* sponsors included Kellogg cereals, which bought the fourth quarter during 1943 and 1944. In 1945, Philco (freezers and refrigerators) bought the final quarter hour and stayed with that time slot for many years. When Kay Daumit (Lustre Creme Shampoo) bought the first quarter hour in 1946, it marked the first time the full hour of the *Breakfast Club* was sponsored and provided the network with its only hour-long daily show to have full network sponsorship. Lustre Creme left the following year and was replaced by Toni (home permanents). After nine months Toni canceled its sponsorship of the first quarter which was picked up within a few days by General Mills (Kix) cereals which signed a one-year contract.

Beginning in 1941, the *Breakfast Club* had no problem attracting sponsors, and some of them, such as Philco and Swift, stayed with the show for many years. A closer examination of Swift's experience as a *Breakfast Club* sponsor provides an interesting case study on the value of the program to advertisers. Swift began its relationship with the *Breakfast Club* in 1941 and was billed $209,310 for the three-day per week run on 75 stations. The following year Swift increased its sponsorship to a five-day per week run on 154 stations and was billed $337,769. By 1950, Swift was buying both the second and third quarter hours and its billing reached $2.25 million which was "the biggest single-show budget in the radio business," according to *Advertising Age*.[9]

Swift did not advertise on any other show during its relationship with the *Breakfast Club* and augmented the sponsorship with an aggressive merchandising campaign. Retail store and newspaper tie-ins offered customers incentives to buy products related to the advertising on the *Breakfast Club*. Swift advertising managers were often pleasantly surprised when they tested the strength of the program to reach listeners, such as the audience pull that asked Breakfast Clubbers to write in for a mystery "something" (peanut butter jar tops/coasters). The only information given about the mystery item was that it came in four different colors. The announcement was aired on the show once a week over a three-week period, and drew 104,000 requests.[10] Contests were another way for Swift to gauge audience interest in the *Breakfast Club*. In 1941 listeners were asked to complete this poem by adding two final phrases:

There was a husband named Bill
Cold cuts he'd command
Swift's Premium he'd demand
_____
_____   11

Each week during the run of the contest, three first-prize winners would receive an RCA portable radio valued at twenty dollars and ten runner-up winners would be given five dollars. An audience pull in 1944 turned out to be too successful: Swift decided to offer charter memberships to the *Breakfast Club*, which were free and entitled card-carrying members to reserved seats whenever they attended *Breakfast Club* broadcasts in Chicago. In addition, members were invited to sign up new listeners to the *Breakfast Club* and by doing so compete for war bonds and war stamps which were to be given to both the new listener and the member. Membership materials included words to the Four Calls to Breakfast plus pictures of the cast and a card signed by McNeill. Listeners were instructed to send in their name and address so the membership cards could be prepared and mailed back.

The response was phenomenal. Nearly one million requests came in from every state and several foreign countries, to the dismay of Swift which had not anticipated the avalanche of mail. Requests for memberships arrived from such well-known people as state governors, and Supreme Court Justice William O. Douglas wrote in requesting memberships for himself and the Douglas family. Processing the memberships would require additional staff and expense to cover postage. Sizing up the situation, Swift decided to call a halt to the promotion after the first week of the drive cost them $50,000. McNeill disbanded the club, but from then on would be greeted regularly by people in the studio audience who kept their membership cards and would proudly show them to him.

Swift could certainly conclude that marketing its products on the *Breakfast Club* contributed to the company's success. In 1941 Swift's revenue was just over $1 million. By 1947, it had grown to nearly $2.25 million.[12] Obviously, other factors also contributed to the company's sales growth, such as the booming post-war economy. Strong sales helped Swift's advertising staff justify staying with the show for a continuous run of fifteen years.

Right behind Swift was Philco, which spent more than $1.5 million on the *Breakfast Club* during 1949, followed by General Mills, which also topped $1 million that year. In the ten years since attracting its first national sponsor, the *Breakfast Club* made a spectacular transformation from a sustaining program to a major revenue source for its network. The total billing to *Breakfast Club* sponsors for time costs on the network during 1949 was an impressive $4,814,049.[13]

Having found itself sponsors, the *Breakfast Club* had to make time for their commercials. From the start, the commercial messages were

CHARTER MEMBER

of the Blue Network

BREAKFAST CLUB

This card certifies that

No. 345508

IS ENTITLED TO SPECIAL RIGHTS AND
PRIVILEGES OF THE BREAKFAST CLUB

THIS CARD IS NOT
TRANSFERABLE

Don Mc Neill

PRESIDENT

Breakfast Club Charter Membership card

written so that they blended cleverly into the flow of the program. During World War II, Swift's advertising reflected the nation's concern about winning the war. A typical week of commercials scheduled for Tuesday "Food Fights for Freedom Day," for Wednesday "Cooperation with Government Campaign Day," for Thursday and Saturday "Product Days," and for Friday "Martha Logan Day," which featured the Swift home economist's tips on how to prepare Swift products. A year after the war had ended, Swift used some of its commercial time to promote a humanitarian effort to help feed hungry Europeans. The *"Breakfast Club* Share-a-Meal Plan" was responsible for collecting nearly forty-eight tons of food that listeners mailed to the Salvation Army headquarters in New York. From there, the food was sent in eleven-pound packages to people in Belgium, France, Holland, and Norway.[14]

McNeill could be counted on to provide sponsors with a solid and clear pitch for their product. His approach was not satirical or combative like some other radio performers, who often denigrated their sponsors. In contrast, McNeill's on-air selling style could be characterized as down-to-earth and sincere, mixed with enthusiasm. One sponsor remarked that when sitting in the studio control booth during a *Breakfast Club* broadcast he was spellbound by the blissful expressions on the faces of the live audience when McNeill began a commercial. The adman said he simply "loved to watch their faces."

Perhaps the key ingredient of McNeill's success as a radio salesman was the way he cultivated listeners' loyalty by showing he had respect for them every day they tuned him in.

One morning in 1945 while talking to a young boy in the audience, McNeill led into a Kix commercial by asking the chap if he liked the cereal with cream and sugar. The boy shouted, "I hate 'em." Not to be deterred, the next day when ten-year-old Tom McNeill paid a visit to his dad's show, McNeill tried the same approach. "What do you think of Kix with cream and sugar?" the toastmaster asked. Tom replied "They're dandy, I eat two bowls every day. It gives me a lot of pep and energy."

"That's fine," said McNeill as he launched into the commercial.

"Pop," interrupted Tom. "Did I say it all right?"

Through the years McNeill continued to have fun with commercials and the studio audience. During the 1960s he was sponsored by Archway Cookies which had been featuring an eating contest with children selected from the studio audience. Each of the youngsters were given four cookies and McNeill was ready to begin the contest when one girl piped out, "I don't like 'em." McNeill replied, "How do you know if you haven't tried them? Do you like some cookies?" To which the girl said, "Yes." The crew scrambled for other Archway cookies, and put them in front of the girl. McNeill asked if she would like to try them. She screwed up her face and said, "They're terrible." More cookies arrived. McNeill asked if she would try them, but each time she said, "No." McNeill ended his ordeal with the observation, "If everyone liked Archway Cookies, they wouldn't need to sponsor this show."

McNeill undoubtedly felt the girl's honesty added believability and reality to the show. That is surely why he also decided not to edit out a young boy's reaction when asked if he drank Kool-Aid. McNeill kept asking his young guest whether or not he liked the drink until the boy finally blurted out that it gave him pimples. Since the show was taped for rebroadcast, the remark could have been snipped out but McNeill let it go as it was.[15]

McNeill rarely made mistakes himself while reading commercials, but one morning in 1962 during a remote broadcast from Chicago's Trade Fair at McCormick Place he fluffed a word. Here is how he read a spot for Frank's Red Hot Sauce:

There are more red peppers per bottle than any other hot sauce you tried. . . . Those peckers—ah—those peppers are picked at their prime, blended, processed, and aged in oaken caskets just like fine sherry.[16]

There were plenty of snickers filtering through the audience and among the cast after McNeill fluffed the word but the program continued normally. McNeill even chuckled a bit before moving to the next feature.

McNeill enjoyed a laugh with the audience but never in a way that would compromise his role as a radio salesman. He even looked the part by coming off more like a marketing executive than an entertainer.[17] McNeill's personality was that of an ordinary and likable chap rather than dynamic, comic, or even lovable. McNeill didn't overwhelm the message he was sending and, at the same time, communicated the type of trust listeners might have in a close friend or neighbor. Advertisers who had been associated with the *Breakfast Club* soon learned the value of McNeill's less-than-dynamic style and were lining up, waiting for available spots on the show.[18] McNeill was committed to having an enjoyable visit with the audience and this approach gave him the freedom to make everything on the show entertaining.

> "Fun Radio" has been my life . . . if it hadn't been fun all these years, I don't think I would have stuck with it . . . and I'm sure I can say the same for our listeners and sponsors. We even make our commercials fun to do, and every one of our current sponsors have asked that we continue to do so. Which, to me, means that our brand of fun radio is moving their products, as well as entertaining our audience.
>
> I have tried to create intimacy with the Breakfast Club . . . make it a program that's there . . . in the home. Tried to make our cast and our personalities real people . . . just like those at home . . . with the same problems and feelings. And our mail tells us that our listeners accept us that way. . . . "We look upon you as members of our own family." . . . How many thousands of times I've read that in letters.
>
> Such a close feeling has developed a loyalty among our listeners that, through the years, certainly has and is paying off for our sponsors . . . and it has certainly made friends for our program . . . and our network . . . and our stations.[19]

Radio Guide magazine conducted an annual poll of radio listeners who were asked to vote for their favorite emcee. The listener poll results showed that McNeill jumped from tenth in 1936 to the poll's most popular emcee in 1940. More citations came from other magazines, when McNeill was selected "Radio's Star of Stars" by *Movie & Radio Guide* (1941) and the Breakfast Club was chosen the "Favorite Morning Program" by *Movie & Radio Guide* (1942).

The recognition received by McNeill and the show made the network and sponsors very pleased that they were in on something that was a solid and long-term success. So the future of the *Breakfast Club* was secured by the fact that it became a major revenue source for its network. What was not certain, however, was who would own that network. In 1941, the Federal Communications Commission (FCC) ruled that no local station could affiliate with a company that operated more than one radio network. The ruling would require NBC to divest either its Red or Blue system. Although the action was challenged by a New York District Court, it was eventually upheld by the U.S. Supreme Court.[20] In anticipation of the higher court's decision, in January 1942 NBC began the process of giving its weaker network a separate identity by calling it "The Blue Network." In addition, NBC began an aggressive effort to attract sponsors to make the entity more attractive to potential buyers. NBC's commitment to find sponsors for programs on the Blue Network contributed to the *Breakfast Club*'s success in reaching full sponsorship. Blue Network revenues practically doubled from what they were in 1941 to nearly $25 million in 1943.[21] The preening worked and NBC found a buyer, industrialist Edward J. Noble, who owned Life Savers, Inc. Noble paid NBC $8 million for the network of 116 affiliates plus three stations. He also owned a New York City radio station, WMCA, and therefore was no stranger to broadcasting. On December 30, 1944, the Blue Network became the American Broadcasting Company and, from that day on, ABC embarked on a long struggle to compete with its two major rivals, NBC and CBS. In the daytime hours, those networks had developed schedules filled with soap operas that had a loyal following of both listeners and advertisers. Unfortunately, ABC had only a few daytime dramas. Rather than endure the expense of building competing soaps, ABC relied on the proven success of the *Breakfast Club* to build audiences and attract sponsors. The *Breakfast Club* provided a reliable revenue stream and, in addition, helped ABC capture an audience for programs that followed it.

5

The Wartime Silent Prayer Becomes a Tradition

For the McNeills, 1941 began as a happy year because their family became complete with the birth of their third son, Bob, on St. Patrick's Day. The mood of the nation that year was influenced by concerns over the hostilities in Europe and the increased likelihood that the country would go to war. Those concerns were shown to be real following Japan's surprise attack on Pearl Harbor on December 7, which resulted in President Roosevelt's declaration of war on Japan the next day. Germany and Italy responded by declaring war against the United States and on December 11 Congress made the same declaration against the Axis powers.

In December 1941, McNeill turned thirty-four and was eager to serve his nation, but a back problem and flat feet, which had kept him from playing sports in school, prevented his signing up for active duty. Like many Americans, he found a role at home that was as important as any part he might have played overseas.

The *Breakfast Club* was one of the first shows to be regularly transcribed and sent to stations maintained by the Armed Forces Radio Service on military bases abroad. The one-hour broadcast was recorded on sixteen-inch platters, which were reproduced and mailed to the stations making up the military base network. These transcriptions were distributed to the Armed

Forces stations two to three weeks after the original broadcast, so the material was still current and a duplicate of the original broadcast, except that the commercials had been edited out. Through Armed Forces Radio the breakfast table was stretched to provide a link between service men and women and their families back home.

War had taken over the national consciousness and this fact was reflected in almost every aspect of the *Breakfast Club*. During one wartime broadcast of the show McNeill greeted a woman in the audience who said she worked the graveyard shift in a war plant, and when she got home would invariably fall asleep while listening to the *Breakfast Club*. Wanting her to feel comfortable, McNeill asked that a couch be brought in and invited her to lie down.[1]

Strangers who were in the studio audience often would be introduced to one another by McNeill during an interview, and when he sensed a good match he would send them away with a gift of a free dinner that night. That's how Harry Eumont and Pat Murry met. Later they wrote McNeill to express their gratitude: "Dear Sir: We're writing you in regard to the meeting of the Breakfast Club on the morning of September 13, 1944 when an Army Lt. met a Cadet Nurse and spent a swell evening as guests of Don McNeill. We had a wonderful time and we have made future plans together."

McNeill, who smoked at the time, encouraged everyone to smoke a new brand, "No Cigarettes," in order to help with wartime tobacco shortages. The specially printed pack advertised: "no butts, no ashes, no ifs, no ands, put plain, no cigarettes." In a more serious vein, the *Breakfast Club* began featuring a series of interviews with war plant workers to encourage civilians to take up the call for more defense employees. Other activities to help the war effort included the National Paper Salvage Drive, which the *Breakfast Club* helped initiate in 1943. At every opportunity, McNeill and the rest of the cast would visit as many military camps and hospitals as their broadcast schedule would allow. By 1943, at least fifteen members of the *Breakfast Club* orchestra and staff had joined the armed forces.

War Bond rallies were common during the war years and the *Breakfast Club* helped organize one of the more successful. It was a National Breakfast honoring American heroes held simultaneously in cities across the nation on July 17, 1942 with the *Breakfast Club* providing the connecting link among the various sites. McNeill originated the show from Chicago's breakfast site, the Grand Ballroom of the Hotel Stevens (later renamed the Conrad Hilton), where over two thousand were assembled. During the event, McNeill interviewed

Illinois Governor Dwight Green, Chicago Mayor Edward Kelly, Army Air Corpsman Lieutenant Thomas Griffin, a Chicagoan who was the flight navigator during General Jimmy Doolittle's April 1942 attack on Tokyo, parents of other war heroes, plus an assortment of people who were invited to the breakfast. These included a sailor who had been aboard the aircraft carrier *Lexington* when it went down in the Pacific in May 1942, railroad workers, Pullman conductors, and volunteers selling war bonds.

Commercial announcements during the broadcast were geared toward the theme of the special program. Swift announced that 90 percent of its employees were participating in a wage reduction program which diverted payroll dollars to help purchase tanks and other weapons. McNeill interviewed a Montana sheep herder who said he made his own breakfast so he would have extra money to buy bonds. McNeill often had trouble during the broadcast moving among the tightly packed crowd in the ballroom. One waitress got impatient with his blocking her ability to serve the table where he was doing an interview and she yelled out that she was carrying "Oscar Mayer sausages." McNeill replied, "I'm a Swift man myself." Singers Jack Baker and Marion Mann plus the Escorts and Betty provided music for the occasion by singing several songs associated with World War I, "Till We Meet Again," "It's a Long Way to Tipperary," and "Don't Sit under the Apple Tree with Anyone Else but Me."

The National Breakfast was successful in raising $25 million in war bond pledges and in the process demonstrated the power and reach of McNeill and his radio show.[2] In the final year of the war, the *Breakfast Club* went to Washington, D.C., to help inaugurate the seventh War Loan Drive for the Treasury Department. While in the capital city McNeill and his wife got more than the usual tourist tour of the White House as evidenced by the note Kay wrote home.[3]

Dear Boys,
    Daddy and I had a thrill we will never forget. Today at 12:30 we were inside the White House—met lots of guards who ushered us into the President's outer office. We met his secretary and saw Ickes come out. Then, we were called in—shook hands with President Truman and had a nice visit with him. He is very handsome and very nice. He showed us a large map of Germany and we saw a beautiful rose garden.

Love,
Mama

The tour continued to several eastern cities where it raised $7 million in bond pledges. Later, McNeill took the show to his hometown, Sheboygan, Wisconsin, and brought in another $621,000 worth of pledges.

A rather unusual bond drive occurred in 1943 in Evanston, Illinois—an author's rally. The *Breakfast Club* originated from the event, and McNeill interviewed several authors including Stanley Johnson, the *Chicago Tribune*'s war correspondent and author of *Grim Reaper* and *Queen of the Flat-tops*. Johnson discussed his experiences aboard the U.S.S. *Lexington* during the Coral Sea Battle of 1942 when it was sunk by the Japanese.

Frequently the show would travel to military camps and hospitals in the Chicago area where they would entertain servicemen and women and give listeners a sense of involvement with the military effort. The psychological support the *Breakfast Club* gave to the war was not lost on the military, which honored McNeill in a number of ways. The Army named him an honorary sergeant major at Fort Sheridan, north of Chicago, and the Marine Corps gave him the title of reserve recruiting officer.

Just as in civilian homes, the habit of waking up to the Four Calls to Breakfast was part of military life. Here is how a seaman second class from Chicago, who was hospitalized at the naval facility on Treasure Island, San Francisco, put it: "Keep us laughing. The Breakfast Club really entertains all of us in our ward and when your gang gives to the War Bond effort it really thrills me." From Austin, Texas, Corporal M. K. Dickler described the typical morning at his air base, "Throughout the barracks every morning it's your Breakfast Club. I've noticed the enthusiastic reaction of the enlisted men not only in our outfit, but all over Bergstrom Field." McNeill's efforts to help sell war bonds were appreciated by the U.S. Treasury Department which awarded him their Distinguished Service Certificate in 1945. That same year the Veterans of Foreign Wars presented McNeill with the organization's good citizenship medal.

The war pushed the country into coming to terms with its beliefs about patriotism and tolerance and McNeill didn't hesitate to let the *Breakfast Club* become a forum for the sharing of those values. One letter he read on the air reflected the beliefs of a listener about why the United States was at war with Germany:

Dear Don McNeill:

I am not a Catholic nor a Protestant, but I am an American. I believe I am as patriotic and loyal to my country as any good

American. But I certainly feel let down when time after time you hear people who continually say we do nothing for our country and we are only parasites and should be annihilated. "That Hitler is doing one smart thing by getting rid of the Jews."

Sitting on a bus I heard a man make that remark. Do you wonder why I am writing you, telling you my story? Asking you to tell our America just what one little Jewish family so far has done.

My oldest son, who was 18 years old, gave his life for his country while on extra hazardous duty on his ship somewhere on the Atlantic Ocean. He died two weeks before Pearl Harbor.

My second son will be going soon as an Army Air Cadet. My husband gave up a fine job to work for defense.

My two youngest boys help gather scrap and made a beautiful Victory Garden. And my little girl, who is 3½ years old, sings "God Bless America."

I am a Nurses Aid and give between 5 and 10 hours a week in a hospital.

Should we be annihilated? Born and raised as Americans . . . doing our little bit, but I think the little bit that means so much with other little bits that are being done. And I know if there is more we can do we will be the first to do it. Yet do you wonder the way I feel that people should say such things? And I know there are other Jewish families that have done as much and more, and get the same slap in the face.

But with it all we still go on singing, "God Bless America."

After three years of American participation in the fighting, the Allied forces were gaining. In the *Breakfast Club's* annual yearbook highlighting the year's events on the program Kay described the excitement related to D-day, June 6, 1944, in the McNeill household.

Before we as much as had a sip of coffee, our smug little world was turned topsy-turvy by a news bulletin we all know was inevitable . . . "under the command of General Eisenhower, Allied naval forces supported by strong air forces, began landing Allied armies this morning on the northern coast of France."

I looked at Don. He started to say something, but only managed to mutter, "This is it!" patted the boys' arms, kissed me goodbye, and dashed for the car.

On the way down to the studio, he told me later, he began to formulate a fitting way to observe this important day. Before he reached the highway he had the formula. First, clear the way for the omission of commercials, play patriotic music, offer up a prayer, stand by for news flashes, and PRAY.

"D" Day is here—the day of deliverance for men who would be free again—the day of liberation. While our first impulse when hearing this glorious news—that the long awaited hour has finally arrived—is one of exultation and thrills, when we stop to ponder for a moment . . . the tremendous implications of what is now happening, we pause . . . we pray.

You mothers, sweethearts, fathers—all of you who have someone near and dear to you this day over there— and the rest of us, too—every loyal believer in our cause of righteousness—MUST PRAY TODAY—that's all we can do. Those of you who are incapacitated who cannot even leave your beds . . . here, you shut-in Breakfast Clubbers must lead us today—in prayer.

O, Great God of Justice! Watch over them today. They have waited so long for this—their hour. You too, dear Lord, had Your hour of pain and suffering before deliverance. May all of our brave sons and daughters, with Your Divine Help have the same fortitude and understanding to keep their spirits in legion with Yours. Until they, too, may see that glorious hour of enlightenment for all men, for which we fight. God, we trust in Thee. We leave our sons with Yours this day. Smile down on them in Thy mercy. We need You, today.[4]

The emotional energy McNeill expressed in that message is an indication of the responsibility he accepted to lead his listeners in supporting the national goal of winning the war. In many important ways, the *Breakfast Club* was helping people to get through the war with good music and fun, plus a bit of nostalgia to help begin the day in a positive way. But reflecting on the strain caused by the war, McNeill felt more was needed,

I believed that prayer—the greatest single force in the world—was urgently needed at this moment while we were at war. Our Breakfast Club mothers, fathers and sweethearts . . . needed a vehicle through which they could spiritually unite with their boys and friends overseas as the last supreme efforts were being made to bring order out of chaos.

Family prayer, I believed, was the vehicle. For 12 years the Breakfast Club family had laughed, sung, marched and reminisced together. Why not pray together?[5]

So on Saturday, October 28, 1944 during the second quarter hour of the show, McNeill asked the audience,

All over the nation,
Each in his own words,
Each in his own way,
For a world united in Peace—
Bow your heads, and let us pray!

There were nearly five hundred in the studio audience that day and each head was bowed, following the example set by members of the cast and orchestra. The prayer brought strong reactions from listeners, which ranged from those who felt it was out of place in an entertainment program to those who admired the courage it took to start the feature. Reflecting back on Prayer Time as it was to be called, McNeill saw it as a temporary feature designed to help the nation weather the war, but when 90 percent of the letters from listeners urged that the prayer be kept McNeill changed his mind. Many had their own need for personal support, like members of Alcoholics Anonymous who used the Prayer Time as a reminder to stay on track with their program. A St. Paul, Minnesota, newspaper columnist wrote about a young woman who worried that she would fall off the wagon by quoting her as saying, "One thing that has helped me stay on keel is Don McNeill's Breakfast Club program. During his moment of silent prayer I always ask God to help me. In two years, He has never failed."[6]

A twenty-four-year-old Ohio farmer wrote that he stopped whatever he was doing to say a prayer along with McNeill. A woman from the same state wrote McNeill that "you may be the only Bible some folks know." Another woman wrote, "My ten-year-old son has been flippant about church going, but this morning during your Prayer Time I looked in from the kitchen and saw him bowing his head over his plate. Thanks McNeill, as only a mother can say."[7] Often parents would send McNeill photos of their children standing silently by the radio praying, presumably during the silent observance.

Typically, Prayer Time would begin about 8:23 A.M., but one morning the schedule was packed with special guests and the segment had not occurred. By 8:40 calls started jamming the network's switchboard complaining that children were ready to go to school but could not because they had not said their morning prayer. The producers scrambled to rearrange the remaining minutes to fit in the silent prayer plus a hymn.

True to *Breakfast Club* tradition, listeners began writing McNeill with suggestions for special prayer themes. As a result of those suggestions, a silent prayer of thanksgiving for all the blessings received during the week was inaugurated on Fridays. Listeners reported that Prayer Time helped them deal with family-related problems, like the mother of five who wrote that she had finally decided to give her husband a divorce, but when she heard McNeill ask for a moment of prayer "for families separated because of misunderstandings" she reconsidered. Her husband returned home the next evening and she thanked McNeill for providing the guidance they needed and, reflecting on her good fortune, suggested that a prayer be offered for "better family understanding."

Saturday, April 14, 1945, was a sad day in America. President Roosevelt died two days earlier and his body was being transported by train from Warm Springs, Georgia, to Washington, D.C. The *Breakfast Club* that morning was a subdued affair with no applause or songs. The program that day reflected the sorrowful mood of a nation which had lost its symbol of leadership. McNeill calmly told about the horse-drawn caisson which thirty minutes later was scheduled to take the president's casket from Union Station to the White House where a "simple Episcopalian funeral ceremony" would be held in the East Room that afternoon. McNeill reported that American flags were at half staff around the world, even on the front lines in Germany and on Okinawa. He then recapped the latest war news which included successful strikes by U.S. bombers at German defenses on the French coast. Ninth Army infantrymen were reported to be running into heavy enemy fire forty-five miles from Berlin. German anti-aircraft guns were being used against ground troops in a desperate attempt to defend the city. Three other American armies were only a hundred miles from the Russian border and the Russian allied troops were nearing Prague and the mountains of southern Germany. In the Pacific War news, he said Tokyo had been battling fires all night after receiving attacks from as many as 450 American B-29 bombers. McNeill relayed that "the Jap broadcasters have informed the home folks that the fighting on Okinawa seems to be changing for the worse" with the enemy losing over 250 planes, one having gone down only two hundred yards from the flagship of Admiral Richard Turner.

McNeill read a poem which he said "was found on several bodies of unknown Yanks who were killed in action" titled "Conversion" by Francis Anger Meyer. In it the soldier tells God how even though he had never known him before, he now feels his presence and is ready to face death.

In the audience that day was a church-school basketball team made up of boys ages ten through twelve. The youngsters had memorized a Bible verse, which they recited in unison. Next, McNeill talked with a woman who was from Vienna, Austria, who proudly told him that she was the first refugee to become a Girl Scout leader. Her husband was active with the Cub Scouts as were their two children. She expressed the hope that America would help make the rest of the world as happy as she has been here. The program ended with a tribute to Franklin Roosevelt read by actor Frederick March in New York followed by live coverage from Washington of the funeral cortege.

Even though the war news was increasingly optimistic, there were still reports of death and loss which made anyone with a family member overseas uneasy. On May 7, 1945, everyone listening to the *Breakfast Club* at home or in the studio felt the significance of the Silent Prayer. Following the day's prayer, Nancy Martin was singing "Oh What a Beautiful Morning" when suddenly the program was interrupted by the sound of striking teletype keys followed by the excited voice of a network newsman in New York who said there were unconfirmed reports that the German army had surrendered. The program was returned to Chicago, and Nancy Martin, still waiting to conclude her song, exclaimed: "It really is a beautiful morning—it really is."

In the spirit of the celebration, McNeill observed, "We've heard the wonderful news and I know we're all straining at the leash. There are those among us, however, whose loss has left them with no cause to rejoice. Let's remember them in the hour of victory in the West and gird ourselves for victory in the East." Ten minutes later another interruption from the Blue Network newsroom repeated the first announcement with additional details on the German surrender. After the network returned to Chicago, McNeill focused the energy in the audience by saying: "Well folks, this seems to be it. Let's stand up and give those cheers we've been holding back." The audience roared.

McNeill signed off that day by putting into words a sense of how the nation was dealing with the good news:

> I think if you could look into the homes of millions of Americans today, you might find a composite picture of a mother on her knees—a wife breathing a prayer—a child not quite understanding, but yet with some strange emotion—some unexplained feeling of awe and reverence. . . . I think today we're all going to talk to old friends. . . . We are going to talk quietly and calmly and reverently and hopefully.[8]

The silent prayer succeeded as an element on the *Breakfast Club* because listeners could sense how sincerely McNeill felt about the need for prayer. His willingness to pray publicly resulted in some listeners projecting their faith onto him. For example, he often received letters that began: "I know you are a Methodist," "You must be a Christian Scientist," "You're Episcopalian, aren't you?" In reality, McNeill and his family were Roman Catholic and members of the Saints Faith, Hope, and Charity parish in Winnetka.

The McNeills were accustomed to praying and when they were confronted with a family scare found even greater consolation in its value. Twelve-year-old Tom woke up one morning in September 1947 complaining of violent headaches and nausea despite being fine the day before. The McNeills located the best doctor available to diagnose Tom's condition and after making his examination, he suggested they all go downstairs and have a cigarette. The physician began by saying "I have some news for you that isn't too good, but I want you to take it in the right way. With the faith you have in prayers, I don't think it will be any problem. Tom has polio."[9] He then asked Kay and McNeill to wrap Tom in a blanket and take him to the hospital near their home. At the hospital they waited for more news, and what they learned was that their son was paralyzed and the likelihood of his walking again was not good. The doctor advised the family to go about their usual routine and even suggested that McNeill keep a golf date.

By the time McNeill reached the golf course he found it difficult to think about anything but Tom and decided to turn around and drive back home. Kay had gone home but soon afterward was drawn back to the hospital to check on Tom. There she found the ward where the boy was taken and could see him through a window lying on a board perfectly still except that he was crying.[10] Resigned that there was nothing to be done, she turned away and left. By now, McNeill had returned from his failed attempt to play golf and they sat down to dinner in silence. According to Kay, her husband became a hero at that moment when he suggested they stop trying to eat and "plan something that would really please Tom." They cleared away the plates and began drawing cartoons and writing little messages and poems to cheer Tom. Everyday McNeill would draw a cartoon and take it to the hospital, and on her daily visits, Kay would report family news to Tom. In addition, both parents prayed regularly for their son's recovery.

One week after the initial attack, the doctor told them that Tom was moving a leg, which McNeill took as a sign his boy would be all right, and the next morning, for the first time, he told the radio audience about the ordeal that he and the family had been undergoing. He asked the orchestra to play a song Tom enjoyed. Then during Prayer Time McNeill asked everyone to join him in thanking God for Tom's signs of recovery. They did and soon their letters, cards, and gifts started arriving, 15,000 of them. Between the prayers and cards, something worked, because within three weeks Tom was able to leave the hospital and continue recuperating at home, where with all his free time he began a stamp collection drawn from the mail he received. Within a month he was completely recovered and began resuming a normally active life. The following year he was well enough to play on New Trier High School's freshman football team. On his first visit to the *Breakfast Club* after the polio scare, Tom thanked his dad's audience this way: "I had everyone scared for a while, even myself, but because of your millions of prayers God did me a swell favor. This polio bug zoomed in and out of me on a non-stop flight."

The advantage of a silent prayer was that it invited anyone and everyone to participate without casting favor on any one faith. The ecumenical prayer was apropos for radio and other non-restrictive groups, which is why it was proposed for a body like the United Nations which was being formed after the war. McNeill, along with others including Florida Representative Emory Price, encouraged the world organization to adopt a silent prayer. In 1947 the U.N. began opening all general sessions with a silent prayer.[11] In time, the practice was also adopted by many college and professional sports teams.

There were other inspiring aspects to the *Breakfast Club* which the show's cast helped plan and participate in. In 1945 they decided to help servicemen who had missed spending the last few Christmas seasons with their families because of being stationed thousands of miles from home. The cast decided to make up for the lost family holiday by having a Christmas in July party for twenty-five servicemen and their families. The warm Chicago weather did not deter the festivities or the emotion on the faces of the servicemen when Santa Claus distributed gifts to their children and wives.

McNeill was not inclined to preach or editorialize on his show, but instead used humor and poetry to get his ideas before the audience. The prayer afforded him a non-verbal way to communicate his commitment to making the world a better place. It was as if the moment of silence (twenty seconds) was his special gift to a harried nation which otherwise would not take the time for contemplation. The prayer continued as a part of every McNeill broadcast thereafter, with one addition in 1961 when he inserted the word *free* into the final phrase, "for a free world united in peace, let us bow our heads and pray."

6

Aunt Fanny
Joins the
Growing Cast

Chicago is a great convention city because it is centrally located, easy to reach, and fun to visit. By the mid-1940s, a major attraction for the thousands of conventioneers was to attend the *Breakfast Club*. Sitting in the audience had become so popular that it was not unusual for there to be hundreds more visitors than the 450 seats in Studio A at the Merchandise Mart could accommodate. One day in June 1941 audience cards indicated that the guests came from twenty-five states.[1] The demand to see the show was so great that the network began requiring guests to write in for tickets at least two weeks prior to the broadcast they wished to attend and, in the summer, four weeks notice was necessary. Printed on the tickets were pictures of the cast plus space for audience members to write their questions, comments, gags, or funny life experiences. Guests had until 7:30 A.M. to claim their reserved seats. When they arrived at the Merchandise Mart, the building's long-time elevator starter, Herman Benning, directed them to the express elevators to the nineteenth floor. As they entered the studio, the audience cards were collected so McNeill and his staff could cull out the most interesting for possible interviews.

One morning McNeill selected a card which read: "I walked up nineteen floors to see you. I get sick riding elevators." McNeill asked the writer to come forward and to his surprise a frail, older woman stood up. The cast scrambled to find a cot so she could rest after her hearty climb to Studio A.[2]

Thumbing through the cards one morning, the staff came across a card without any comments, but with an eye-catching signature, Norman Rockwell. It immediately sparked McNeill's interest since the illustrator had been a role model for McNeill, who studied cartoon artistry in high school and college. McNeill strode into the audience and asked, "Is Norman Rockwell here?" Sure enough, a thin arm raised and they had a delightful on-air chat.[3]

Every morning McNeill went into the audience with a live mike, which could backfire if he didn't keep alert to what guests might say or do. By contemporary standards, the concerns seem unnecessarily squeamish, like the day McNeill announced he was going to interview two young servicemen who were celebrating something (they both were on their honeymoon) and asked them to identify themselves. When a sailor and a soldier came up to the mike, McNeill asked one of them if he knew what he had in common with the other. Seeing a funny, shy look come over the young man's face, McNeill moved the microphone behind his back before the man spoke so no one in the home audience could hear his answer. Listeners never learned what the two couples shared unless they wrote in for a copy of the annual *Breakfast Club Yearbook*, "Don's Other Life," which reported the serviceman's response, "Are they expecting?"

Over 130,000 copies of that yearbook were sold to listeners who wanted to learn more about the show and see photos of the cast. One letter requesting the 1942 yearbook should have caught the mail room's attention. It was addressed to "Mr. Don McNeal" and read, "Will you kindly send me your Breakfast Club Book, in payment of which I am enclosing one dollar." It was signed John Edgar Hoover and was written on the letterhead of the Federal Bureau of Investigation.

Listeners could depend on having fun every time they tuned into the *Breakfast Club*, in part because McNeill had plenty of help in the humor department. Although he could deliver a pretty good monologue of one-liners, his usual style was to be part of an interplay with other characters on the show. The character who embodied much of the fun associated with the program was Sam Cowling, who was first heard on the program as the lead singer and guitarist for the Three Romeos in 1937. Cowling began his radio career as a singer on a number of major stations including WLW, Cincinnati, and WHAS, Louisville, and within a few years migrated to NBC, Chicago, where he appeared on Garry Moore's *Club Matinee*.

By the time World War II was underway two of the Romeos, Lou Perkins and Gil Jones, had left for active duty and Cowling began to show more promise as a comic than as a singer. Cowling certainly looked the part, standing five feet, seven inches and weighing over two hundred pounds, but even more than his looks was his seemingly effortless ability to come forth with a funny quip, gag, or story. Also, much of his humor became visual for the studio audience, such as his daily leading of the kids and brave adults during March Time. Cowling would lead the entourage down aisles, across peoples' feet, out and in studio doors until the whole assemblage was in chaos. The scramble he created made the ritual a truly funny and human event for the studio audience which was also communicated to listeners at home.

The contrast between McNeill and Cowling was dramatic. Aside from their differing heights, McNeill was dignified and debonair while Cowling acted clumsy and comical. The differences between the two were made clear to the studio audience when, seconds before air time, the warm-up announcer would introduce McNeill as "the man you probably came to see" and as McNeill greeted the audience Cowling would shout, "Take off your shoes and loosen your girdles" before being laughingly pushed away by McNeill. The slight shove would propel Cowling onto the lap of an unsuspecting woman in the front row. The studio audience's laughter would be picked up just as the program began—an enticement for the home audience to stay tuned to the merriment.

As a result of his forays into women's laps, Cowling's face was soon covered with blotches of lipstick, his tie and shirt were soon disheveled. His daily antics were like a clown's behavior on the periphery of the main ring and served to keep the studio audience amused and involved with the show. When Philco sponsored the fourth quarter, Cowling would ruffle the announcer, Bob Murphy, at the microphone just as the segment was about to begin. While the orchestra played the Philco theme and as Murphy prepared to read his introduction, Cowling and singer Johnny Desmond would grab the script from Murphy's hands. Murphy would frantically take part of it back, but Cowling and Desmond would snatch the lion's share. Cowling and Murphy would end up holding a tiny wedge of paper and at the right moment would shout "Philco" into the microphone and the show would continue while the audience watched with amazement that the opening went so smoothly.

Cowling's transition from singer to comic didn't please all Breakfast Clubbers. A loyal listener wrote McNeill as follows:

For the past several weeks I've been in a hospital with 14 broken ribs. As a result I've had a chance to give more attention to my favorite radio program, the Breakfast Club, and I'd like to make a suggestion. Why don't you let Sam sing more? I don't know how his voice may sound in your studio, but by the time it gets out here, it's a wonderful cowboy tenor.[4]

The loyal listener was U.S. Supreme Court Justice William O. Douglas, who maintained a lively correspondence with McNeill, offering suggestions and observations about *Breakfast Club* lore and especially Sam Cowling.

By nature, Cowling was a very funny man. He wrote his own material and in 1943 Cowling began a *Breakfast Club* feature, "Fiction and Fact from Sam's Almanac," in which he drew from his ability to create deadpan humor out of inverted quips, puns, and satire. His material often dealt with marriage:

> Your conscience is what makes you tell your wife before someone else does.
>
> The best way to keep a husband is in doubt.
>
> A man should work eight hours and sleep eight hours, but not at the same time.
>
> In Paw Paw, Michigan, if you are facing East and want to face West, turn around.
>
> The best way to make a picket fence is to give him a sword.
>
> The best way to get out of cleaning a rug is to beat it.
>
> The best way to drive a baby buggy is to tickle its feet.
>
> It is a well-known fact that if you eat vegetables for 87 years you won't die young.
>
> It is almost impossible to play cards on a boat if someone is sitting on the deck.[5]

Cowling typically read four entries from his Almanac and each was punctuated by a raspberry squeal from the brass section of the orchestra. Regular listeners could detect a parallel theme between the Fiction and Facts and Cowling's repartee on the show about mothers-in-law, weight, drinking, and sloth. Although Cowling wrote the bulk of his material, listeners knew his taste and frequently sent in their quips, which, if they were good enough, he would use on the air.

Another *Breakfast Club* singer who turned comic was Fran Allison, who began her career on radio as a singer but showed an even stronger talent playing a rural spinster. Three days a week McNeill would ask rhetorically, "How would you like to meet your old friend Aunt Fanny?" and she would stride in wearing a long 1890s-style dress. Aunt Fanny would always arrive a bit out of breath with a story or strong opinion to share with "Mister MackNeel." Her routine was usually interrupted three or more times by "phone calls" from her friends back home around which she developed her comedic storyline. One morning McNeill noted he was glad she was back after having a minor operation and wondered if "they found out what she had?" She replied, "Well, yes, within a dollar or two." In the middle of discussing the surgery, she was interrupted by the ring of a telephone. McNeill answered and then obligingly turned to Aunt Fanny and said, "It's for you." Aunt Fanny shouted "Hallooo" into the mouthpiece and ended up listening to the caller, Nettie Kennicutt, talk about her operation. Saying goodbye, Aunt Fanny hung up and resumed telling McNeill about her experience but another phone call from another home-town friend, Orphie Hackett, stopped her. After listening to a third caller, Aunt Fanny hung up and told McNeill, "If the next caller asks what I had out, tell her the telephone," and to the strains of "Bird in a Gilded Cage" Aunt Fanny made her exit.

One morning when the *Breakfast Club* was visiting Los Angeles Aunt Fanny told McNeill about her trip to the Santa Anita Race Track.

> It's a beautiful place, but I couldn't understand why they spoiled the view with a big board out in the front yard just for the horses' social security numbers. The horse show was so bad, some people took tickets back to windows to get their money back. Other people were so mad they tore their tickets up. Funny thing, though, I saw those same people go right back and buy new tickets.

The urbane McNeill would smile patiently while Aunt Fanny gossiped on about her friend Bert Beerbower's fondness for alcohol or her problems finding Lutie Larson a birthday present since the only thing that would fit her would be a handkerchief. When the McNeill family was moving into a new home, Aunt Fanny was prepared with housewarming presents such as a feather mattress or a set of flowery slipcovers which she was going to install personally. McNeill wasn't at all thrown by her style, since he relied on slightly daffy women to liven up his early radio shows. McNeill wrote the sayings of a mythical Angelian Glutz into his early *Breakfast Club* scripts. Betty Winkler played his dumb stenographer in the ill-fated *Pontiac Show* in 1934 and McNeill often reflected on Juliet, a dumb dame, during his repartee when he starred on *Tic Toc Time* from St. Louis.

Allison's characters were purely fictional, or at least that was her intention. One morning she told everyone about her possible good fortune that she had heard about in a letter from her cousin Ross Biggers in Oklahoma City, who wrote that her uncle had willed her an oil well. The only problem was that the well was underneath a post office. To Allison's surprise, the deputy sheriff of Oklahoma City, a Ross Biggers, wrote that people told him about hearing his name mentioned on the show. Biggers also informed her that oil had been discovered under the governor's mansion.

Some chance connections were more strongly communicated, as when Allison was informed by a Lutie Larson to stop using her name on the radio or risk a lawsuit. And one day a letter arrived from Iowa saying Aunt Fanny's friend, Bert Beerbower, had passed away. The same sort of reality feedback came Aunt Fanny's way from listeners who would share their home-grown remedies for poison ivy or lumbago. She reportedly received over 250 suggested household cures for the hives.[6]

It was no wonder that Aunt Fanny conveyed reality over the air—after all, Allison was born and raised in La Porte City, Iowa. In her hometown it would not be unusual for someone to talk the way she did in her Aunt Fanny role. Indeed, someone who is ill could be described as "miserable bad off" or a man who was kindly as being "the best man who ever walked in shoe leather." As in much good comedy, her observations about life were extreme but tinged with some truth. Her old chum, Hettie Hornbuckle, was having problems with her husband and the furnace. According to Aunt Fanny, "when Hettie watches one, the other goes out." After spending a day at the beach, Aunt Fanny commented, "I never knew there were so many kinds of people," and she saw one woman wearing a four-piece swimsuit that "was a two piece till she bent over."

Allison's career in show business followed her first career as a teacher. After completing a degree at Coe College in Cedar Rapids in 1927, she took a position teaching in Schleswig, Iowa. She might have stayed in the job, but after being in the classroom four years she learned that her salary was to be increased from $100 to $102 a month.

She not only wanted more money but the satisfaction that comes from doing what she liked and was good at. At Coe, Allison had studied music and enjoyed performing, so she grabbed the opportunity to sing on a Waterloo radio station. One day the station's announcer, Joe DuMond, surprised her when he said, "Guess who just dropped in, Aunt Fanny! Come on up here and tell us what's new." Her quick wit and grasp of the local idiom prepared her for the ad lib routine that followed:

> Well Mister DuMond, I dropped by to see Daisy Dosselhurst yesterday and her Junior came in to the door and I said real nice, "Junior, is your mother home?" "No, she ain't," he said. "Is your father home?" I asked. "No, he ain't," he said. Well I heard about enough ain'ts, so I said, "Where's your grammar?" He answered quick, "She ain't here, either."[7]

Her comedy act was funny and became a regular feature on the Waterloo station, but singing was her main draw and in 1937 she was invited to audition for a staff position at NBC in Chicago. She passed it and was assigned to be a vocalist on the *Breakfast Club*. Soon she also found work singing commercials and acting in several comedy programs including *Clara, Lou, and Em* and *Sunday Dinner at Aunt Fanny's*. These other interests pulled her away from the *Breakfast Club* in 1939.

One of the people who listened to Allison's audition at NBC was a music publisher's representative, Archie Levington. They became friendly and in 1942 were married a few months before he began active duty in the army. During the war when he was stationed at Mineral Wells, Texas, Allison joined him, but after a year found herself missing the fun and challenges of being on radio. She moved back to Chicago and stayed with a friend, Nancy Martin, who was then a singer on the *Breakfast Club*. Occasionally, Allison would accompany Martin to the broadcast and sit in the audience where McNeill would spot her and conduct a spontaneous interview.[8] Her quick wit and sparkle undoubtedly convinced McNeill to make Aunt Fanny a permanent member of the cast in 1944. She fit into the routine of the show perfectly in that her comedy blended well with Cowling's and McNeill delighted in her discussions about the foibles of her home-town friends.

Allison had made friends with a Chicago artist, Burr Tillstrom, who thought she was the perfect human to talk with his puppets on a television show he was creating for WBKB-TV. The result was the pioneering children's show for adults, *Kukla, Fran, and Ollie*, which set a standard for television entertainment that few programs could ever match. They worked without a script, but instead sketched a rough idea for each show. Often Allison would come into the studio all enthused about something that had happened to her and it would become the focus for that day's show. Tillstrom created other puppets like Madame Oogelpuss, Fletcher Rabbit, and Beulah Witch much like Aunt Fanny's Ott Ort, Toodie Teeter, and Eulty Norks to enlarge the humor of any issue or topic. The Fran which Allison played on television was the mirror opposite of Aunt Fanny, in that she was the foil for the assemblage of puppets and the nonsense they created. Not only was Fran attractive, but she was also a polite listener who exercised restraint in expressing her opinions—in contrast to the bombastic spinster Fanny. The charm of these portrayals is that the careful listener/viewer could detect a bit of Fanny in Fran and vice versa.

Another *Breakfast Club* cast member who made a professional transformation was Cliff Petersen. He joined the show in 1936 as a member of a singing group, the Escorts Plus Betty. In addition, he drew from his Scandinavian roots to play "Yust Plain Gertson" who could discuss the merits of "lutefisk" and sing with a screeching Swedish lilt. Petersen left the show in 1943 to pursue interests in New York, but returned to Chicago the following year to become part of the network's production staff. In 1945 he was named producer of the *Breakfast Club*, a position he held for the remainder of the life of the show. It was his fingers that snapped the cues which ensured that the station breaks and commercials ran properly. Petersen was a handsome man who stood over six feet and always dressed in a stylish suit and tie. Except for the blond hair, he didn't look like someone who would belt out songs like "I Yust Go Nuts at Christmas." He also sang in a more straight fashion when he joined the other vocalists as part of the *Breakfast Club* chorus.

McNeill drew upon these cast members to help invigorate the show with witty sayings or clever features, but probably the most enduring source of support for the toastmaster came from the orchestra. Indeed, it was the twelve-piece musical group that provided the major source of entertainment when the show began in 1933. In those early years, McNeill would talk with conductor Walter Blaufuss about the musician's interest in European travel and Continental cuisine. Orchestra members were the unseen audience that McNeill made asides to and listeners could hear their response to his barbs.

Whenever McNeill had an occasion to mention the city of "Sheboygan," the orchestra would shout in unison, "My Old Home Town!" Besides adding to the humor of the show, orchestra members played their musical parts well, with a richness and variety.

Many of the musicians on staff during the 1940s had played with some of the more well-known groups in the country. The orchestra's concert master, Oscar Chausow, played with Leopold Stokowski before joining the network's orchestra. He and two other staff violinists, Bowen David and Ben Senescu, had played with the Chicago Symphony. Violist Ethel Hand had a background of playing with the Chicago Women's Symphony. One of the most well-known musicians in the group was Ennio Bolognini, who played cello with the Chicago Symphony and was conductor of the Waukegan Symphony. Bass player Jack Shirra was formerly with Hal Kemp's band. The trumpet section included Jimmy Sims, who used to play with the Dallas Symphony, and Don Jacoby, who played first trumpet for Les Brown's band. Trombonist George Jean played with the Casa Loma band and saxophonist Louis Cohen played with Benny Goodman. Drummer Tommy Thomas was one of Chicago's best-known music teachers and had published several articles about his drum techniques.[9]

Typically, the orchestra played ten songs a day on the show in addition to the forty or more musical cues which served as the structure for the various segments and commercial breaks on the program. The workday for a musician assigned to the *Breakfast Club* began around 7:00 A.M. with a pre-show rehearsal and ended with another rehearsal for the next day's show which concluded by 11:00 A.M. With those hours, no wonder the musical staff was stable over the years. Two musicians held the record for longevity on the show, pianist Bill Krenz and trumpeter Eddie Ballantine, who were in the orchestra on the *Breakfast Club's* first broadcast. Krenz stayed into the final year the program was on the air while Ballantine remained until the very end.

When music director Walter Blaufuss became ill in 1942, Harry Kogen, Rex Maupin, and Joe Gallichio took turns temporarily leading the orchestra. Blaufuss passed away in 1944 and Ballantine, to no one's surprise, was named director since he had been head arranger for the orchestra since 1934 and had a distinguished musical background. At Cornell University he studied engineering during the day while earning tuition money playing the horn with student bands at night. After two years of leading a double life between math and music, the latter won out when Ballantine left Ithaca to join the Lloyd Huntley orchestra as a vocalist and trumpet player. He eventually got the ear of Paul Whiteman, who recommended him for a position on NBC's staff orchestra in 1931. After passing an audition, he began a long career as a radio musician, arranger, and composer. In his spare time, Ballantine wrote a number of popular and classical works including "Romance Is Everywhere," "Suite for String Orchestra," "Boogie Woogie Made Easy," and "Rushing around on Rush Street." He also made time in a busy work schedule to study music at Northwestern University. Ballantine took his studies seriously and with the help of one of his professors, Clair Omar Musser, made musical history on the *Breakfast Club.* Musser's specialty was designing concert marimbas and one he fashioned for Leopold Stokowski was literally a giant, standing over six feet with tone pipes that looked like those found on the big Wurlitzer organs. It replaced the ten-string bass viols in Stokowski's orchestra with a tone that was considered as rich as that offered by the stringed instruments. Ballantine decided the monster marimba would liven up the *Breakfast Club* and July 26, 1944, it made a radio debut on the show. His relationship with Northwestern continued and, after eleven years of fitting in classes around work and family obligations, Ballantine earned a Bachelor of Music degree. He didn't completely forsake his earlier academic training; in 1943 he took a war-related job as an engineering technician for an electric company in Chicago. Balancing the jobs proved to be too demanding and after a year he resumed his role as a full-time musician.

As is true in many industries these days, radio stations are trimming staffs and utilizing automation to handle routine business and technical chores. It is hard to imagine that in the 1940s and 1950s over forty people were employed as part of the *Breakfast Club* staff. The number of musicians in the orchestra would grow from twelve to twenty-two and then shrink below a dozen, but the number of on-air talent and administrative staff would remain fairly constant over the program's life.

Few radio personalities had the bench strength that McNeill could draw from during every broadcast. The orchestra and singers could be counted on to evoke emotional feelings from romance to patriotism and the comics could help save a limp joke or enliven a bland interview. The toastmaster's job was obviously crucial in tying elements together and being the center-stage attraction, but he had plenty of help.

7

"McNeill for President"

The *Breakfast Club* would strike first-time listeners as a program with a lot of running gags and inside jokes. The comedy grew out of the relationships among members of the cast and the audience as much as the content of the humor. Cowling and Aunt Fanny were funny, but playing off McNeill's genial reserve gave their bits a greater impact. He provided an intriguing mix of qualities in that he looked like a banker but had the ability to speak with the emotion of a preacher, the common sense of a philosopher, and the conviction of a salesman. Add to these traits his ready enjoyment of a joke or pun and the result was a master of ceremonies who could handle almost anything that might come his way.

McNeill had a clear view of his strengths as an entertainer. He often commented, "I don't act, I don't sing, I don't dance. I'm just not a performer." He would play his clarinet on the show, on occasion he sang, and once, with Beatrice Kay he danced, but these sides of McNeill were rarely shown. What he offered was a gentle, affable, and humorous view of life not unlike Will Rogers but tinged with an aura of Norman Rockwell. In an essay he wrote in 1940 titled, "Personality Versus Gags," McNeill demonstrated his insight into comedy, and at the same time made it clear that he was not a comic like those heard cavorting on radio every night:

"Say something funny—make me laugh!"

Yeh, they'll say it to you, too, my friend, if you're a comedian.

Your intimates will say it to you when you're off the air, and your listeners will do likewise when you're on the air.

It's like being a lion-tamer and every time you meet someone have him say, "Go on, tame me a lion. Let's see you do it!" You could respond, "I'm sorry, the lion is busy." But then you'd have all the earmarks of a comedian, and people would again beg "Go on, say something funny, make me laugh"—so where are you?

So you're better off not being much of a funny fellow. If people don't expect a hilarious witticism to roll from your lips every time you open your mouth—when you do say something funny, un-expected like, you've got something there, besides your uppers.

It's taken me ten long years on the wireless to find where I belong—and I hope the answer isn't equidistant from two plow handles. I'm not exactly an announcer, not exactly a comedian—just a messer of ceremonies. I know I can't sing—I have one of those toothpaste voices—you squeeze it and it comes out flat. I know I can't tell funny jokes all the time be-cause I can't afford a staff of gag writers—and then too, I get tired of hearing the same jokes on other shows. But I do know that I can be myself on the air—if that means throwing in a Martin Lewis pun, on the least provocation—I'm sorry—but what can I Lewis? If that means mentioning my two kids and wife (same one all the time—never changes) whenever I happen to think of something that happened at home I want to mention it. I'm sorry again, but oh you kid.

After all, I'm married, I don't care who knows it, I like to talk about it—but I would have stopped long ago, if I didn't think listeners rather enjoyed hearing someone who wasn't ashamed of the fact that he's happily married, even though it means one darned thing after another. After all a bachelor's life is one *undarned* thing after another. There I go again. . . .

After drawing these conclusions for myself—I've decided to just be myself on the air: it'll either be that way in the script, which I write myself—or I'll be ad-libbing as I usually am not too funny, not too serious—not too anything I hope—especially a word rhyming with Frowsy. Every so often, when the mood strikes me, I'll repeat my favorite story about the time my little son, Tom, was learning to talk. One day I said to Mrs. McNeill—"Why does he say Mamma all the time? Why doesn't he ever say Daddy? After all I'm around here too." "Yes, I know," she said. "I wasn't going to tell him who you were until he was a little stronger." Dear reader, I can just hear you telling me "Say something funny, McNeill, make me laugh."[1]

The personality McNeill projected worked well on radio and brought him increased national recognition. *Radio Daily* readers voted the *Breakfast Club* as their favorite daytime variety program two years running in 1944 and 1945. *Tune In* selected the show as one of the "outstanding radio programs" of 1944. *Radio Mirror* reported that McNeill's show was its "Readers' Favorite Audience Participation Program" of 1948. Another accolade came in 1942 when St. Bonaventure College and Seminary awarded McNeill an honorary Doctor of Letters. ABC Radio took the cue by giving McNeill a five-year contract in 1945. In October of that year, the *Breakfast Club* dropped its Saturday show, which must have agreed with McNeill's sleeping schedule.

Across the nation, *Breakfast Club* fans came in droves wherever McNeill and company took their show on the road. In 1945, ABC's New York offices received over 75,000 requests for tickets to attend the show's week-long War Loan campaign in the city. On that same tour, when the show originated in Richmond, Virginia, one woman fan offered fifty dollars for a ticket to see the broadcast.[2]

McNeill and his gang demonstrated their appeal whenever they made public appearances during their War Loan drives. Based on the success of those trips, the *Breakfast Club* began making regular visits to cities across the U.S. New York City was a frequent destination; however, in 1946 the visit there was anything but routine. Arrangements were made to broadcast from Madison Square Garden where Ringling Brothers and Barnum & Bailey's circus was performing. The circus put on afternoon and evening shows so there was no conflict with the *Breakfast Club's* early morning schedule. In fact, the radio show audience would be welcome to remain in the Garden and to watch the circus crew as they rehearsed for that day's performances.

What nobody anticipated was the size of the crowd that was eager to see McNeill and his *Breakfast Club*. Well before dawn, hundreds of women began a vigil in long lines that wrapped around the entrance to the arena. Several had been there since midnight. Police erected barriers and patrols on horseback made sure the throng didn't disrupt traffic, as a total of 17,000 persons jammed into the Garden that morning. After a warm-up of several acts from the circus, a fanfare trumpet blast announced the arrival of McNeill who was perched atop a giant float inscribed with a sign hailing him as the "King of Corn." Cowling and Aunt Fanny made their entrances from the luggage compartment of a clown car already packed with midgets. Singer Jack Owens was tied to a rope and hauled up to the trapeze perch for one of his songs. The size of the crowd limited the degree of intimacy that could be achieved during the show, but McNeill climbed into the scoop of a steam shovel so he could interview guests in the balcony. Prayer Time took on a new look with search lights scanning the bleachers while everyone bowed their heads. Clown great Emmett Kelly joined McNeill at the close of the show and broke his legendary silence by asking, "When do we eat?" What made the Garden broadcast even more memorable was a police chase during the show involving a robber who tried to hide in the crowd.[3]

Being introduced as the King of Corn did not go against Mc-Neill's sense of himself, and whenever asked he unabashedly confessed to liking corn and being corny. The definitions he used to define corn explain his attitudes toward both the subject and himself:

> Corn is the remark that comes to a lot of people but they're too timid to say it. Corn is the knack of having fun in a clean, spontaneous, friendly way with "just us folks." . . . Corn is Junior delivering the Gettysburg Address at high-school commencement and Sis playing Handel's "Largo" at a church social. Corn is all the things that John Steinbeck overlooks and most of the things Sinclair Lewis ridicules.[4]

Other times, McNeill simply defined corn as "something funny that makes you groan because you didn't say it yourself." That's how he defined corn while being interviewed on national television by Edward R. Murrow during McNeill's guest appearance on *Person to Person* in 1958. Murrow didn't bring the subject up, McNeill did. He was not shy about offering his views about corn with gusto and without equivocation.

> Every normal person likes corn. . . . Cynics and sophisticates think they hate 'corn,' but that's only because they've developed their own peculiar brand. The tombstone of many a sophisticate bears a 'corny' epitaph.[5]

The corny side of McNeill was out there for all to see. When he was a guest on several network nighttime shows he came off as a bit of a genial bumpkin from the hinterland. When he made a guest appearance on the *Chesterfield Supper Club and Hildegarde* network radio show in 1946, McNeill claimed to be taking notes on how to make his show more sophisticated like that of his host's. When Fred Allen planned to have McNeill as a guest on his show in 1947 the two collaborated on the best approach to take for the visit. Allen's letter (as the comic typed it using all lower-case) to McNeill suggests the scenario of the sketch between the two:

> the gem we came up with for you involves a routine of talk where i meet you in a lunchroom. for some reason i am up early one morning. we meet and you don't know me since you only associate with people in morning radio and you have to go to bed at six p.m. to be able to get up early enough to work every day. i have never heard of you since i am up at night and never rise before noon. you never heard of amos and andy, benny, hope or any of the other nighttime shows. you tell me how much fun you have broadcasting on ferries and in ball parks etc. and you are surprised that i am still doing the old style broadcasting indoors.
>
> i tell portland that you have so much fun i want to see how you put on your show. i am sick of my drab routine and want to have a program like yours. i supposedly disguise myself to appear in your show. we reproduce the opening of your program with commercial, singing, etc. you interview two of our stooges and then you question me. as we are talking there is a shot and the program turns into a murder mystery. it may sound a trifle involved but we can work it out and when you look it over we can add anything you may want to put in later.[6]

McNeill's guest appearance on the *Fred Allen Show* on April 27, 1947, essentially went as Allen outlined. The two entertainers have a chance meeting in the Automat where Allen was convinced that working on a morning program would be good for a change. Following the scene at the Automat, the *Breakfast Club* theme began and so did a satire of the show.

> DON: Good morning, good morning, Breakfast Clubbers! Ah, it's a bright sunny morning here in New York, and I'm glad to see so many of you here from all over the country. Over there we have a group of Boy Scouts from Ashtabula, Iowa.

CAST: (*Cheers*)

DON: They'll be up here at the microphone later to tie some knots for us. Over in the corner is a pair of geologists from Waterbury. They have a two-ton rock we're bringing to the microphone in a minute. And now, waiting for us, is a gentleman who is ninety years old! He roller-skated all the way to New York from Cedar Rapids, Iowa.

Just before beginning the morning March around the Breakfast Table, there was a scuffle between an usher and a man in the audience who was not from out of town and, therefore, was about to be thrown out of the studio. McNeill asked the New Yorker how he managed to get a ticket to the broadcast and the man said he asked his cousin in Des Moines to write in for it. After getting rid of the interloper, McNeill asks a woman (Minerva Pious) her name. She replied "Beulah Bodenheim" and then retorted, "What's the next question?" She was convinced she had come to a quiz show and stood ready to take a pie in the face, dance with a bear, or even get kissed by an announcer. McNeill assured her none of those things occurred on his show. He noticed another guest, Fenton Upjohn, from Old Rochelle, who volunteered to lead the day's march. McNeill called for the music to begin, but three gunshots stopped the proceedings. The Bodenheim woman screamed that her husband was slumped over next to her. Fenton Upjohn rips off his disguise and announces that in addition to being Fred Allen, he is also One Long Pan, private detective. After some clever questioning, Allen discovered that one of the shots came from the interloper who meant to hit McNeill but missed and the other two were practice rounds from a sound effects man getting ready for his job on another radio show, *Gang Busters*.

The Bodenheim woman confesses to murdering her husband saying she had enough of his demands.

I been supportin' the family with what I win on quiz shows. All week I bring home nylons, stoves, pressure cookers, and Snickers. . . . Last week, the *Breakfast Club* comes to New York. We think it's another one of them quiz shows. Me husband starts naggin' me to try my luck on it. Get on the *Breakfast Club* he keeps sayin'. I bring three gunny sacks figgerin' on a big haul. So what happens—yer givin' away nothin' but a free march around a breakfast table! Durin' the time wasted here, on some other program I coulda knocked off a refrigerator!

McNeill ended the bit by admonishing her that "you have not acted in the true spirit of the jolly Breakfast Clubber."

Fred Allen had an acerbic wit that provided ironic truth to most of his comedy. Quiz shows were definitely on Allen's mind when McNeill was his guest. In his book, *Treadmill to Oblivion*, Allen wrote that,

> Give-away programs are the buzzards of radio.
> As buzzards swoop down on carrion so have give-away
> shows descended on the carcass of radio.
> Like buzzards the give-away shows, if left to pursue their scav-
> enging devices, will leave nothing but the picked bones of
> the last listener lying before his radio set.
> Radio used to be a medium of entertainment.
> The give-away programs have reduced radio to a shoddy gam-
> bling device.[7]

Allen's radio show had enjoyed many years of strong listener loyalty largely due to Allen's persona and his clever scripts and funny characters, but in 1948 ABC scheduled a quiz show *Stop The Music!* on Sunday nights opposite Allen on NBC and Edgar Bergen and Charlie McCarthy on CBS. The quiz program was an instant smash, in part because it gave away big prizes. Listeners were afraid to leave home, let alone not tune in the program for fear of missing a call from host Bert Parks and the chance to win cash and plenty of merchandise plus a try at the "mystery melody" and its $20,000 prize. As Allen's ratings began to tumble, he fought off the inevitable with a novel insurance offer which guaranteed that anyone who was tuned in to the Allen show and missed an opportunity to win "a refrigerator, a television set, a new car, or any amount of cash prize" will be reimbursed by the National Surety Corporation up to $5,000.[8] The next year NBC canceled Allen. CBS gave Bergen and McCarthy a hiatus for a season, putting them back on Sundays the following year. Allen never returned to radio with his own show.[9]

McNeill coped with the quiz show craze with better luck. He always maintained that the *Breakfast Club* never gave away anything, not even breakfast. In September 1947 McNeill was talking with a woman from Wilmington, Illinois, Rose Kral, who kidded him about not giving away anything on his program. McNeill turned the issue over to his audience, asking them to write in with their opinions about prizes on the *Breakfast Club*. It was no surprise to McNeill when nearly all the mail ran against having giveaways on the show, and it gave him an idea which went contrary to the concept of audiences getting something from a radio program—it was the "reverse giveaway." Listeners were asked to do the giving, with their presents going to help needy people in the Chicago area. The campaign was launched in the fall of 1947 and by the time it ended on November 7, $10,000 worth of donations were received from six hundred people in twenty-four states, filling Studio A in the Merchandise Mart with clothing, food, household items, a refrigerator, and a stove. Every member of the cast made a contribution, including a sewing machine from McNeill, a half-dozen house-dresses from Aunt Fanny, and 6,000 pounds of coal from the orchestra.[10] The goods were then loaded onto trucks and distributed to families identified by the Cook County Bureau of Public Welfare as in need. The reverse giveaway embodied the spirit of the *Breakfast Club* to help those less fortunate and demonstrated the skill McNeill possessed in presenting himself authentically as an entertainer who cared about other people.

Judging from the response of McNeill's fans, he struck the right balance between being a jovial personality and a concerned citizen. Whenever the cast made personal appearances or took its annual treks to several cities for special broadcasts, the demand for tickets was high. Ever since they packed Madison Square Garden, the *Breakfast Club* cast was in demand to make personal appearances across the country. By 1947, the *Breakfast Club* cast had given evening performances in more than fifty cities east of the Rocky Mountains. Typically, there was an admission charge for these shows and the sponsoring organization gave the proceeds to a philanthropic group such as the Boy Scouts or to help McNeill inaugurate a summer camp for needy children. During a twelve-month period in 1947–1948 the *Breakfast Club* had received 462 requests to make personal appearances from organizations in thirty-six states, Hawaii, and Canada. The cities visited in 1947 with approximate attendance figures were:

February 15	Oklahoma City	12,000
June 7	Youngstown	6,500
June 14	Harrisburg	4,000
September 13	Wichita	4,000
September 27	Grand Rapids	4,500
October 4	Springfield, Ill.	5,300
October 24	Flint	6,000
November 28	Duluth	3,300
December 8	Tulsa	5,500

In addition, the *Breakfast Club* cast traveled to New York City twice in 1947, where the show originated from the 58th Street Theater. While there, the show made two side trips to do a broadcast from Brooklyn and another from Atlantic City during a Philco dealers' convention.

As plans were being laid for the *Breakfast Club* to commit to a travel itinerary in 1948, a plan emerged that coincided with the election campaign being waged that year. McNeill would be nominated as a "laugh party" candidate for president and the campaign would take him to the cities where the staff had decided to make personal appearances. McNeill's candidacy purportedly evolved as the result of his being drafted by the studio audience during an April 1948 broadcast. In response, he articulated a platform which included the following: every listener had to be "up" by the time the *Breakfast Club* hit the airwaves; every household would serve a complete breakfast seven mornings a week; husbands would prepare the family's breakfasts on Saturdays and Sundays; and no newspaper reading would be allowed at the breakfast table.

The orchestra wrote a special campaign song titled, "Don McNeill for President," which paraphrased George Gershwin's "Wintergreen for President" from the musical *Of Thee I Sing*. Woody Woodpecker became the official mascot for the campaign to "Put McNeill behind the Wheel." For a variety of reasons, Philadelphia was chosen as the city where McNeill would be officially nominated. It was where both the Democrats and Republicans planned to hold their conventions that summer, but more importantly, since the coaxial cable which carried television signals had gotten as far west as Philadelphia, it was the logical place to hold major events which were suitable to the new medium. Not the least of the reasons was that Philadelphia was the home base of *Breakfast Club* sponsor Philco, which owned one of the city's local television stations and was a major manufacturer of television sets. It was felt that bringing the *Breakfast Club* to town for a special simulcast on radio and television might stimulate Philco sales. The sponsor chartered a presidential train car to bring McNeill and the cast down from New York. When the train arrived at the Broad Street Station there was a welcoming celebration followed by a parade downtown where an estimated 25,000 spectators were waiting.

On May 12 the *Breakfast Club* originated from the Academy of Music in Philadelphia, with 3,200 people in the audience. In addition to the national radio hookup, anyone with a television set in Philadelphia, New York, Baltimore, or Washington could watch the proceedings. A kinescope[11] recording of the event reveals that most of the effort by McNeill and the cast was exerted toward putting on their radio program and only scant attention was given to the television cameras. The audience was visibly coached when to applaud and singers and announcers were shown running to get positioned in front of microphones, holding scripts that were casually tossed on the floor after being read. The cameras merely looked in on a radio program that had its own routine.

McNeill received encouraging comments from one viewer, Fred Allen, who wrote, "You screened very well and the action, songs and comedy came off surprisingly well in that medium. If any film scouts see you in television you will probably get some offers to go to hollywood."[12] Another reaction came from ABC's executive vice president, Robert Kintner, who was convinced the show had great potential for television and asked McNeill to "turn over in your mind the potentialities of televising the 'Breakfast Club', beginning in the Fall, when WENR-TV [Chicago] will be on the air and when television will really begin to hit its stride for the 1948–49 season."[13]

The campaign theme proved to be an interesting gimmick for comedy sketches with Cowling dressed as a political manager, and for a clever Swift commercial. Ostensibly to save time, McNeill gave his campaign pitch while announcer Don Dowd sold some bacon.

> McNEILL: Citizens of America, my great grandfather made a good politician, my grandfather made a good politician, my father made a good politician, and I would make—
> Dowd: Good bacon. Every single package of Swift's Premium Bacon contains—
> McNEILL: 50 million Frenchmen. Now as to this question of foreign relations, I have this to say. If I am elected, I promise you that every patriotic American by next year would be—
> Dowd: Sizzling in the skillet. Swift's Premium Bacon is an appetizing invitation to a brighter breakfast. In fact, a lady from Peoria recently said she had—
> McNEILL: 75 thousand children under six years of age and it is my belief that these children are old enough to be—
> Dowd: Kissing their husbands at breakfast. Remember, you'll start the day off with a bang if you eat several—
> McNEILL: Atomic bombs. And in closing let me remind you that the last time I ran for public office—

DOWD: Swift's Premium Bacon won. When homemakers were
    asked to select their favorite bacon they said that they—
McNEILL: Won't shave their long, gray beards till I'm in
    office.

From Philadelphia McNeill's campaign swung south, with a stop
in Atlanta where he promised to "get the country out of the red and
the Reds out of the country" to a crowd of 8,000 at the Municipal Auditorium. The orchestra obliged McNeill when he said he'd replace
the "Missouri Waltz" with "Rambling Wreck from Georgia Tech."

Another opportunity for campaigning was in New York City,
where the *Breakfast Club* performed in front of world's largest radio
studio audience on May 6 when 1,500 people crowded into Studio
8H at Radio City. More were waiting to get in, but fire marshals
wouldn't allow standing, so the overflow was taken to another studio.

While McNeill was in New York he made another guest appearance on Fred Allen's show and used it as an opportunity to build
upon his comical presidential campaign. In preparing for his guest
shot, McNeill wrote Allen about a gimmick he was planning to use
on his program that sounds like a bit that might be seen any night on
David Letterman's television show.

> On our first show in New York next Monday one of the mem-
> bers of the cast is going to accuse me of not being well enough
> known so I am going to announce that I will be standing on
> some corner on Fifth Avenue at a certain time during the day
> and first person who recognizes me will be my guest on the show
> the following day. We will probably keep that thing running for
> the two weeks we are in New York.[14]

In the broadcast, Allen heads for Fifth Avenue in hopes of finding
McNeill and being interviewed on the *Breakfast Club* the next day.

ALLEN: Mr. McNeill, I hope I'm the first one to recognize you.
McNEILL: Yes. You're the lucky winner.
ALLEN: Gosh, Mr. McNeill, how did you know I was looking
    for you?
McNEILL: I can tell you're a typical Breakfast Club listener.
ALLEN: Really?
McNEILL: You come from a small town in the middle west.
    You have a wife and three point two children. You have an

Acme Mutual Forty-year Endowment Policy which expires
at the age of seventy-five and guarantees you twelve dollars
a week and absolute security as long as you live. You read
three comic books a week and you're rooting for the
Dodgers to win the pennant. In other words, you're the average man.

ALLEN: Wait a minute! I'm not from the middle west, I have
no insurance, I like Jersey City in the International
League, and I'm not the average man.[15]

When McNeill discovered Allen also had a radio show, "Break
the Contestant," the two ended up as quiz master and contestant on
that program. For every wrong answer, Allen, as Lomax Nishball, had
to remove an article of clothing. He missed every question and as the
show ended he was wearing nothing but pink bloomers. Obviously,
Allen's battle against quiz shows in the ratings race continued to
dominate his and his writers' minds. The closing skit was reminiscent
of the culmination of the long-running feud between Allen and Jack
Benny which had begun in 1937 over wisecracks Allen made about
Benny's violin playing and came to a head in 1946 with a skit titled
"King for a Day." Benny, the contestant, won the show's grand prize
which was a pressing of his suit, and the show ended when he
stripped to his shorts so the steam pressing machine could do its job.
Seeing a man stand in front of a crowd in his underwear is not particularly shocking by today's norms, but the excitement communicated in
Allen's voice and the audience's reaction during the show added to
the impact of the skit.

McNeill had his own sort of feud going with another morning
radio man, Tom Breneman, who was host of *Breakfast in Hollywood*,
which followed McNeill's program on ABC. Breneman catered to
women in the audience by giving guests orchids and looking for the
woman with the most outlandish hat, which he would don. In what
was a friendly rip-off of Aunt Fanny, Breneman portrayed a hayseed
character, Uncle Corny, who would tell stale jokes. On a broadcast in
1946, an eighty-eight-year-old woman told Breneman he was "grand."
He replied, "You're smart," but she said, "No." He asked if she ever
listened to Don McNeill and when she said no, he retorted, "Now I
know you're smart."[16]

When Breneman began his program it was broadcast from Sardi's
restaurant in Hollywood. The show proved to be very popular and
Breneman decided to buy his own restaurant to house the daily program.

It was rumored that McNeill was interested in acquiring a restaurant in Chicago that he would use for his radio show. In 1947, Chicago columnist Irv Kupcinet reported that McNeill was one of the bidders for a defunct nightspot in the city, the Copacabana.[17]

To keep the "feud" going, McNeill told his audience that if anyone was planning a trip to Hollywood they should drop in on Breneman and "break some dishes" because "Breneman deserves all the breaks you can give him." Breneman returned the favor by asking his listeners to gather all the broken dishes and glasses from around the house and mail them to "Don McNeill, Merchandise Mart, Chicago."[18] McNeill took the joke well, even if the network's mail room was flooded with the rattling packages. The sparring was in good fun, and when McNeill and his wife were in Los Angeles in February 1948 they dropped in on Breneman at his Sunset and Vine restaurant and were interviewed on the show. Two months later, just before going on the air, Tom Breneman died and the next day on Memory Time McNeill offered a eulogy to his colleague.

> May he be lovingly remembered
> So long as there are radios to dial
> And orchids and good neighbors live in sunshine
> So long as people still can laugh and smile.
>
> We are all so speedily forgotten
> When life on this earth must end—
> But don't forget—Tom Breneman.
> Yesterday we lost a friend![19]

The McNeill presidential campaign continued on the air with a daily stumping for Fourth Party votes in all the states, during which the candidate promised little beyond putting a "louse in the White House" and claiming that his *record* was unclear because (American Federation of Musicians president) James Petrillo had invoked a ban on *recordings* before he could come up with one. During a strategy dinner session in Highland Park near Chicago, McNeill was advised that he needed to convene another party convention to determine whether or not the country will accept his "corn standard." Instead of going back to old Philadelphia, it was decided to go to New Philadelphia, Ohio, a town of 13,000 people in the east-central part of the state noted for being a manufacturing center of pretzels and Swiss cheese.

On Thursday, August 12, the McNeill for President entourage boarded a special train car and left Chicago's North Western Station bound for Ohio. When it got to Canton there were an estimated three thousand folks waiting to see McNeill as he stepped off the train in a drenching rainstorm. The *Daily Times* of New Philadelphia reported that a few months earlier when President Truman came to Canton only about thirty people turned out to see the Democratic presidential candidate. McNeill briefly addressed the crowd and when a woman asked to see his feet he promptly put them up on the train's observation platform and asked to see hers. The rain stopped as the party headed for New Philadelphia in a caravan of about a hundred cars, while eleven private airplanes from nearby airports gave them an escort from overhead. The route went through several Ohio towns, including Massillon, Navarre, Strasburg, Columbia, and Dover.

Meanwhile, in New Philadelphia, another crowd of mostly women estimated to be five thousand waited for the caravan to drive the twenty-nine miles from Canton. The women had been waiting for nearly two hours and were miffed that they merely got a glimpse of McNeill when his car briefly stopped at the Hotel Reeves before going to a private home where he was to spend the night. The *Daily Times* reported that the large mass of onlookers refused to leave the hotel vicinity and local officials persuaded McNeill to return and address the crowd from the hotel's balcony. He cheerfully told them, "I've had a grand welcome in New Philadelphia, my old hometown," which was what he said on stepping off the train in Canton earlier in the day. Then McNeill returned to the private home where he joined Kay and their three sons, who had just arrived from Chicago, before going to bed. Back at the Hotel Reeves members of the *Breakfast Club* cast attended a press party with reporters sent from nearly every newspaper, wire service, and radio station in Ohio. The musicians meanwhile went to the junior high school's gym where they held a brief rehearsal for the next day's show.

Mayor Robert Lukens proclaimed Friday, August 13, as Don McNeill Day in New Philadelphia and requested that all businesses remained closed until 10:30 A.M. during the convention proceedings Friday morning. In addition, an effort was made to decorate all the storefronts along the town's main business district with bunting and flags.

Fortunately, the rain didn't return, since the "convention" was to be held in an outdoor amphitheater in the city's Tuscora Park. When the 9:00 A.M. broadcast began all 3,200 portable chairs were filled with adoring fans, including Mrs. Thomas Herbert and her husband, the governor of Ohio. Hundreds more people stood on the wooded hillside to watch the broadcast and be part of the largest crowd in the history of the 144-year-old town. Planks in the Fourth Party platform were read. One promised to issue a new seven-dollar bill with Lana Turner's picture on it to help deal with post-war inflation—since things were so expensive, voters should at least have the pleasure of kissing their money goodbye. If elected, the candidate promised to stage treasure hunts at Ft. Knox, Kentucky, and levy a tax on all serious political speeches. He interviewed an eighty-seven-year-old woman, and when she told him she had two daughters and seven sons, he promptly kissed her.

When it came time for McNeill's acceptance speech, he told the crowd he was withdrawing for several reasons. He said his having five hours of national radio time every week at an early hour when no one can think gave him an unfair advantage over other politicians. He said Washington is DC and his alarm clock was AC, so he'd never be able to get up on time. Since the presidential term is only four years and he had been on the *Breakfast Club* for the last fifteen, he felt the job offered too little employment security. McNeill concluded by "singing"

I feel that a load is off my chest.
I'd rather stay here with our Breakfast Club fun,
In other words I do not choose to run.

I realize that now is the hour
To get the heck out like Ike Eisenhower.

I've got my reasons why I quit this race,
I realize the Breakfast Club is my place.

I leave the White House to Harry or Tom,
They can struggle with Congress,
I'll stay where I um.

Following the broadcast there was another parade from the park to the city's court house where the mayor gave McNeill the keys to the city and appointed various cast members to honorary positions. After lunching at the Reeves Hotel, the cast was given an opportunity to enjoy some local recreation. McNeill went fishing, others swam or golfed. The day ended with a dinner at the country club, with the *Breakfast Club* orchestra providing the music, before the party was driven to Canton to catch the train back to Chicago.

8

After the Merchandise Mart

The routine of the *Breakfast Club* was upset the first week in October 1948 when it moved from its original home in the Merchandise Mart to a theater ABC had leased in the Civic Opera Building. The shift was prompted by NBC's need to find suitable studio space for its television operations, and the large radio studio which the *Breakfast Club* used was an ideal candidate for conversion. ABC had similar needs for television studios and decided to use the Little Theater in the Civic Building for both radio and television programs. The theater's stage was fairly deep and easily accommodated the cameras and lights required for television. In addition, the main seating section plus a small balcony held 836 people, which was about twice as many as could fit into Studio A at the Merchandise Mart.

The *Breakfast Club* had been using the theater for nearly a year when a member of the studio audience was startled by what she saw, and it was not on the stage. The woman noticed a mouse near her seat and let everyone know about it. Then, just as quickly as it appeared, the creature was gone, and was not to be found. The next morning, singer Patsy Lee brought her cat to look for the elusive mouse without success. The following day McNeill brought his hunting dog to give the theater the once-over. Still no mouse. Traps were set, but the bait was untouched. In desperation, McNeill summoned big game hunter Frank Buck to see if he could catch the pesky mouse. Buck arrived by week's end to join cast members and the audience in the mouse hunt, but before the "bring 'em back alive" adventurer could prove his worth, the excitement ended when Cowling pulled a mouse from his pocket.

The mouse caper was typical of the humor that spontaneously occurred on the show. The cast was encouraged to find material that would enliven the morning routine. McNeill helped each performer contribute to the merrymaking in the way they were most comfortable and able. In the process of sharing ideas and humor with McNeill, the cast showed more of themselves to the listeners and engendered more fan loyalty.

During the years he sang on the show, Jack Baker had attracted a loyal following. When he turned the tables on his *Breakfast Club* fans and asked for their autographs, over 100,000 signed greetings arrived. In 1944, when he decided to join the armed forces, the goodbyes were long and emotional.

Baker's replacement was Jack Owens, who rejoined the *Breakfast Club* after having recently moved his family back to Chicago. Not long after his return he created a unique singing style which his wife inspired. Helen Owens was sitting in the studio audience one morning and he picked up a portable microphone, walked over to her, and began singing "Love Is the Sweetest Thing" specifically to her. The studio audience's reaction to the serenade was so enthusiastic that each morning he continued to walk into the audience and sing to women, earning a nickname, "The Cruising Crooner." Everyone seemed to enjoy Owens's forays into the audience, including Helen, until the media critic at the *New York Times*, John Crosby, saw the 1948 telecast from Philadelphia and wrote his reaction.

> I strongly object to a singer named Jack Owens who cruises around the audience singing love songs to the girls. By radio this is painful; by television it is excruciating. Mr. Owens kisses the women, musses their hair, and sits on their laps. Why some irate babe hasn't broken his neck is beyond me.

It is likely that Crosby wouldn't approve of Sam Cowling's landing on women's laps either, but such clowning didn't bother the critic in the same way. When Owens left the show in 1949 to concentrate on song-writing his replacement was Johnny Desmond, who had sung with Bob Crosby's orchestra and during the war with Glenn Miller's band in the Army Air Corps. The band had played weekly over the

British Broadcasting Company's network and Desmond was reputed to have become a favored singer of Princesses Elizabeth and Margaret. Although Johnny didn't cruise as he sang, his style had a definite appeal to women.

Another male singer who attracted a lot of attention didn't follow the usual path to becoming a singer. Instead, eleven-year-old Bernie Christianson was merely sitting in the studio audience and by chance McNeill interviewed him. During their conversation, the boy asked if he could sing "Galway Bay" to his grandparents in Minnesota. He did and within the next few days McNeill received so many cards and letters praising Christianson's singing that the boy was asked to come back. Listeners were not only taken by his voice, as he could sing both tenor and soprano, but, most likely, were touched when they heard that he had overcome polio, a lung ailment, mumps, and a ruptured appendix, all in one year. After more than five thousand listeners wrote in asking to hear him sing again, Christianson became the replacement singer when Jack Owens went on a week's vacation in 1949 and then was hired to sing on the show twice a week. His schedule was such that he could make morning rehearsals, be on the show, and still get to his sixth grade classes at Cornell School on Chicago's south side.[1]

Two singers who had shared the female spot since 1939, Nancy Martin and Marion Mann, decided to leave in 1946, prompting a search for their replacement. Finding the right singer was a challenge because, in addition to having talent, the person had to appeal to the audience, plus get along with the staff.

While the auditions were underway to find the new female singer, producer Cliff Petersen heard someone on a San Francisco radio station who sounded just right for the show. Patsy Lee had planned to be a dancer and had performed in California theaters as part of a dancing act since she was fourteen. She was noticed as a singer after winning several beauty and talent contests. Gradually she switched from dance to singing when she got offers to perform on radio stations in the San Francisco Bay area. She was nineteen years old when she signed on as the *Breakfast Club's* female singer in 1947 and quickly became a favorite of both the audience and the other members of the cast who welcomed her like a new member of the family. Lee also became very close to one of the administrative staffers, Jean Reynolds, who introduced her to Rick Lifvendahl who had just completed service in the military. Sometime later, the couple married, moved to California, and had two daughters. In 1956 Rick Lifvendahl died in an automobile accident. Years later one of their daughters married Reynolds's son.[2]

As in any organization, the cast exerted some influence over the show, but not in such an organized way as was done in 1948. ABC thought it would be useful to know the cast's preferences as plans were being made to celebrate the *Breakfast Club's* fifteenth anniversary with an alumni party on the air. The performers and musicians were asked to identify their favorite guests on the show during the previous year. Their responses reflected a preference for unusual but ordinary visitors rather than well-known celebrities. For example, the choice for best all-around guest was a six-year-old boy from Akron, Doyt (Butch) Akom, Jr., whom McNeill picked out of the audience one morning. Akom's card said he had a story to tell and within no time he was helping with interviews, kissing Patsy Lee, reading commercials, and conducting the orchestra.

The favorite non-celebrity guest was Chicago tavern keeper, Bill Mahoney, who sang and told Irish stories during annual visits to the show on St. Patrick's Day. Mahoney first visited the show in 1941 when he was working as a street car motorman and made news by heroically capturing a robber who had just killed the owner of a jewelry store. The next most popular amateur guest was a Chicago woman, Adelina Jackson, who during her visits to the show identified herself simply as Mrs. Smith and proceeded to chatter away telling McNeill about all her troubles. A retired Shakespearean actor, Robert Abbott of Chicago, was next on the favorites list followed by the McNeill family's milkman, Ed Houellen, whose contribution to the show one day was the result of a refrigerator survey he conducted.

Topping the crew's list of favorite celebrities visiting the show was former Breakfast Clubber Bill Thompson followed by actors Dennis Morgan and Jack Carson, both Milwaukee natives. Morgan had worked with McNeill at a Milwaukee radio station in 1932. Next was actor and veteran Harold Russell who won an academy award for his acting in the motion picture *Best Years of Our Lives*, which chronicled how three soldiers struggled to put their lives together following the war. Other celebrities mentioned included golfer Babe Didrikson Zaharias and the actor who provided Donald Duck with a voice, Clarence Nash.

The youthful favorites, in addition to the overall winner Butch Akom, included a Chicago paperboy, Nick Comvitchi, who told McNeill he was saving his earnings to help bring his mother to America from his native Greece. The next favorite choice was a skeptical lad,

Bill Munns of La Grange, Illinois, who spent a full morning watching the show before he became convinced that the *Breakfast Club* was not rehearsed. Another favorite was Cub Scout Carey Otis on assignment for his school paper in Wilmette, Illinois, who concluded that "after watching Don McNeill broadcast, I'm going to give up writing and be a radio man. It's better than working."[3]

The in-house research project concluded by asking the cast to identify their favorite program feature during the preceding year. The responses reflect a preference for familiar guests and family-related features. First choice was the *Breakfast Club's* Reverse Giveaway which asked listeners to provide presents for needy people. Second was the annual Christmas-time visit to the program by the McNeill family. Third in popularity was McNeill's fortieth birthday party for which he dressed in a Lord Fauntleroy suit and the cast donned childish costumes.

It should be of no surprise that visits by Kay and the three McNeill boys were popular with the cast. Indeed, hearing real families in the morning had become very popular on radio. In addition to *Breakfast at Sardi's* (*Breakfast in Hollywood*), there was a well-known local morning show on WOR, New York, *Breakfast with Dorothy and Dick*, featuring columnist Dorothy Kilgallen and her husband, actor-producer, Richard Kollmar. Similar husband and wife teams were heard on stations across the country and offered listeners a chance to experience what seemed like real discussions and conflicts around the family's kitchen table.

Over the years, *Breakfast Club* audiences heard virtually no McNeill family squabbles other than good-natured kidding among the boys. Listeners could vicariously experience the growth of the McNeill family and compare it with that of their own offspring. Beginning in December 1935 when fourteen-month-old Tom McNeill made his first appearance on the show, the family typically was heard during the Christmas holidays and often was featured on the *Breakfast Club's* anniversary shows in June. During these visits, Kay and the boys would read commercials, sing with Aunt Fanny or Sam Cowling, and participate in interviews of studio guests.

The family almost didn't make their Christmas visit on December 20, 1946, when an Evanston policeman pulled McNeill's car over for speeding. McNeill explained to the officer that he and his family were trying to get to the studio by 7:30 A.M. to prepare for the eight o'clock show. Instead of getting a ticket, they got an escort downtown, and later on the show McNeill thanked the policeman for his assistance along the road. McNeill undoubtedly was nervous because he had found himself in the same situation nine years earlier. In 1937 he had been stopped for speeding while headed to the studio with a car filled with presents for underprivileged children. The officer's ticket writing had made McNeill late for the first time since the *Breakfast Club* began. The Evanston officer's escort, however, brought them to the studio in plenty of time. During the broadcast, Kay McNeill and the boys read a dramatization of Commodore Perry's exploration to the South Pole which cleverly evolved into an ad for Swift's ham and bacon. Imitating their father, the boys went into the audience and asked folks about the qualities of their refrigerators compared to what the new Philco offered. Their prowess as performers was evident when they sang an ad for Luster Creme Shampoo which borrowed a melody from a then familiar Pepsi Cola commercial.

During Prayer Time, McNeill asked all children, including his own, to bow their heads and pray. Kay McNeill read a Memory Time poem asking for harmony and peace in the world that should begin in everyone's home. Next came the Sunshine Shower which was initiated in 1946 at the suggestion of Ole Olsen of the comedy team Olsen and Johnson when he was filling in for vacationing McNeill. Olsen quickly captured the spirit of the show and in doing so left a memory of his visit by suggesting that Breakfast Clubbers send written greetings to people in hospitals and institutions. Olsen called the request a Sunshine Shower and thereafter it became a regular feature on the program. During the December broadcast, Bob McNeill gave the Sunshine Shower, asking that listeners send their cards to the Children's Home in Marion, Indiana.

The family's visit was a bigger success than anyone anticipated. Days before the broadcast, McNeill had mentioned that his wife and boys would be guests on the special Christmas program. Audience ratings for that morning as tabulated by the leading audience research firm, C. E. Hooper, Inc., showed the *Breakfast Club* scored its highest rating ever. In addition, Hooper's telephone surveys showed the December 20 show among the top ten daytime programs that day.[4]

ABC's executives noticed the high level of audience interest in McNeill's private life and decided to rewrite his contract which had been negotiated just a year earlier. A new, four-year agreement recognized Kay McNeill's importance to the *Breakfast Club* by stipulating that she would make regular appearances on the show. The new contract gave the McNeills freedom to explore media opportunities beyond radio such as motion pictures and television. That provision

McNeill house in Winnetka, Illinois

didn't really do McNeill any good, because in 1947 when he was approached by a studio to star in the Arch Obler screenplay, *Breakfast in the Country*, the network refused to spend the money necessary to move the *Breakfast Club* to California for the five to six weeks required for the shooting.[5] ABC may have been reluctant to relocate the *Breakfast Club* but it had no hesitancy in signing McNeill and his family to a generous contract. He had demonstrated an ability to keep listeners interested and sponsors happy.

The program's fifteenth birthday celebration in June 1948 was special in that it originated in the backyard of McNeill's Winnetka home. More than two hundred people crowded under a huge tent to watch the remote broadcast. Many of them were friends and neighbors of the McNeills or related to the cast. In making out the guest list, Kay McNeill counted fifty-four children in the families of cast and orchestra members and most of them came to the yard party. The tent proved to be a necessary precaution because of heavy rains that morning right up to air time.

During the show, McNeill interviewed several children and wives of the cast members, most of whom were sporting "Don McNeill for President" buttons. The youngest guest whom he interviewed was six-month-old Donald Bennett, son of Jim Bennett, McNeill's personal representative and Kay's brother. Tom McNeill showed off his piano playing ability for his school friends. As the weather improved, the wife of announcer Ken Nordine, Beryl Vaughan, told McNeill her worries about being out on his lawn. The radio and film actress said she was concerned the sun might pop her freckles out. The sun appropriately came out during the daily hymn which featured all the children singing "America the Beautiful." McNeill checked with Jack Owens's wife, Helen, to see if she objected to her husband's singing a romantic ballad to some other wives in the audience. She replied, "Let nature boy have his fun." Following the broadcast everyone sat down to a late breakfast consisting of the food they were asked to bring themselves plus hams which Swift provided.

This was not the first time the *Breakfast Club* had been broadcast from the McNeill home. In their first home-broadcast in 1935 the McNeills were living in a modest residence in Evanston. Once in 1938 McNeill treated himself to doing the show from his bed with the cast in the studio downtown. The next home origination occurred in 1945 when a Christmas morning broadcast featured cast members and their families opening presents. The broadcast originated in a home the McNeills designed and had built in one of Chicago's more upscale suburbs, Winnetka. In 1950 they would move into a larger home also in Winnetka. Where the McNeills called home improved with the fortunes of the *Breakfast Club* to attract sponsors.

In April 1943, McNeill had signed a three-year contract with the Blue Network which guaranteed him $250 per week plus extra payments for every quarter-hour segment of the program that had sponsors. If a sponsor purchased a segment once a week, McNeill received a $200 fee, but that fee rose to $750 if the sponsor bought the segment all six days of the week that the program aired. Under this pay formula, when the Breakfast Club achieved full sponsorship, which it did in 1946, McNeill's pay would grow to $169,000.

McNeill's agreement with the Blue Network provided for two weeks of paid vacation a year, during which the network would hire guest toastmasters who would bring their own style to the show. In 1947, actor Walter O'Keefe was hired to be a substitute toastmaster. Although reluctant at first, primarily because he had never heard of the morning show, he decided to take the assignment when his agent informed him of the fee he would receive. In reminiscing about the experience, he said the show was one of the most exquisite he had ever experienced, largely due to producer Cliff Petersen's handling of the broadcast's minute details. By the third day of his week as toast-

Sam Cowling and the March through the audience

Fran Allison as the humorous Aunt Fanny

Don's specialty, interviews with ordinary people in the audience

Autograph signing for Breakfast Club fans

Helping the needy in Chicago with the Reverse Giveaway, 1947

Breakfast Club cast during a train stop in Vancouver, 1953

Don's fortieth birthday celebration, 1947

Overwhelming crowds for the Madison Square Garden broadcast, 1946

Don's grand entrance at Madison Square Garden

master, O'Keefe said he called his agent and asked for a daytime show on the coast. Within ninety days he was host of the quiz show, *Double or Nothing*, where he stayed for the next five years. O'Keefe credited the *Breakfast Club* with giving his career a boost, and he also was generous with his praise for McNeill whom he had never met before the vacation stint in Chicago, adding that anyone who can attract and keep people as good as the *Breakfast Club* crew must be pretty good himself.[6]

For the second week of McNeill's vacation, ABC brought in someone who was familiar with the format of the show because he had been the *Breakfast Club's* first Swift announcer. Durward Kirby left the show in 1943 to join the Navy and after the war was transferred by NBC from Chicago to New York where he began a spectacular career, first as the host of *Honeymoon in New York* on network radio, then on television with the *Garry Moore Show*. Kirby was a gifted showman with a knack for spontaneous humor and repartee. In his biography, Kirby recalls McNeill's management of ad libs.

> After I worked the show for a couple of weeks, Don invited me to sit at a large, round breakfast table and contribute to some of the goings on. . . . Don had a large, leather bound, indexed portfolio which he brought to the show each day. It was on the table immediately in front of him. Don might say to me, "Well, Durward, what did you do over the weekend?"
> "I went fishing with a couple of guys."
> "Did you catch any?"
> "Nope. We got skunked."
> Now during this give and take, he would open the book to the indexed letter "F" and there would be jokes about fishing. And he would read, "You didn't get any bites, huh? Well, this friend of mine went fishing and he got nothing but bites. His body was covered with mosquito bites when he got home."
> As he hit the punchline, he would raise his arm as a signal to the orchestra, and when he let the arm down, they would play the next tune. That way no one could top him.
> When I subbed for Don, I would ask him to loan me the book, but there was no way he would even consider letting that joke book out of his sight.[7]

It was clear that both McNeill and the *Breakfast Club* were successful. The show had achieved full sponsorship and increased audience ratings. McNeill couldn't help but feel vindication that his approach to the audience was working, most likely because his style was to enjoy a laugh but not at some else's expense. When he became serious it was done to uplift and inspire, not command or rage. He could and did sell with conviction, but not with crassness or sarcasm. Finally, he was interested in and paid attention to his audience, which McNeill had no trouble defining:

> the trade press writes nice things about the show calling it as American as a three ring circus, county fair, or a crop of corn . . . and I hope the program will continue to reflect just that . . . not the America of the tabloids, divorce court, or sophisticates just ordinary people . . . friendly, religious Americans who are happy and proud of their work. They have made the Breakfast Club what it is today.[8]

The values which McNeill defined for himself, his family, and career would provide focus and strength for the opportunities and challenges he would face in the ensuing years. The fact that the audience continued its loyalty to the *Breakfast Club* is an indication that it accepted him and those values.

9

The *TV Club*
(1950–1951)

After the war, the few experimental television stations that had begun broadcasting in 1940 returned to the air. Beginning in 1945, a scramble was underway by radio station owners, newspaper publishers, electronics manufacturers, and motion picture companies to obtain television frequencies. Television was still a dream for the average American, but its future was clearly a bright one, while radio was seen as a medium that was facing a change and not one for the better. An NBC vice president, Merlin Aylesworth, was pretty grim about what he called "ear radio" in 1949:

> I predict that within three years the broadcast of sound, or ear radio, over giant networks will be wiped out. Powerful network television will take its place, completely overshadowing the few weather reports and recorded programs left to the remaining single, independent ear radio stations. And stars who are now big in ear radio will be the best in television.[1]

In 1946, anyone with a television set in Chicago could watch whatever was offered on Channel 4, WBKB-TV, or nothing, since it provided the only regular television service available in the city. When retailer Marshall Field wanted to sponsor a television program to show off some of its women's apparel, the concept of *Don McNeill's Dinner Club* seemed like a natural, especially since the store had used McNeill a year and a half earlier on a trial video program that was the first use of an established network star in an all-television show. The experimental series had a twenty-six–week airing on Wednesday nights. Building on the night club theme, each week viewers were taken to various Chicago nightspots which were featured in film footage. McNeill and Sam Cowling appeared in a make-believe night club visited by models wearing the sponsor's clothes. The series did not please the local reviewer for *Billboard* magazine who complimented McNeill on having "a few good jokes" but not much else.

> Thruout [*sic*] the program McNeil [*sic*] acted as if he were engaging in a lark. Some might say his actions reflected the nonchalance of a truly great and self-confident performer. But McNeil carried his "I don't care" attitude too far, especially when he made light of present-day video, comparing it to radio in its infancy. Considering that McNeil is getting more than $500 per performance and that the series is costing Field's about $65,000 (including promotion costs), McNeil's attitude, which seemed to express a feeling that he was superior to the video medium, was out of place. He should have taken his work more seriously and put on a real show that did not have the fluffs and mistakes this one did.[2]

The series could boast that it made history when it originated one program from the roof of the University Club with five hundred in the audience and, in doing so, produced the city's first remote telecast. The live audience probably exceeded those watching at home, since Chicago only had an estimated four hundred sets in 1946.[3]

The *Breakfast Club* could not ignore television, and in September 1948 the cast was invited to help inaugurate ABC's new Chicago station, WENR-TV, with a nighttime special from the Civic Theater. The reaction by the critic for the *Chicago Daily News* was such that any reader would conclude that the program was the first of many to come. "Don McNeill, Fran Allison, Sam Cowling, Jack Owens and Patsy Lee all are brimming with talent and do a smooth, graceful job of entertaining. ABC has a gold mine of television stars in those five alone, and we hope they are on the air regularly soon."[4]

The fact that the *Breakfast Club* would become a television show was a foregone conclusion according the show's *Yearbook of 1948*. While acknowledging that an experimental broadcast in Philadelphia and others were successful, the yearbook indicated that the cast was not entirely pleased with the results. Furthermore, since New York was the only city providing morning programs on television, it was unlikely that a video *Breakfast Club* would be seen in many markets. The option of doing an evening show caused some concern for the cast which already had a full schedule preparing for five hours of morning broadcasts every week.

The same year ABC signed on WENR-TV in Chicago, it opened television stations in New York and Detroit, and the following year two more stations joined the fold, one in San Francisco, the other in Los Angeles. Owning stations in five major cities was evidence that the nation's newest radio network had decided to be a major player in television despite a looming problem: ABC was losing money fast. Not only were the startup costs for television high, but the revenue stream was slow. Advertisers were understandably reluctant to buy time on the new medium with so few sets in use. The predictions for television were glowing, but the reality for ABC was gloomy. A former ABC executive, Sterling "Red" Quinlan, wrote that venturing into television produced an $8 million loss between 1947 and 1950.[5] ABC couldn't sustain the television losses much longer while, at the same time, trying to make itself attractive to possible investors or buyers. Revenues from radio, particularly fully sponsored programs like the *Breakfast Club*, helped offset the red ink. McNeill's contract would expire the next year, and the prospect of his being hired away by a rival network worried ABC. Since they already had a personality with a proven success record on radio, it made sense to use him on television plus ensure he wouldn't jump ship. ABC responded to these realities by drafting a contract to keep McNeill with the network and his *Breakfast Club* on the air for the next twenty years. Never before had a network signed a radio performer to an agreement which ran that long, and it was evidence of how valuable ABC felt their morning personality had become. McNeill and the network's vice chairman, Mark Woods, signed an agreement on June 19, 1950, in New York, which guaranteed that the *Breakfast Club* would continue until 1971 unless both parties agreed to a cancellation. In addition, ABC signed McNeill to an exclusive television contract which included his being featured along with members of the *Breakfast Club* cast in a weekly nighttime show that would begin in the fall. Under the terms of the contract, McNeill was to appear on the *Breakfast Club* nine months of every year from Chicago plus two weeks from New York City and an additional two weeks from locations around the country. His annual vacation would consist of a generous eight weeks.

Written into the agreement was the stipulation that Kay and the three McNeill sons would continue to make appearances on the *Breakfast Club*, but not in a way that would interfere with their normal life. Commenting on this provision, McNeill said that the "boys will not assume the roles of professional actors . . . that their appearances will be on a sporadic basis."[6]

Press reports speculated that the contract meant McNeill would take home at least $250,000 a year just for the radio show. Television shows would mean that he would have even higher earnings. One columnist explained McNeill's spectacular success in his unfaltering appeal to the heartland:

> McNeill's seventeen years with the same show is not so much a phenomenon as a revelation of human nature. The backbone of his audience is found in communities of 30,000 to 40,000 people. On the air his personality comes over with a warm, friendly, good neighbor sincerity, which apparently goes right to the hearts of his regular listeners. In addition to the cheerful and optimistic atmosphere, and gags which come right out of the fields of Iowa, standard program features include a daily prayer, poem and inspirational story.[7]

Another critic, Dwight Newton of the *San Francisco Examiner* was effusive in his praise for the *Breakfast Club* in a column published a month before the twenty-year contract was announced.

> I love the Breakfast Club and I guess I'm not the only one because tomorrow ayem it celebrates its 5,000th consecutive broadcast, and it takes a lot of lovers to keep a program on the air that long.
>
> The program is clean, sincere, supercharged with energy, packed with expert talent, continually refreshed by new faces, new stories.
>
> The secret of its success may lie in Don McNeill's attitude toward his important radio assignment: "Running the 'Breakfast Club' is better than working."[8]

McNeill would soon be working very hard, as plans for an evening television production were being drafted, but for the moment he had to wind up his New York City broadcasts. On successive mornings that week, the *Breakfast Club* originated from a variety of locations, giving thousands of New Yorkers a chance to see the cast in the flesh. They performed in the Ritz Theater, on the deck of the U.S.S. *Enterprise* at the Brooklyn Naval Yard before an audience of over 3,000, and finally on board the *Queen Mary* which was docked at Pier 90. The next day, McNeill, his family, and advertising executive Ralph Bergsten and his family returned to the *Queen Mary* to begin a six-week European vacation.[9] McNeill kept a diary of the trip, writing as the voyage began:

> June 23, 1950—Means a lot to me, that date. Just 17 years ago, after a stifling night in a cheap hotel, I let a radio audience have their first listen to a scared but earnest young man. Now, 5,045 broadcasts later, the five McNeills and seven pieces of luggage (thanks to nylon and Kay) and the three Bergstens are on the Queen Mary bound for Europe. Sudden thought before retiring—this trip might go faster if it didn't drag three night clubs, two theaters and a bowling alley along with it.

Back in Chicago, radio and motion picture star Don Ameche took over the toast-master's duties for which he was well prepared. Ameche was a quick study and sharp on the air, but in addition he had a midwestern background that served him well on the *Breakfast Club*. He grew up in Kenosha, Wisconsin, and attended schools in Iowa and Wisconsin before beginning a career in acting. Ameche was at ease interviewing housewives and especially youngsters, since he and his wife had six children, ages six to seventeen years.

When McNeill returned from his longest vacation ever, there was much to be done. During the next month and a half he and the *Breakfast Club* cast would begin rehearsing for the premier of *Don McNeill's TV Club* which was set for Wednesday, September 13. The program was billed as being "A Variety Family Show" which made it similar to the morning show but different in its effort to reach the entire family rather than concentrating on housewives. The first option to sponsor the show was given to the current advertisers on *Breakfast Club*. Philco became the sole sponsor for the venture, buying time on sixteen stations for "live" transmission Wednesday nights and delayed kinescope airing on twenty-three others.

The show was the property of Don McNeill Enterprises, Inc., which consisted of twelve people hired to help with producing, writing, publicizing, and administering the show. The *Breakfast Club* crew was augmented with technical people required for television plus others who could make creative suggestions, such as writer Paul Rhymer, the comic genius behind *Vic and Sade*. McNeill was clearly in charge of the program and put many hours into its planning, which, by his own calculation, took five times as much time and worry as his daily radio program. For example, two nights a week he stayed at a downtown hotel in order to be able to attend late rehearsals for the television show and be ready for the First Call to Breakfast the next morning. Family man McNeill would leave his suburban home early on Monday and not return until late Thursday.

Comparing the effort and personnel required for the hour of radio with the demands of television makes the point. Thirty-six persons put the *Breakfast Club* on the air each morning, while eighty-eight were used for the *TV Club*. Both shows originated in the Civic Theater and shared the same staff, cast, and orchestra members, but with television came twenty-five video and audio engineers, eleven technical assistants, ten stage hands, and six artists and shop crew members. Rehearsal times for the two shows further demonstrated the different approaches taken with the two media. An estimated 1,037 hours were expended each week to rehearse and produce the *TV Club*, which was about twenty times what was required for the *Breakfast Club*.[10] Planning each week's *TV Club* used up over 100 man-hours, with another 145 devoted to set design and construction. How different from the *Breakfast Club*'s hour-long pre- and post-broadcast rehearsals.

With television came the challenge to make everything visually interesting, as each song was seen as a mini-production with a set and costumes for the singer as opposed to their street clothes and performances in front of a mike, music stand, and orchestra for radio. Commercials were produced live in a separate studio on the forty-second floor of the Civic Building where three cameras stood ready to show Philco's refrigerators, televisions, and ovens at work. Aside from using cast members from the morning program and some of the same concepts such as audience interviews, the evening show had the trappings of an elaborate and expensive production in contrast with other television experiments going on in the city.

Chicago, which twenty years earlier had brought small-town life to the nation on radio, was experimenting with something called the "Chicago School of Television." Like its audio genesis, Chicago-style television was often intimate and natural. *Time* magazine explained that the programs reflected the realities facing their producers. "Lacking big budgets, elaborate equipment and big-name talent, they are forced to shortcut the elaborate. They specialize in what they call 'simplified realism' and 'ad-lib' drama. By banning studio audiences they can use the four walls of every set."[11] One of the best examples of the genre was embodied in a half-hour variety show NBC aired Sunday nights called *Garroway at Large*. Beginning in 1949, Dave Garroway and a stock company of singers, dancers, and comedians put on a relaxed show in a studio without a live audience. Everything on the show seemed real, if not spontaneous, with a minimum of fuss and no pretension. *Garroway at Large* ended after two seasons when the sponsor pulled out, but most likely the show would not have continued much longer as Garroway was off to New York to begin preparations for NBC's new morning television program, *Today*.

The *Breakfast Club* clearly was in keeping with the folksy tradition of the Chicago School, but the *TV Club* attempted a more sophisticated style. Undoubtedly, the selection of British actor and Hollywood producer Ivor McLaren as the *TV Club's* producer played a part in shaping the show's style. In addition to owning his own film production company before the war, McLaren had produced and directed over 650 television shows. ABC felt his experience was needed to build successful programs on its nascent television network.

The premiere broadcast of the *TV Club* had plenty of homey touches, beginning with McNeill's entering the theater from the lobby, patting women in the audience as he walked toward the stage, and stopping to kiss an elderly woman. Later in the show he asked everyone to shake hands with the person behind them. He interviewed a seventy-two-year-old man and his fifty-four-year-old wife from New Orleans who surprised all with their energetic jitterbugging. McNeill boasted that his new show had everything a viewer could ask for including "dancing girls" (showgirls from Chicago's Chez Paree did a short kicking routine), "wrestling" which cued Sam Cowling and Philco's hefty announcer Bob Murphy to come out in tights, and "puppets" which brought Cowling back, this time fitted with strings as he mimicked a marionette's amble. Borrowing from the *Breakfast Club*, Cowling led a march through the theater which ended in predictable chaos. The morning Prayer Time was carried over too, but only after McNeill read a letter from a woman who wrote, "I hope you will give up on that foolishness of a 'moment of prayer'" because millions of people will be offended. McNeill said that prayer was in the preamble of the U.S. Constitution and it would be part of his show too, then proceeded to ask everyone to bow their heads.

Screen star Gloria Swanson was the featured guest for the premiere and, besides receiving $5,000, got the royal treatment including two rooms at the Ambassador East Hotel, one for herself, the other for her maid. Having such a star brought attention and excitement to the new show. A few minutes before the broadcast began McNeill received a telegram from an old Swanson friend, the patriarch of the Kennedy family, Joseph Kennedy. It read: "Dear Don my very best to you on your premiere tonight and with you and my favorite actress Gloria on your program it can't help but be a smash hit."

The critics offered mixed reviews. For several, Swanson was seen as a definite plus, such as *Variety's* critic who liked a skit in which McNeill played a Latin lover to Swanson's femme fatale.[12] One Chicago writer wondered why more wasn't made of the film star's recent comeback in *Sunset Boulevard*. Larry Wolters of the *Chicago Daily Tribune* found the show had a Chicago touch in that, "it's simple, it's folksy, it's wholesome, it's easy going," and predicted success in the midwest, but wondered about whether it would go over in Manhattan. He also commented on what he saw as "staged spontaneity" in what was purported to be an ad-lib show.[13] Val Adams at the *New York Times* found McNeill's performance mechanical, "He offered little or no warmth which a television camera demands. . . . It is only natural that Don might become lost in mechanical routine after so many years behind a radio microphone, but with television the shades are up and a change of habit is in order." Adams concluded that the *TV Club* was simply a duplicate of the morning show "which was better heard and not seen. It just doesn't seem to me appropriate as an after-dinner liqueur."[14] Chicago writer Jack Mabley praised the production for making a skillful adaptation to television. Mabley concluded that, unlike most audience participation shows, "McNeill's agents . . . have a knack for spotting people who are not living clichés and McNeill has a genius for drawing them out."[15]

A trio of critics had McNeill's full attention, Tom, Don, and Bob McNeill were reserved in their judgment, but their friends weren't. The boys told their dad what was wrong with the show and dutifully reported the word in the neighborhood, which was "Gee, does your old man stink!" McNeill would bring their suggestions to the studio where one director had the temerity to say to the boss, "Whom am I doing this show for—your ten million viewers or the McNeill boys?"[16]

Show number two featured Victor Borge who, according to critic Wolters, saved the program from being "stuck on dead center." Wolters felt the cast was too restrained, especially McNeill, who should "unlax" and "get out of those double breasted suits and into something more casual."[17]

After several more weeks on the air, the stylistic differences between New York and Chicago were made explicit when Janet Kern wrote "An Open Letter to Don McNeill" in her column for Hearst's *Chicago Herald-American.*

> Let's face it, Don, you've got a problem. You're just a little bit bashful, aren't you? It makes you kind of cold and unapproachable in person until you warm up, slowly. All your warm friendliness is in your voice on radio . . . but it doesn't come over to studio and TV audiences. Come on, Don, relax a little!
>
> Why try to compete with the New York variety shows? They're not your type, and they're not for your fans. . . . Those folks who think Prayer Time and Cowling humor are "corn" just won't like you, no matter what you do.[18]

Whatever the show's problems, their solutions had to be fitted around the deadline of producing the next *TV Club.* McNeill and his staff did not dismiss the critics' observations and toward the end of the first season prepared a press packet which admitted some of their show's failings.

There were rough spots at first. After an auspicious and most successful debut on September 13, the extravaganza dipped a little. But McNeill and his TV Clubbers worked hard to iron out the kinks. Some changes were made in the back-of-the-scenes personnel; experiments were made with camera angles; the format was changed ever so slightly to make a better balanced production.[19]

The backstage shifting occurred in November when Gerry Morrison moved from being a writer to producer, replacing Ivor McLaren, and Ed McKean was hired as chief writer. Both had experience. Morrison, an Iowan, had produced bandleader Wayne King's television show. McKean had migrated from his native Kansas to Hollywood where he wrote for Edgar Bergen and Art Linkletter.

By December, the *TV Club* was "back on the tracks," according to *Variety's* critic who liked the "curtailment of audience interviews" and praised McNeill's more relaxed, friendly manner on camera.[20] Judging from *Variety's* review, McNeill may have been taking critic Kern's letter to heart by trying to appear more comfortable on camera. McNeill's wardrobe expanded somewhat with the suit and tie giving way to an occasional sport coat and open shirt. Also, some elements closely associated with the morning show were woven into the *TV Club*. Aunt Fanny started visiting every other week and Kay McNeill made an appearance December 13 when she helped "re-decorate" the *TV Club* set by tearing down a plain formal backdrop in preparation for a warmer club room look which arrived the following week. Former Canadian jockey Jimmie Darou and his wife Gertrude came by on one show to bring McNeill up to date on his life since his last visit to the *Breakfast Club*.

The *TV Club* made two road trips, one to New York City, where Beatrice Kay was a guest, and another to Los Angeles, where Ronald Reagan and Carmen Miranda were featured. The guests on the show were mostly drawn from show business: Eddie Anderson (Rochester), Joan Blondell, Billie Burke, Joe E. Brown, Leo Carillo, Barry Fitz-gerald, Rhonda Fleming, Ann Harding, Boris Karloff, Arthur Lake (Dagwood Bumstead), Diana Lynn, Raymond Massey, Marie Mc-Donald, Patricia Morrison, Ann Sheridan, Herb Shriner, Cornelia Otis Skinner, and Dorothy Shay. One night Johnny Lujack and the Chicago Bears were guests along with the McNeill boys. In another show, Jack Dempsey and Joe Louis dropped by to demonstrate their boxing skills in a ring set up on the stage. McNeill served as referee for the sparring and demonstrated his knowledge of boxing in a most unusual interview setting.

The tireless effort and enterprising features were not paying off with the critics, the network affiliates who didn't carry the show, or the sales expectations of the sponsor. Philco announced that effective March 1951 it was cutting its sponsorship of the *TV Club* in half.[21] It is difficult to find the reason for the decision, considering the fact that competition from other network shows which were scheduled against the *TV Club* was inconsistent and varied from month to month. Philco Corporation's sales and earnings dipped slightly in the first nine months of 1951, but the company anticipated it would "have an-other successful year," most likely in anticipation of robust revenues during the Christmas season.[22] The larger problem was the number of stations which opted to broadcast the show. *Variety* wrote that Philco wanted thirty stations to carry the program "live," but the network was only delivering about half that number.

While he was in New York in June, Philco signed McNeill to a new agreement for the slimmed-down *TV Club*, cut to thirty min-utes, every other week. During an interview over WJZ-TV, New York, McNeill talked about his views on television compared with radio. He admitted being reluctant to put the *Breakfast Club* on television, saying he worried that the medium would not pick up all the "move-ment, the color, the warmth" of the show. It was only after studying the 1948 experimental simulcast from Philadelphia that McNeill said he felt a format could be found that might allow his radio show to work on television. Once the *TV Club* series began, McNeill said, "We continued to experiment, learning by trial and error . . . we elimi-nated much scenery and arty effects." In a mea culpa, McNeill con-fessed, "I had to make myself over to get rid of a seeming stiffness of manner."[23] The problem he must have seen was that the changes were coming too late.

July and August were off months for the show and the time was used to get ready for the second season plus import another new pro-ducer, George Cahan, from ABC's Hollywood office. He replaced Leonard Holton, who had been in the producer's hot seat for the final months of the first season. As they were making preparations for the fall opener, the *TV Club* crew could not have helped but be influenced by an item in *TV Forecast* titled, "Please Come Back Don McNeill."

Don you just weren't yourself on TV. People who have listened to you for 17 years didn't recognize you at all. You acted a little stiff, a trifle formal and cool.

It didn't help any, either, when your Breakfast Club gang got out of their working clothes and put on some starchy manners.

But showmanship won out. You fooled us all, Don, all the time we thought you were roped and hog tied by script writers you were lying in the weeds plotting and planning. Your last 3 shows were great, really great.

Here's why. You tossed all the fancy stuff overboard, took off the girdle and swung easy. You grabbed the mike and whooped it up with the studio audience. It was the same, great old Breakfast Club routine all over again and everybody loved it.

TV needs you Don. It needs your entire happy gang, too.[24]

The September 1951 kickoff show had comedian Joe E. Brown in the guest spot who came on strong with his bumpkin routine and a monologue on matrimony. *Variety's* critic said McNeill handled ban-tering with his old friend Brown "naturally and effectively" but panned the emcee's efforts with some of the gag material.[25] When it shed thirty minutes, the new *TV Club* also dropped features that were reminiscent of the *Breakfast Club*. Time restraints confined Patsy Lee and Johnny Desmond to a single song apiece and Cowling's role was simply to do a walk-on in the opening. The guest list was paired down to interesting people rather than celebrities, perhaps as a way to save expense. For example, one week's guest was the director of New York's Hayden Planetarium. Aunt Fanny continued her visits on alternate shows.

Late in November, Philco announced it was dropping its sponsorship of the *TV Club* largely because of the number of stations carrying the show shrunk from sixteen to ten live hook-ups and twenty-three to twenty stations using kinescopes to air it on a delayed basis. In response, McNeill told *Variety* that he was withdrawing from television "completely for the time being" and that he asked ABC not to look for sponsors to replace Philco.[26] On radio, Philco continued with their running sponsorship of the fourth quarter of the *Breakfast Club*. For some cast members like Patsy Lee, the end of the *TV Club* was a relief from the dawn to dark rehearsals and the challenge of having to memorize songs.[27]

McNeill speculated that eventually he might want to get back on television, perhaps with a simulcast version of his morning show. He told *Variety* that some of the blame for the *TV Club's* demise could be attributed to the networks. "I hold a dim view of Chicago's future as a television production center unless the networks take positive action soon to provide top facilities and to prevent the movement of good production personnel to the two coasts." McNeill expressed his frustration with the realities of performing on television which required that he relinquish control of his show to "property men, stage hands, electricians, and camera crew." He wanted to be in charge, and radio gave him that control in the palm of his hand. The master interviewer also noticed how "guests who are warm, human personalities when they are interviewed on radio have a tendency to freeze up and lose their color as well as their voices when they're confronted with a battery of spotlights, lenses, and theatrical props."[28]

The final *TV Club* on December 19 was somewhat bittersweet with Victor Borge making a return visit, comedian Gil Lamm, and Aunt Fanny. No discernible theme was evident in the show. During his good-byes, McNeill confidently told his audience that although the *TV Club* was ending, some day he would return to television.

Over at NBC, Dave Garroway met a similar fate when the sponsor of *Garroway at Large*, Congoleum-Nairn, dropped out, purportedly because of rising costs. Armour Meats had the option to take over, but with the understanding that NBC would guarantee a minimum number of stations that would carry the Sunday night series.[29]

The network either could not or would not find enough stations to carry the innovative program. After another potential sponsor failed to sign, the network did not aggressively seek other buyers.[30] Another indication that the networks were not committed to developing the midwest as a production center was the failure of NBC to follow through with plans to expand its television studio space to accommodate additional network shows. The people who made Chicago a creative television market were feeling the pull to leave. Garroway's director, Bill Hobin, asked to be reassigned to New York where Garroway would soon be headed to get ready for his *Today* show stint.

Chicago continued to supply network television with its special brand of programming in the early 1950s, including the children's show for adults, *Kukla, Fran, and Ollie*, an evening soap opera *Hawkins Falls*, Studs Terkel and his friends on *Studs' Place*, Marlin Perkins from the Lincoln park Zoo in *Zoo Parade*, Don Herbert as the forerunner of Bill Nye's *Science Guy* in *Mr. Wizard*, and the long-running, Sunday afternoon favorite, *Super Circus*. Some of these shows won major awards. Each was built with an economy of scale that arose from a tight budget and was fashioned with a simple honesty toward the viewer without a trace of arrogance, perhaps in part because everyone involved was new to television and a little scared.

Television had penetrated about one-third of the nation's homes by 1951, which resulted in a major downshifting of network radio programming. The ratings for nighttime shows dropped precipitously from 1948 to 1951 and with them dropped the charges to sponsors for buying time on the programs. For example, the Hooper Rating for Jack Benny's Sunday night radio show went from 26.5 in 1948 to 4.8 three years later.[31] Ratings for daytime radio shows, however, continued to hold their audience, possibly because listening could be done while working and daytime television programming was relatively undeveloped.

Thus, when McNeill finished his last *TV Club* broadcast on December 19, 1951, he could take comfort in knowing that his showmanship ability would be appreciated the next morning on the *Breakfast Club*. His twenty-year contract was still intact, guaranteeing him an income of about a quarter million dollars annually and making him the highest paid broadcaster in Chicago.[32] McNeill's unparalleled success in radio affirmed his ability and instincts about entertaining, but the requirements of television were so draining and demanding that putting it aside must have been a relief.

Some shifts in the corporate structure of the network were getting everyone's attention at ABC. Edward Noble was looking for a way to save or sell his network, which was struggling to stay afloat because of the high costs of getting into television. Noble had brought in additional investors to help pay the bills, but that strategy was not going to make the network competitive. The radio side was making money while television was pushing the firm deeper into the red. CBS was interested in buying ABC, as were International Telephone and Telegraph, General Tire and Rubber, and United Paramount Theaters, a company formed after a 1948 Supreme Court decision forced the big Hollywood film producers to spin off their theater chains into separate companies, thereby divorcing Paramount Pictures from United Paramount Theaters. United Paramount president Leonard Goldenson and Noble began talking about a merger early in 1951. Goldenson balked at Noble's $25 million asking price for ABC; however the five television stations the network owned and operated made the deal attractive enough to conclude. They signed a merger agreement in May 1951 only to begin what would become an extended waiting period while the Federal Communications Commission prepared for hearings to decide if the deal should go through. The first witnesses were called in January 1952, and by then the stock of both ABC and United Paramount had begun to drop. Former ABC insider, Red Quinlan, described the situation as bleak for the upstart network:

> By now, ABC knew it had but one year to live. Its borrowing power had been extended to the limit. Its debt had jumped from 7 to 11 million dollars. Edward Noble had personally signed a note for 4 million. Paydays were met at the last minute. If the merger was denied, ABC clearly was facing bankruptcy.[33]

Somehow ABC made it through another year, and in February 1953 the FCC announced it had approved the merger. Now the network had resources which would enable it to produce and buy television programs comparable to those on CBS and NBC. It would take the fledgling network the next twenty years to gain parity, but the battle had begun.

10

Breakfast Club
Road Trips

In preparing a story about the *Breakfast Club*'s fifteenth anniversary in 1948, *Chicago Tribune* columnist Larry Wolters asked McNeill why he thought his show had lasted all those years and why hundreds flocked to the studio every morning to witness the broadcast. McNeill's reply showed he had a clear image of his studio audience:

> I think it's just a case of old friends meeting for the first time. Most of these people have heard me off and on for fifteen years—their children have grown up with me—and I guess it's only natural they want to see the guy they have had for breakfast in their home for that long.
>
> I hope to continue the Breakfast Club indefinitely. I think I have probably found my niche in life in this program—natural, friendly, neighborly contact with people and no prepared script.[1]

The show clearly established itself as a way to reach a national audience from Chicago, and the early hour didn't prevent a parade of celebrities from dropping by. Some of the better known visitors included Bob Hope, Gene Kelly, Jimmy Stewart, Gregory Peck, Jane Russell, Burt Lancaster, Lucille Ball, Desi Arnez, Jack Webb, Eddie Fisher, Ernie Ford, Louella Parsons, and Groucho Marx. Marx complained to a writer researching a story for *Collier's* magazine that he never got any breakfast when he was on the show. Nor did Marx much care for the broadcast's early hour. "You know they get up in the middle of the night to put on that program? I don't see how McNeill does it. I think he stays home and sleeps all morning. I think that's really George Jessel up there, putting on an Ohio accent."[2]

Jerry Lewis was wide awake when he appeared on the show and livened things up when he massacred commercials and grabbed Eddie Ballantine's baton, taking the band to places it had never been before. He really got everyone's attention after setting a script on fire while Bob Murphy was reading it. Murphy couldn't finish the spot and failed to give a station break cue to over 275 stations along the network.

Danny Kaye made his entrance to the *Breakfast Club* pretending to be sleepwalking. When he "woke up," he told everyone in the audience they were "mad, mad, mad" for being up at that hour. Kaye became enamored with a spot for ironing board covers and throughout the remainder of the show gave the client a plug. He also plugged UNICEF and its efforts to help children in developing countries around the world.

One guest lost a bet and ended up walking/hitch-hiking 820 miles from his home in Texarkana, Texas, to Chicago. Elmer Feagins and his wife were having breakfast one morning and listening to the *Breakfast Club*. Mrs. Feagins, who was planning a visit to Chicago, told her husband that when she got to Chicago she would just walk into the studio and chat with McNeill. "Yeah, I'll bet," replied Feagins, who said the show was probably rigged. "If you do, I'll walk or hitch-hike all the way to Chicago." With a story like that she naturally made it on the show and gleefully told McNeill the details about the bet she had just won. Plans were made for her forty-seven-year-old husband to take his vacation from his job as a locomotive fireman with the Missouri-Pacific Railroad so he could make good on his bet. Feagins told a reporter with the Texarkana *Gazette* that half the people he worked with thought he would not go through with it while others thought he was crazy to even try. He explained that everyone seemed to enjoy the gag and he was getting a lot of fun out of it, too. A six-day trek was scheduled so he would arrive in time for the *Breakfast Club's* eighteenth anniversary broadcast on June 22, 1951. Publicity about the bet made Feagins an instant celebrity in Texarkana, where he was asked to lead the local rodeo parade as a send-off to his journey which took him to Little Rock, Memphis, St. Louis, Springfield, and Peoria. The entire cast had fun sending Feagins presents during his march. McNeill wrapped up a pair of size thirteen shoes in case Feagins's feet became swollen, Aunt Fanny sent a boxed lunch, and Patsy Lee packaged an oversized thumb. He finally reached Chicago on Friday morning, June 22, and walked into the Civic Theater during the broadcast to be met by McNeill, and to his surprise, the whole Feagins family, which included five children and a daughter-in-law.

Another Texan got more than he bargained for when he was interviewed by McNeill one morning. Tom Joseph, a member of the Texas state legislature from Waco and a bachelor, told McNeill his nickname was "bedspread" because he had been turned down by so many women. McNeill made an impassioned plea to anyone looking for a suitable husband to write in and invited Joseph to come back to the *Breakfast Club* in a month when he would arrange to have an entire studio audience composed of eligible women. "Bedspread" kept McNeill up to date on his prospects and all the proposals he began getting, including one that paid off, resulting in his marriage. Joseph became a minor celebrity, making guest appearances on Garry Moore's *I've Got a Secret* with his story of how his bachelorhood ended after over six hundred girls proposed to him by mail.

Educator and poet Mark Van Doren (father of Charles Van Doren, who became notorious after being a contestant on a rigged television quiz show) was sitting in the audience one morning. When asked what he thought of the show, Van Doren told McNeill it was "silly, not funny" and a "waste of time." Earlier, the cast had led into a commercial with a satire of the balcony scene in *Romeo and Juliet*, and perhaps the scholar took offense at any lampooning of Shakespeare. Audience mail received after the Van Doren appearance turned out to be solidly in favor of the *Breakfast Club's* level of erudition.

When they were not entertaining visitors in Chicago, the *Breakfast Club* cast members continued their tradition of traveling around the country and sometimes found themselves in the news. A western trip in February 1951 marked the first ever *Breakfast Club* broadcast from Los Angeles. As usual, Kay McNeill was along, and shortly after checking into the Beverly Hills Hotel, she went for a walk to stretch her legs after the long train trip from Chicago. While she and a friend were strolling down Sunset Boulevard, they saw a man dart out from a store and right behind him was another man yelling he had just been robbed. Kay ran after the two men, despite the fact she was wearing high-heeled shoes. The trio attracted the attention of a cab driver who joined the chase and successfully collared the suspected robber who was carrying a knife which he had threatened to use on the shopkeeper. After all the excitement, the women decided to take the taxi driver's offer of a ride back to their hotel rather than walk.

Since the Hollywood visit included ten morning shows and one *TV Club* broadcast, the network reasoned that they could satisfy most fans with one of the dates, but when the demand for tickets ran as a high as 10,000 a day ABC was taken by surprise. In an effort to get more seats, the network booked the Earl Carroll Theater Restaurant with a capacity of 1,200 for most of the broadcasts and scheduled the final program in the 7,000-seat Shrine Auditorium. Every morning, more people were lined up in front of the theater on Sunset Boulevard than could be accommodated, which often created traffic snarls. Housewives made up most of those waiting, and some had come a hundred miles to see McNeill and his troupe. Mrs. D. L. Berkey from San Diego told United Press International that "I've listened to him for 18 years . . . all that time I've listened to Don and looked at my husband. Today I decided to skip my husband and just look at Don."[3] Hollywood columnists were speculating about the chances McNeill might make California a permanent home for the show and one quoted Kay as saying "she'd settle down right now if Don would give the word." She added that "he wants to come eventually but thinks the two older boys should not be uprooted until they finish high school."[4]

The routine of taking road trips continued in January 1952, when the *Breakfast Club* chartered a plane for an eight-city tour of the southeast, beginning in St. Louis where more than five thousand fans started lining up two hours before broadcast time. Stan Musial was a guest on the show and good-heartedly took a ribbing about his Cardinals being at the bottom of their league that year. Next stop was Louisville, followed by Nashville where the scramble for tickets was such that all were sold within two days. The War Memorial Building broadcast featured *Grand Ole Opry* star Minnie Pearl. Birmingham was the next city and again the tickets went so fast that a family from Memphis who had tried to attend the Nashville broadcast and had driven to Birmingham failed to get tickets again. They did manage to catch the show in the next city on the tour, Atlanta. From there it was on to several Florida stops beginning with Jacksonville, followed by St. Petersburg where the biggest crowd of the tour filled the city's Coliseum. Connie Mack, long-time manager of the Philadelphia A's, was the featured guest. All 2,700 tickets were gone on the first day, so the cast decided to make an unusual appearance after the broadcast by playing a softball game with the local Quarter Century Club's Kids and Kubs team. An estimated five thousand persons watched as the teams played an abbreviated two-inning game. Cowling was catcher and Aunt Fanny and McNeill took turns as pitcher. Ballantine singled and announcer Jack Callahan doubled, bringing Ballantine home. Despite the radio stars' efforts, one of the seventy-five-plus year olds got on base with a walk and was brought in on a double, tying the score. The tour concluded with several broadcasts from Miami.

Later that year, the cast packed again for an eastern trip that included Pittsburgh, Philadelphia, Washington, and Baltimore. The Baltimore broadcast was complicated by a fire that erupted in the Hippodrome Theater where the show was to originate a few hours later. A bare light bulb fell against a curtain, igniting the fire which destroyed the equipment required for the radio transmission. Even though the blaze was quickly extinguished, there was little time to find a new location and, more importantly, the gear required to produce the show. The local ABC affiliate, WFBR, secured another theater and provided enough equipment to put on the show for the two thousand persons who were resourceful enough to find the alternate location. The cast performed on a platform that had been placed over the theater's orchestra pit, which put McNeill and the singers closer to the audience than was usual. McNeill decided the setup contributed to his having a closer sense of rapport with the audience as well as made it easier to get people on mike quickly for interviews. Thereafter, whenever possible, the cast performed closer to the studio audience. Their eastern trip concluded in New York with a broadcast from Radio City where they had a visit from two of the *Breakfast Club's* most loyal fans, Jimmie Darou and his wife.

When war broke out in Korea in 1950, the *Breakfast Club* continued its tradition of supporting the armed forces. A special $10,000 fund was created to cover travel expenses to make arrangements for the families of seventy-three wounded veterans to spend Christmas together. Family members took advantage of the offer by being with veterans at seventeen military hospitals across the nation. Some of the vets and their wives and children were guests on a special broadcast of the show. The news that month from the war was grim, as United Nations forces were forced to retreat to the 39th parallel. McNeill reported the events on December 29 in a rare *Breakfast Club* news summary following the first song of the morning:

In Korea the Communists are attacking along a 150 mile line. It is not clear if this is the expected big push. Commander Ridgeway is confident we can handle the situation. In Red China,

Communists issued seizure orders for all American property and bank accounts. Effect on Americans to the tune of 150 million bucks. In the U.S., labor shortages exist in some areas. The Labor Department is setting up thirteen new regional committees to find workers. Civilian employees at two California Naval shipyards go on forty-eight hour work weeks next month. The government announced tighter bank credit controls. The government is the sole importer of rubber and hoarding has been forbidden on fifty-five essential materials. Three more production cutbacks in the auto industry and we can see how economic mobilization is being felt in the U.S.

Reading the latest war news continued to be part of McNeill's morning ritual and on Monday, November 27, he began with the report that 100,000 U.N. troops were in retreat from Chinese and North Korean forces that were 200,000 strong. Since the war began, both sides had their share of victories and losses, but now that Communist Chinese forces entered the battle the situation turned for the worse. Putting down the news copy, McNeill looked at the studio audience as he spoke about the war news.

We have faced such crises before. We faced it in Pearl Harbor in December, 1941. I feel that such moments serve to bring us closer together. We will overcome it as we have done before.

You know friends, we here in America are the most prosperous people in the world. But all too often, we are inclined to think of our riches only as material, while disregarding the spiritual. We cannot afford to do this, for without spiritual values, everything else is meaningless. The great men who founded our country realized this. America was dedicated to freedom under God. And as God's help was needed to establish this nation, so it is still needed to sustain the nation and the people in it.

We all want peace. But we cannot have peace—world peace or personal peace—without God's aid. And the way to get His aid is to go to Him and ask Him for it.

I can't think of a better time than right now with the future of the nation hanging in the balance. So I ask you, each and everyone of you, to go to the church or synagogue of your choice today and pray. Take your problems to church—millions leave them there.

The Korean War ended with the signing of an armistice on July 27, 1953, in Panmunjom, but for years afterward there were repeated violations of the agreement. U.S. forces were used to maintain the border between the two Koreas in an effort to minimize intrusions from the North. On March 19, 1956, McNeill read a letter he received from an American soldier who was helping to enforce the truce, Tim B. Nelson of the 2nd Artillery:

> I am a forward observer in an artillery observation post overlooking the Demilitarized Zone of Korea. Every morning my men and I listen to your program over radio "Vagabond." This morning you were telling about the engineering wonders in America. When you finished "America The Beautiful" was sung. Our conversation stopped immediately and everyone listened. It is strange how that one song did more to bring home to us and raise our morale than anything we have heard for a long while. We all come from the Midwest and the picture of the waving grain is very familiar to us—perhaps if we could see and almost smell "home" a little more often as we did today our Korean tour would become a more meaningful experience. Only those who have been away from the states can understand the feeling that sometimes comes over us—a feeling that we have never lived anywhere but here in Korea. Our routine is so strong: Many times our thoughts are so stagnant that it is wonderful to be brought back to the reality of what we are here for and what we have to return to. Thank you so much for helping us out and making our job seem a little more necessary.

Hearing McNeill's voice and his message about the American strength, combined with familiar music, had a powerful effect on the soldier, as his letter indicates. It's likely that the soldier grew up listening to the show with his family which would make for powerful associations.

Despite its being on the air for nearly twenty years, the show continued to sound fresh and succeeded in attracting new listeners and winning kudos. In 1952, *Radio TV Mirror's* audience poll selected McNeill and the *Breakfast Club* as the "variety show of the year." The next year the show was selected as the "favorite non-serial show" by the magazine's poll and in 1954 its "favorite daytime (radio) variety program." Another publication, *Motion Picture Daily*, reported that the *Breakfast Club* was chosen by a poll of radio editors as the "best morning radio program." The program was securely established on the radio landscape as one which met the needs of the audience, the network, and its sponsors.

If the morning show was at the center of McNeill's professional life, his family was second to none in his personal life. Therefore, it was not unusual that the *Breakfast Club's* annual Christmas shows in 1951 and 1952 were broadcast from the high school attended by the McNeill boys, New Trier. A year earlier, the school was featured in a special edition of *Life* magazine on U.S. education in which New Trier was described as being a "public high school at its best." In 1999, *Life* revisited the topic and New Trier noting that the students' taste in clothing had changed in forty-nine years but not the school's tradition of excellence.[5] As an example of student garb in 1950, the article ran a photo of New Trier junior Tom McNeill wearing one of his dad's Hawaiian shirts.

During the 1951 *Breakfast Club* broadcast, New Trier students made up the bulk of the audience in the school's auditorium and McNeill was well versed on their favorite teachers, hangouts, and frustrations at the school. Sam Cowling showed up in a New Trier basketball uniform. In 1952 Don and Bob McNeill helped with the fun and when introduced began saying names of some of their classmates aloud. When asked about the recitation, the boys said for each name read they received a quarter. Don helped with a commercial for O'Cedar polish with a rhyme about shining his teacher's desk. Bob gave the Philco commercial by admitting to setting his clock radio so as to wake up at 3:00 A.M. and listening to ship and police bands. Reflecting on those broadcasts, Bob remembered having anxiety whether or not the show would go well. He also remembered being teased a few years later when he was playing on New Trier's basketball team. When he was shooting free throws, opposing players would chant, "Good Morning Breakfast Clubbers." Despite the distraction, Bob said he managed to make 80 percent of his shots. Whatever distress he felt about his dad's show coming to the school was balanced by the positive attitude the teachers showed toward him as an extension of the program which they obviously knew about and enjoyed.[6]

McNeill interviewed some teachers and students including the son of announcer Don Dowd, who talked about his being on the school's swimming team. New Trier's choir sang a medley of Christmas carols and Kay McNeill provided a Memory Time tribute to the high school saying the students "will remember for the rest of their lives the friends and lessons they learned there."

11

Himself's
Hideaway—
The Perfect Retreat

On June 23, 1953, the *Breakfast Club* turned twenty, and to celebrate the event, McNeill began several months earlier asking listeners to send him the names of their children who were born during the hour the show was first broadcast in 1933. The responses were starting to arrive in January when the cast boarded a train for a tour of the north and northwest. Along the way, they were met by folks who identified themselves as *Breakfast Club* babies in Minot, North Dakota, Shelby and Havre, Montana, and Spokane, Washington. The cast was also greeted by loyal fans who were bearing homemade pies, cakes, and cookies in response to a brief aside McNeill had made on the air about having to give up home-cooking during their upcoming trip. After a swing up to Vancouver, British Columbia, the train stopped in Seattle for a January 20 broadcast scheduled for the city's Civic Auditorium. That was also the day Dwight Eisenhower would be sworn in as president and the staff had concerns that, since the inauguration would be covered on television, the chances of filling the giant auditorium that morning were slim. To the surprise of many, the hall was packed with over eight thousand Breakfast Clubbers that day.

More *Breakfast Club* babies came to say hello when the train stopped at Portland, San Francisco, Oakland, Pasadena, Long Beach, and Hollywood. Later that year, McNeill made a return visit to his alma mater, Marquette University in Milwaukee, for a look around campus and to produce a *Breakfast Club* broadcast from the school's student union. Another road trip that year was designed to help the American Red Cross when the *Breakfast Club* cast encouraged over two thousand members of its audiences in Cleveland, Detroit, Youngstown, Pittsburgh, Rochester, and New York City to donate blood. The McNeills found time for a vacation in Hawaii and, in honor of the trip, McNeill wrote a song, "I Could Never Learn to Hula" which he sang on the show, only once, after returning from the islands.

As June 23 approached, plans were made to get several of the twenty year olds born during the first broadcast to Chicago for the anniversary show. Arrangements were made to have twenty of them and their families flown in from seventeen states and Canada. Just before the anniversary program, the *Breakfast Club* once again changed its origination facilities, from the Civic Theater to one of Chicago's older downtown hotels, the Morrison at Madison and Clark Streets. The move freed the theater for productions by the local ABC television affiliate, WENR-TV. The Morrison was built before the turn of the century, but had been enlarged with several additions, including a forty-six–story tower built in 1927 which gave guests views of Lake Michigan and the city's skyline. In 1930 the Morrison became the home of Cook County's Democratic Party, one of the nation's most effective political machines. The Democrats were still in residence when the *Breakfast Club* moved in.

As a reminder of the *Breakfast Club's* beginning, the anniversary show started off with "Too Much Mustard" with Bill Krenz playing the same ragtime piano he did in 1933. The first quarter of the show was devoted to the twenty Breakfast Club babies and their families who came to the program, each telling the circumstances of their being born in 1933. An additional baby came the farthest: he was a sailor from Okinawa, Japan, Ben Round, who was joined by his mother from Syracuse, New York, whom he hadn't seen in over a year. McNeill saluted twenty-one other babies who were not in the studio but wrote in saying they wanted to be part of those recognized as being born during the first show in 1933.

Announcer Bob Murphy read a proclamation from Chicago Mayor Martin Kennelley making June 23 Don McNeill Day in honor of the program's longevity and what he and his program had meant to the city. McNeill handed the citation to his parents, who with his sister, Agnes Donohue, were among the 1,500 in the audience. The spotlight then turned on the McNeill family and especially their sons: Tom, who would be a sophomore at University of Notre Dame; Don, a senior at New Trier High School; and Bob, a sixth grader. The McNeill boys began debating with their dad about which one of them would take over the show when he retired.

Memory Time gave McNeill a chance to reflect on how the *Breakfast Club* had changed over the past twenty years and some of the highlights he had experienced. During her remembrance, Aunt Fanny credited McNeill with having the ability to bring "brightness, happiness, and comfort" to so many people because he woke up cheerful which meant he went to bed with a clear conscience. She asked him to close his eyes because she had been wanting to do something for a long time, and would be embarrassed if he didn't close his eyes. He did, and she kissed him on the cheek.

Just as the hour came to an end, McNeill announced that he decided to "pop for breakfast" for the first time in twenty years, which cued a parade of Morrison Hotel waiters to file into the room with food and a four-foot birthday cake for McNeill and the cast to cut and share with the audience. In truth, in the early 1940s McNeill had served rolls and coffee to the studio guests, but the experiment ended when many in the audience said they came to see a show, not to eat.

The anniversary simulcast was not McNeill's first return to television, because he had appeared on NBC-TV during the coverage of the political conventions in Chicago the year before, which was allowed in his contract with ABC. Every morning during the Democratic and Republican conventions, Philco sponsored McNeill's *Convention Sidelights* report. His assignment was to find unusual situations and people at various locations around the city using a mobile video unit. One morning he and Bob Hope were at the Brookfield Zoo "interviewing" a donkey and an elephant. On various mornings, he staged a fashion review with Pearl Mesta in front of Buckingham Fountain, rode rides at Riverview Park, interviewed cattle buyers at the Stock Yards while riding horseback, and delivered delegates to meetings by horse-drawn tally-ho. Television technology allowed viewers to experience McNeill and his guests aboard a yacht in Lake Michigan even though the camera was on shore, since a Zoomar lens provided a picture so close that viewers felt they were on the boat. They saw the true relationship of the camera when it zoomed to a wide shot. Considering McNeill's day began well before his convention reports, it made for a hectic couple of weeks for him to rush from the *Breakfast Club* to the site of one of these *Sidelight Reports*. Critic Janet Kern accompanied McNeill on one of his busy mornings and was impressed with his handling of the pressures and confusion of the schedule.[1]

McNeill's staff helped him both maintain and survive a busy schedule, especially his secretary, Mary Canny, who had been with him since 1942 when his previous assistant had joined the WAVES. Canny was a native of Ottumwa, Iowa, who had designs on becoming an actress, but soon after joining the *Breakfast Club* staff forgot about the stage and delved into the task of keeping the show and its boss running smoothly. She recalled that her first meeting with McNeill began with lunch at the M & M Club in the Merchandise Mart. Afterward, they walked into the show's small office that was bursting with unopened mail and papers which had accumulated since the previous secretary left several weeks earlier. McNeill looked around the room and said, "Mary, organize this stuff, will you? Just—well, just take off your hat and go to work!"[2]

From that moment on, Mary not only became a member of the *Breakfast Club* family but was crucial to its daily functioning. Her day would start at 5:30 A.M. to be ready for a 6:15 ride from Sam Cowling or Cliff Petersen to the office to pick up messages, scripts, and commercials. Then they would go to the studio to go through audience cards, sorting out the best ones for McNeill to consider for interviews. Her earlier interest in showmanship helped during those rare times when an announcer failed to show up on time, giving her the chance to read the commercial. Following broadcasts she would attend a post-show breakfast meeting and then get back to the office for the routine of phone calls and mail which often ran as high as 10,000 items a month. Canny described her boss as being easy to work for because, as she put it, he was a psychic. When she was bothered by something and wanted to dump it on him he was able to diffuse the problem with ease.

> In the first instant he senses my state of mind, in the second, he grasps the problem, and in the third he's making some wisecrack which dissipates my irritation swiftly as sticking a pin into a balloon. I laugh, go back to my desk, and settle things easily.[3]

When McNeill's mood would turn quiet and remote, Canny and the staff collaborated to help bring him around. For example, Petersen would put on a Swedish dialect and talk with no one in particular or Cowling might pick up a mop and begin some janitorial duties around McNeill's desk. It was a big loss in 1953 when Canny decided to leave McNeill and accept a job with *McCall's* magazine in New York. She died unexpectedly in 1958.

People discover ways of easing their stress or periods of moodiness, and ever since he was a small boy, McNeill found solace in the out-of-doors. As a youth, he would be taken to his family's summer cottage on the Fox River near Princeton, Wisconsin. Built by his grandfather, it was a simple log cabin without electricity, where he often would sleep out in the woods overnight. His father and grandfather would regularly take him along on their hunting and fishing expeditions, which had become a way of life in the McNeill family. Grandfather McNeill had worked to further conservation by stocking lakes and streams years before the state had established a fish and game commission. In 1940, McNeill and his wife created their own log cabin on some land on small Sylvan Lake northwest of Chicago. The cabin worked as a retreat, but McNeill wanted a larger, more private place to enjoy fishing plus the solitude that nature can provide. He found it in a forty-five–acre tract of wooded land near Barrington, Illinois, which was a forty-minute drive from his Winnetka home. A man-made lake with an island was added and stocked with large-mouth bass and bluegill, plus a comfortable, informal home near the water with enough bedrooms so the family could spend weekends in the country. He named it "Himself's Hideaway," signifying the true purpose of the retreat, which was to offer McNeill a place to get close to nature and recharge his energy for his public role. Here is how he expressed his love for the out-of-doors, and especially fishing:

> Comes the first blush of Autumn, it's out in the field with my German short-hair for pheasants. Comes the first breath of Summer, it's the golf course. But come any time—fishin'. I'm lucky having my own bass lake, but if they're not hitting, I'll hit the road: Canada for wall-eyes and northerns, Florida for bone fish and tarpon. So, forgive me, but fishin's my favorite sport— from pole to pole.

Himself's Hideaway became what McNeill called "every man's dream of where he'd rather be than working." He got so much out of being there that he wanted to make it available as sort of a mini-camp to boys who would benefit as he did from the outdoor experience. The Boys Clubs of Chicago liked the idea of giving underprivileged boys ages ten to fourteen a chance to take advantage of McNeill's generosity. Over a hundred boys representing all nationalities and religions in the city were selected by the Boys Clubs to attend the July and August weekend camps. McNeill covered such expenses as providing a screened sleeping area, a mess tent, food, and a supervisor to plan the outdoor activities for the campers. In exchange, the boys were expected to keep their sleeping area tidy, do the dishes, and dig their own worms for fishing. Each camp session consisted of ten boys plus two adult leaders.

McNeill shared his knowledge of fishing with the boys and helped them learn-by-doing. He and his sons would accompany them on hikes through the woods and join them in other sports including swimming, boating, archery, softball, basketball, badminton, and horseshoes. For many of the boys, the weekend trip to Himself's Hideaway was their first trip beyond the city limits. To make sure things ran smoothly, the camp had rules such as no one being allowed to leave the property nor could any visitors enter. The experience would end early Monday morning, when the campers were driven by bus to the Loop so they could make a guest appearance on the *Breakfast Club* before returning to their homes. McNeill saw the camp as such a success that the weekend boys camp became a tradition at Himself's Hideaway for many summers.

It is clear that McNeill took pleasure in seeing the boys enjoy the same things he found satisfying when he was growing up. He never forgot the struggles of his own youth and wrote about them indirectly in a Memory Time titled, "The Kid Who Always Struck Out."

> There's usually one on every team from every neighborhood.
> A boy who can't quite make the grade; a lad, misunderstood.
> His heart and soul in every play, he tried for every fly,
> But he just can't field like the other boys;
> The ball goes zooming by.
>
> And when his turn comes at the plate, the other side will shout
> "Put 'em across—this guy can't hit!"
> He's the kid who always strikes out.
> You'll never know the bitter pain nor the tear drops in his eye
> As he stands there lost and awkward as that third strike goes by.
>
> Each game for him is a bitter draught, no fun and laughter there
> He wants to be like the other lads without a worldly care.
> But his whole world crashes at his feet,
> He's a mass of gloom and doubt

He'd like a hole to crawl into, each time that he strikes out.
His teammates somehow seem to sense that he can't quite
    make the grade.
There's indifference there, a sickly green and then smiles so
    quickly fade.
He could stay home, all alone, and give up the game, of course
But he wants so hard to be one of them;
It's a constant driving force.

So he grits his teeth and buoys his hopes;
He's the last kid each side chooses.
Then it starts again—his bungling hands,
And of course his ball team loses.
You watch the kid.
You can't help admire the spirit in that breast.
As he stumbles on and fluffs again and fails his every test.
And you somehow feel there'll come a day in another world
    perhaps
Where he'll get a chance and come flying thru like the other
    lucky chaps.
In the Great Beyond you can see him grin as the angels cheer
    and shout—
For that home run he's smashed o'er the Pearly Gates—
The kid who always struck out.

McNeill read the story on the *Breakfast Club* September 7, 1961, but he had told the story several times before, once with a video dramatization on the *TV Club* which featured a boy nervously shouldering a bat. McNeill encouraged his own boys' participation in sports and with his wife, like many suburban parents, spent Friday nights and weekends driving to nearby schools to be in the crowd watching their sons' baseball, basketball, and football games. At home there was backyard basketball, table tennis, billiards, and living-room bowling. In this atmosphere, the boys grew up knowing that their family was more important than anything else in their father's life, even his work. The best example of McNeill's putting his family ahead of a career was his reluctance to move to New York or Hollywood to take advantage of television opportunities in those cities. McNeill felt his sons' education and development might be adversely affected by a move to either coast, so he stayed in Chicago.

An article about McNeill in *Radio-TV Mirror* reached a conclusion which echoed what other writers said about this family man,

> To Don McNeill, the big things in life are simple: The satisfaction of raising a family, watching your children grow, being part of their lives and having them want you to be a part of theirs. The greatest thing, according to Don, is to see what you've done growing up in your children.[4]

Examples of this attitude were evident throughout his private and public life. When he turned forty-six on December 23, 1953, McNeill's present was to take the day off, so Kay McNeill and the boys did the show. A telephone on the desk was connected to one beside McNeill's bed if they needed help from the toastmaster, but none was needed. Instead, at the end of the show McNeill called them to say how well everything went and that he was going back to sleep.

12

1954–1955
Radio-TV Simulcast

By 1954, over 55 percent of the households in the United States had television, and those sets were "on" an increasing amount every year. NBC made the first attempt to lure early morning viewers with its *Today* show in 1952, and although the concept for the program eventually proved to be successful, its first producer admits "for one year we died on the air."[1] At that same time, CBS was attempting to find an audience for its *Morning Show*, first with Jack Paar and then a variety of hosts including Will Rogers, Jr., and Walter Cronkite, who was teamed with a puppet lion named Charlemagne. At midmorning, CBS found success in 1952 when it began simulcasting Arthur Godfrey's network radio show. In the early morning slot, ABC decided to counter with a video version of the *Breakfast Club* from Chicago. In fact, ABC had seriously considered beginning the video version in 1952, but the show's radio sponsors balked at having to pay an additional $4 million for the video addition.[2]

As the number of television homes increased, so did the network's appetite to invest in the medium to attract and keep advertisers. ABC's plan to simulcast the *Breakfast Club* was resurrected in 1954 with an approach that would keep the radio show intact and make sure it was unaffected by the addition of television cameras. Nor would those cameras have much impact on McNeill and the cast, according to comments he made to the press just as the simulcast was about to begin.

McNeill anticipated that "the camera will pick up what happens the same way it picks up the United Nations. We'll pretend it isn't even there." Obviously, he did not plan to quadruple his workload the way he did for the *TV Club* four years earlier. Reflecting back on that experience, McNeill decided that less was more when doing television: "We made too many concessions to TV. We tried to do, without a studio audience, the kind of show that requires one. And we dropped from our basic formula—'Be yourself.'"[3]

During interviews, McNeill was noncommittal when asked about reports that Arthur Godfrey considered him a competitor. In 1953, the *Chicago Sun Times* had carried a story about Godfrey becoming irate after learning that his bandleader, Archie Bleyer, had signed recording contracts with McNeill. Bleyer owned Cadence Records, which was chosen to produce an uplifting song featuring McNeill's narration and a chorus of one thousand teenagers. Another agreement involved Cadence's producing recordings of *Breakfast Club* singer Eileen Parker. Reports were that Godfrey accused his bandleader of treason.[4] McNeill's reaction was simple: "Arthur and I have been very friendly and I've been informed, indirectly, that he still feels the same."[5] Furthermore, McNeill indicated he had no intention of expanding his television work into another nighttime venue.

For the television side of the simulcast, ABC spent $155,000 to transform the Terrace Casino in the Morrison Hotel into a television studio. Four cameras were set up, one with a Zoomar lens to capture closeups of McNeill and the singers, while other locations were above and to the side of the stage which allowed pickup of McNeill's forays into the audience. The set was nonexistent except for a tufted panel behind McNeill's desk, which soon was replaced by a curtain on which was drawn coffee cups and saucers. Three chairs were placed in front of the desk for interviews on the stage. The cast performed at a standup microphone or from a small table near McNeill's desk. Behind these setups was room for the band. Commercials were staged in a small studio set up in the hotel or, when a kitchen set was required, in the Civic Building.

The most complicated part of the simulcast was covering the television feed while commercials were running on radio. The radio spots were recorded in advance, and so that they did not sound any different from the "live" program, they were cut in front of the studio audience after each broadcast for the next day. Door prizes enticed the audience to remain in their seats while commercials were recorded, which typically took about forty-five minutes. During the show, separate announcements were necessary to billboard the radio-only sponsor, and elaborate time cues were required for the cutaways to play the recorded commercials. These spots ran nearly two minutes, which was enough time for McNeill to conduct interviews for the television audience. While doing interviews, he could see a reverse clock which was a long, lighted box with window panels that displayed the elapsing time beginning with two minutes, one minute, and then every interval of fifteen seconds to zero. After one minute and forty-three seconds, the radio commercial would end and the band would play a musical button, which blended the simulcast together. The "digital" clock must have helped, because according to the director, Lynwood King, they never missed running the radio spots. Usually McNeill ended the interview by the time the band began playing, but if not, the music was somewhat jarring, which he acknowledged with the remark, "They just play whenever they want to." A few sponsors, including Swift, Philco, Quaker Oats, Staley Starch, and Mutual of Omaha, bought time on both media, making this arrangement unnecessary.

On February 17, 1954, a week before beginning to simulcast the show, a practice videotaping of the radio show was made. As the announcer began his opening: "From the Terrace Casino of the new Morrison Hotel in Chicago, it's time for your family to join the millions of families from coast to coast and listen to America's favorite, Don McNeill and his Breakfast Club," studio cameras panned photos of the hotel's tower and front plus the city's lakefront skyline near Grant Park. Superimposed overlays headlined the cast members, which included Johnny Desmond as the male singer and Eileen Parker, who had taken over the female singer role when Patsy Lee left to get married and Peggy Taylor went on a European singing tour.

McNeill appeared comfortable with the cameras and, although he gave them plenty of eye contact, was clearly not overwhelmed by their presence. He moved smoothly from his desk to the audience and occasionally to a map to summarize the national weather forecast. Radio listeners most likely could not detect any difference in the style or content of the show. The video-rehearsal broadcast had all the elements of a typical version of the show, such as McNeill's interview with a Lucerne, Indiana, woman who had had a busy morning before coming to the broadcast. She got up at 2:00 A.M. to kill the skunk that was attacking her chickens.

A man from Alameda, California, told McNeill that Aunt Fanny would enjoy visiting his town and a short while later, when Aunt Fanny arrived, she told him that one of her old neighbors actually moved to Alameda. Immediately, the phone started ringing as Aunt Fanny's friends called to correct her pronunciation of the name of the man who moved to California and exactly where he had moved. One caller said he went to Anaheim, another said Azula, and the last one said her friend was in Alcatraz for bank robbery.

The *Breakfast Club* turned twenty-one on June 23, 1954, and to mark the milestone the McNeill family was on hand to talk about the present and the future. Tom McNeill said that in twenty-one years he would be forty, married with five children, and hoped there would be peace in the world. In twenty-one years, son Don said that he would have a family life patterned after that of his mom and dad and would regularly take his six children to visit their grandparents. He also hoped Prayer Time would continue on the show. Bob planned to be working as a lawyer in twenty-one years and with his wife raising their seven children. He also anticipated listening to the Phillies as they won another pennant. After hearing these predictions, Kay said she simply wanted to be alive and well so she could care for all those grandchildren.

No regular *Breakfast Club* listener tuned in expecting to learn about the affairs of the day, but on this broadcast the issues raised by Senator Joseph McCarthy burst into the morning routine. It began when McNeill interviewed the Chief Counsel for the U.S. Senate's investigation into charges by Senator McCarthy that Communist sympathizers were in the army. Raymond Jenkins was a trial lawyer in Knoxville, Tennessee, when he was tapped to be counsel for the subcommittee's probe of the charges in what became known as the Army-McCarthy hearings. During a break in the hearings, Jenkins had stopped in Chicago on his way home. With his typical whimsy, McNeill invited members of the audience to play investigator and ask Jenkins some questions. One woman obliged by asking him what he thought of Senator McCarthy's legal aide, Roy Cohn, who had become a very visible member of McCarthy's investigating team. Jenkins avoided answering the query and instead volunteered his thoughts about the *Breakfast Club*. He told McNeill there were two things that impressed him about the show: the moment of silent prayer and the "sense of pride your wife had in her eyes when your three sons walked down the aisle." They reflected such positive values, Jenkins said, that he had "no fears whatsoever about our country. . . . I have no apprehension whatsoever."

McNeill took his usual vacation time that year and the guest hosts were Peter Donald, Walter O'Keefe, Walter Kiernan, and Dennis

James, all familiar names to the radio and television audience. By the time they were brought in to do the show, a routine had been established for the simulcast by director Lynwood King and his crew. Before coming to ABC, King worked as a stage manager and for *Garroway at Large* and *Kukla, Fran, and Ollie* at NBC and had produced the Philco spots that McNeill did during the political conventions in 1952. As King described it, his job with the *Breakfast Club* was simply to put a radio show on television and do it with the least possible strain on the cast.[6] His workday would begin at 4:30 A.M. to ensure the television commercials were properly rehearsed. At about 7:30 A.M., he'd look over the shoulder of McNeill and the producers to see what interviews were planned. King's camera operators were charged with getting shots of everything that happened, including March Time through the aisles and spontaneous interviews with studio guests.

One of the trips the cast took that year was to Florida where they spent the first of two weeks at the Dade County Auditorium. The first day's broadcast from the facility was interrupted when a lighting bolt struck the remote truck and took the show off the air for several minutes. For the second week's broadcast they moved pool-side to the Di Lido Hotel along Collins Boulevard. More traveling later in the year took the show to New York, where it began a Mystery Guest feature which asked local listeners to identify famous people by their voices only. McNeill would call listeners at home and let them hear the voice of the guest who was in the studio. A correct answer was worth $1,000. The guests for the week included Jackie Cooper, Nat King Cole, Vaughan Monroe, and Celeste Holm. The day Holm was the guest, there might not have been a toastmaster had it not been for Kay McNeill being willing to substitute for her husband who was struck with influenza. The Mystery Guests feature was also used the next year when the program originated from Hollywood. While there, the broadcast originated from the same sound stage where movies like Lon Chaney's *Phantom of the Opera* were shot. Due to the time zone differences, the crew, cast, and audience had to be in the studio by 4:00 A.M. every morning during the week. Among the celebrity guests that week were former *Breakfast Club* singers Patsy Lee and Jack Owens.

When the show returned to Chicago, changes occurred among the singers. Johnny Desmond left to perform in clubs and eventually on Broadway and in motion pictures, while Eileen Parker decided to leave when she married. Their replacements already had well-established careers. Dick Noel, who became the regular male singer, had been singing on the Ruth Lyons radio show in Cincinnati and had cut several records. The female singer was Betty Johnson, who had been making guest appearances on network television shows, but long before that grew up as a member of the Johnson Family of singers from Possum Walk Road, North Carolina.

In a later interview, Johnson said, "It all began in Chicago," because that is where she got the kind of exposure that helped her records get noticed.[7] When making personal appearances, she still opens her show by singing "Good Morning Breakfast Clubbers" and people in the audience respond because "they remember the *Breakfast Club*." All the credit for the success of the *Breakfast Club* goes to McNeill, according to Johnson. She admired his great sense of timing and knowing when "enough is enough." During the two years she worked on the show she never really got close to McNeill, who she said would typically communicate with the cast through his secretary. One day, however, McNeill called her into his office after he discovered that she was being approached by NBC to be a guest for a week on Jack Paar's *Tonight Show*. McNeill began the meeting by saying, "You have a job on this show for the rest of your life, people love you." He added that although she was doing well as a singer on local television in Chicago, "You really don't have the looks for national television." She retorted that she knew about her looks, but was busy working hard to save, send some money back home, and buy a farm. Finally, McNeill admitted it came down to the fact that he just didn't want her to leave the show. She got the week off to take advantage of the television offer, which led to her being on the *Tonight* show for the next four years. Her replacement was a runner-up for the Miss America title from Oklahoma, Anita Bryant.

After the simulcast had been running only eight months, there were indications ABC was wavering in its support for the early morning telecast, while at the same time desperately trying to build its programming base. ABC's strategy for the *Breakfast Club* was to attract a sizable number of viewers and sponsors at the start of the day which would carry over to mid-morning and beyond. Advertisers bought time on the basis of the cost to reach a thousand viewers, and ABC was at a distinct disadvantage by having only fourteen stations which regularly carried its programming compared seventy-one for NBC and seventy-four for CBS.[8] The larger the audience, the lower the cost to sponsors to reach each viewer with their message. Production costs were the same, regardless of the number of stations carrying the show, but with fewer affiliate stations, ABC's potential audience was smaller than that of its competitors.

The national Nielsen rating for the *Breakfast Club* in May 1954 was 2.8, which represented 443 thousand of the nation's 30 million homes.[9] By comparison, the May Nielsen's for NBC's *Today* show was 4.2 or one million viewers tuned in during the half hour just before the *Breakfast Club*. These relatively modest ratings prompted the few sponsors who originally signed on to signal their intentions to bail out. Swift dropped its television time, leaving Philco and Quaker Oats as the simulcast's regular video sponsors. When it became evident that Quaker was going to leave, ABC-TV president Bob Kintner expressed his doubts about whether the simulcast could continue much longer without more sponsors.

McNeill wrote Kintner in December to assure him that he and the *Breakfast Club* staff were doing everything possible to improve the situation and quickly.

> We are changing both singers on the show in an effort to bring in fresh faces, record stars, etc. Also, we are holding daily meetings on TV production problems on the show in an effort to get every single ounce of entertainment value; and, generally, have been knocking ourselves out.
>
> While I am very cognizant of the fact that the show is now a most costly one for the network, I can think of nothing worse for the network or myself than to have it go off television for any reason. Whatever the reason, the columnists and public would label it a failure. Not only would this knock the props out of your plans for daytime TV programming but I am afraid it would have a dismal effect on the radio show.
>
> It's a sad paradox that here we've got a TV show that is a good as any daytime show on any network, but until we get a really whopping rating—nobody buys because of that "cost-per-thousand" stuff, when it should be "how many people out of a thousand can you sell?" I'll bet any advertising man a thousand dollars that I, or any of the other well-known daytime TV personalities, can sell more people out of thousand on a product than "I Love Lucy" can with five thousand.[10]

One plan to salvage the show was to allow sponsors to buy minutes rather than quarter hours, as was the rule on the radio version of the show. To help with this sales strategy, McNeill wrote Kintner that he and every member of his staff would make calls on agencies and their clients to promote the new approach. Kintner replied that he was trying to keep Quaker on board with price discounts, but they still were likely to cancel by the end of February. He also addressed the realities of the "cost-per-thousand" issue:

> Most certainly, sales should be the true barometer of the broadcast media. But most of the daytime advertisers look upon the sliderule as gospel. They need circulation and exposure to make sales and must get these "at a price." Unfortunately, the Nielsen ratings make the BREAKFAST CLUB costs prohibitive in the agencies' eyes and, while ARB ratings are much more favorable, Nielsen is still the bible of the soap trade.[11]

Kintner and his boss, Leonard Goldenson, were busy putting the new network's prime-time schedule together and broke new ground by building alliances with the motion picture industry to produce television series in their studios. Their first major deal was with Walt Disney and resulted in the weekly family show *Disneyland* in 1954, and a year later the afternoon series, *Mickey Mouse Club*. Warner Brothers and ABC teamed up to produce adult westerns such as *Cheyenne*, *Kings Row*, and *Casablanca* for the 1955 schedule, beginning a genre that would serve the network well for the next decade. Sports offered another programming opportunity, starting with the 1954 NCAA football season.

ABC's money worries were eased somewhat by the fact it ended 1954 with nearly double the profits of the year before, due to the fact that it sold twenty-one hours of its prime-time schedule versus about half that number in 1953.[12] Continuing to build the evening schedule was the primary focus of Kintner and his executives who undoubtedly saw the *Breakfast Club* as an expensive venture that the network could not afford.

Just as it had done twenty-three years earlier, Quaker Oats played a pivotal role in McNeill's career when it dropped its sponsorship. In 1932 without a sponsor, the *Two Professors* were forced to hit the road looking for work, but in 1955 McNeill had a successful radio show to fall back on. Hearing McNeill was different from seeing him, according to former general manager of ABC's Chicago station, WBKB-TV, Sterling "Red" Quinlan.[13] "He did not have a commanding essence on television," said Quinlan, who equated McNeill's fate on television with that of ABC commentator, Paul Harvey. Both thrived on radio, but neither had the chemistry required to succeed on television. One long-time observer put it this way, McNeill "sounded like your brother, but didn't look like him."[14]

With the news that the simulcast was over came protests from *Breakfast Club* fans who not only were going to miss McNeill on television, but were angry about the way television was being programmed. Emma Lerch of Columbus wrote McNeill that,

> My indignation burns high, and I am ashamed for the "powers-that-be"; but it was ever thus. I am tempted to keep my TV set off for a week in deference to your program's passing [and] perhaps forsake those delicious Quaker Oats and hearty Aunt Jemima pancakes because they have the audacity to believe those swizzle-stick figures.

Robert Bailey of Greenville, South Carolina, was more emphatic in his letter to ABC, New York:

> WHO IN HEAVEN'S NAME DO YOU THINK you are to decide that a scroungy bunch of New York entertainers should determine that a country of 160 million people don't care for the clean, wholesome, friendly, and ALL*AMERICAN entertainment that Don McNeil [sic] and the BREAKFAST CLUB provide. This is the one morning program—in fact one of the few any time of day—that I let come into my home without a worry as to its freshness, richness, and cleanliness.
>
> If you don't have a sponsor, either get off your fat, lazy bottoms and look for one; or keep the show going as a public service.

McNeill wrote Bailey telling him that of the 10,000 letters he received about the cancellation, "I treasure yours as one of the greatest." McNeill concluded by saying he hoped to be back on television in the fall "in some manner or other."

The cast took the cancellation of the simulcast in stride, according to Dick Noel, who admitted he did not like the 50 percent cut in pay that accompanied the end of television.[15] He said that like any professionals, he and his colleagues continued to do their best work everyday.

13

Taking Pride
in America

When the *Breakfast Club* stopped being televised, there was no longer the need for a room as large as the one it had been using in the Morrison Hotel. Therefore, in December 1955, the show moved a few blocks away to Randolph and Clark and into the College Inn of the Sherman House. The first Hotel Sherman was built by the father of the Civil War general, William T., and served as one of the city's premier hotels until it burned in the great fire of 1871. When the new Sherman was built, its owner gained prominence for his hostelry by having excellent entertainment in the restaurant, the College Inn. The Inn quickly became a fashionable nightspot and by the 1920s began featuring some of the city's best jazz performers, who previously had only been heard in clubs on Chicago's south side.

A few weeks before the move, McNeill drafted memos to the cast in which he outlined his goals for each one, plus reminding them of their importance to the continued success of the *Breakfast Club*. The memos reveal McNeill's scrutiny of every detail of the show and his instincts for successful showmanship.

He wrote Betty Johnson that her singing left "little to be desired." What he felt needed some encouragement was for her to speak "up" rather than "down" in order to better reflect her basic good nature. He also asked her to mingle with the studio audience before the show to enliven it for the broadcast while at the same time build her confidence. He didn't want her to be shy about making comments during the show and suggested that when she had something to contribute she should simply raise her hand and he would call on her. He advised her to think up "kickers" to use as a gag or closing line of a song to raise audience involvement and interest.

Dick Noel was encouraged to use kickers in his songs, too, as well as keep up his good nature and aggressiveness, but with caution:

> Don't, however, be overactive to the point of ludicrousness as it then tends to have the opposite effect on the audience. I mean if, for instance, you race around too rapidly, they clam up and say to themselves, "This guy isn't natural—he is putting on an act."
>
> Also, if you don't understand something someone says, don't ask for it to be repeated. You are there to add comments, if necessary. The audience isn't interested in your education on the show.
>
> Remember, I am tremendously interested in you and your progress and in building you into a real character on the show. The better you are, the better it makes me look.[1]

Noel recalled enjoying the challenge of coming up with a crazy song lyric every week, and after a while he created a character whom he called Boris Beatnik. Boris's main objective was to inject the latest hip jargon into his language so as to confuse McNeill.

McNeill's letter to Sam Cowling encouraged the comic to think up and execute funny bits during the show, but to guard against being overcome by moodiness.

> Before the show, you should spend your time between the Porterhouse Room and our backstage room. I think in kidding around with the audience before the show and talking to them individually, you will dream up some cute bits of business for yourself.
>
> You have developed an unconscious tendency to fit your mood to mine before the show at times and, whereas I frequently get a bit bogged down in assembling comments, announcements, gags, cards and letters I want to use, you should let me worry about that and as much as is humanly possible be the irrepressible gadfly that the audience expects.
>
> As I have told you before, I think you have always been and still are most helpful in doing things for others and damn lazy in doing things for yourself.
>
> I would like to see you supply yourself with a little kicker or two *each morning* as you do on some mornings. It really pays off

for you on the show and it is something you can often carry through with.

Don't forget your character on the air—the gadfly, interrupter, overhelpful bungler, Kmukls.

Cowling's creative mind kept churning out skits, poems, and a comic song that got some attention nationally, "Dorothy Hermershimer."

Producer Cliff Petersen was given encouragement and suggestions about his responsibility for contacting convention groups and visiting celebrities. He also had responsibilities for making the music more entertaining:

> The other area in which I would like to see more activity on your part is in helping the singers with little novelty song presentations. You know the value of showmanship and contrast and sometimes it is only the addition of a special phrase before the climax of a song that lifts it out of the "just another song" category into a rouser or perhaps just gives a song a reason for being on the show with a lead-in intro.

Announcer/writer Eddie McKean was reminded about the need for keeping commercial copy tight and flexible.

> Your Number One Job—livening up commercials. Remember to use the cast, if possible, at times. Use different slants. Audience interviews, if possible. Don't try to get in all copy points. Not announcerish. If they turn out too long, cut and tighten. Remember—shorten, tighten, lighten, brighten to one minute— not 1:15 or 1:30. I would much rather have them too short so I can ad lib around them because too fast a pace destroys the personal commercial feeling of them entirely.
>
> Remember all the advertisers stress they want my own style of believability, sincerity and cleverness much more than strict copy points. This is what will keep us all working.

McKean did all that plus find time to come up with clever features like a horse trading puzzle which kept the cast and audience busy thinking for several days. "You buy a horse for $70, sell him for $80, buy him back for $90 and sell him again for $100. How much money do you make, if any?" After getting a wide range of answers, McNeill asked a CPA for an expert's solution, which was simply to treat the deal as two separate transactions that produce a profit of $10 each for a total of $20.

A few staffers received a second page with their memo in which McNeill was gentle but firm about cast members imbibing before and immediately after the show.

> I would appreciate it if you would refrain from patronizing the dispensers of liquid refreshments in the Sherman during the morning. There will be too many hotel guests and personnel involved in our show who observe same.
>
> I think it is helpful on occasion to reduce these things to writing such as it is—what there is of it. Let's really give them the old 1–2 in the Sherman. You can be a tremendous factor in putting even more life in the old show than she has got now.

The fact that cast members would be drinking at 9:00 A.M. is understandable considering their days began four hours earlier, so a "drink" at lunchtime would not be so unusual. Another issue was the fact that the demands of broadcasting and the lifestyle it fostered often correlated with excessive drinking. Certainly, the memo was not going to stop anyone from enjoying a cocktail after the show but it did send a message that the boss was not about to be embarrassed by any member of the cast's inappropriate behavior.

The overall tenor of McNeill's staff notes was to invite cast members to fully participate in the planning and execution of the show, which they did, enabling the show to remain fresh sounding. Members of the audience and guests, too, made their imprint on the show. During an interview in 1950, a woman told McNeill he was getting a bit heavy around the waist. He took her comments to heart and immediately began an exercise program that was so successful that a few days later he reported having lost two pounds. Unfortunately, the strenuous regimen resulted in his landing in Evanston Hospital with a slipped disk, causing him to miss his first broadcast in four years. Ten days later, when he was finally out of traction, he returned to work wearing a neck brace, which became part of his wardrobe for some time afterward.

Occasionally, cultural topics added variety to the show and were woven into vignettes and commercials. Memory Time was often a vehicle for providing focus for special features, such as McNeill's raising the issue of teenage dating in 1954 by asking listeners what limits should be placed on the hours young people are allowed to keep. He then reported the results of the survey over several days. Another *Breakfast Club* campaign during the 1950s promoted teenage safe driving.

Teenagers were a news topic during the 1950s and the stories were typically related to concerns about juvenile delinquency. The Secretary of Health, Education, and Welfare, Oveta Culp Hobby, admitted to *Newsweek* that the problem was real, based on the dramatic rise in juvenile court cases between 1948 and 1952.[2] Chicago Juvenile Police Officers conceded in 1954 that they were losing their battle to prevent youth crime, as the case load in the city's family court kept expanding. Leading the list of youth crimes were auto thefts and school vandalism. Chicago police were surprised to find girls imitating their boyfriends by organizing street gangs and donning leather jackets and tight jeans. Philadelphia's City Council was thinking about implementing a 10:00 P.M. weekday curfew and a law empowering police to break up large numbers of youths congregating at night. Before the council could act, police were drawn into battles with youth gangs angry about the proposals.[3]

As much as to say not all teens are bad, McNeill invited the New Trier High School Choir to perform on the *Breakfast Club* and one of their songs, "Make America Proud of You," expressed an optimism that confronted juvenile delinquency. It had been written by two established composers, Lois Steele and Jack Fulton, who envisioned the song to be sung by teenagers to other teens. McNeill liked the song and was particularly impressed with the spirit displayed by the young people when they sang it. He felt the song could spread the same upbeat feeling about young Americans to the nation.

Fred Waring arranged the music so it could be sung by a chorus of one thousand, which was made up of students from New Trier and Evanston High Schools plus Chicago-area Boy and Girl Scouts. Archie Bleyer supplied a thirty-piece band as well as the services of his Cadence Records to produce a recording of the song. McNeill provided narration over the youthful chorus which he read in a manner that was simultaneously low key and emotional:

> Here is a song for young America to sing and to believe in, because, young Americans, it is a simple song about you and by you. It's about the way you think and the way you live. The way to play it smart. Sing it as you tell the world that you're in business. The business of making a liberty-loving, self-respecting success of yourself, and that you're proud of it. It is your answer to those who deride your generation.

This is your theme. Maybe I'm not the star of the team nor the brain of the class, but I can be on my own honor roll with my conscience. There's nothing old fashioned about living right. It is the only way to take God's happiness on earth. And that's why you sing and mean it, every word. Our country is the greatest. You are proud to be an American. Play it smart. Sing it out. Make America Proud of you.

The recording was made Saturday, February 11, 1956, at Chicago's Medina Temple and eleven days later, on George Washington's birthday, McNeill gave it an inaugural playing on the *Breakfast Club*. Disk jockeys across the nation were sent complimentary copies of the record with an admonition from McNeill to let it be heard.

I don't plug records—ordinarily—but this is different! Aware of the important voice you have in your community, I call your attention to a disk that will put another civic feather in your cap.

This recording is the first positive, affirmative approach in song to the delinquency problem.

A thousand fresh young high school and Scout voices sang Fred Waring's arrangement with me in this Cadence Recording session. . . . It is the first time I ever had a 4-hour lump in my throat.

Every cent of profit from the sale of this record will go to the Boy Scouts and Girl Scouts of America.

Our reward will be in hearing this song played on the air . . . and played and sung in every Junior High and High School in the country.

That's why I can plug it without compunction!

It is difficult to determine to what degree the song accomplished its goal of fighting juvenile delinquency, but it did raise a "sizable" amount of money for national Scouting groups over a number of years after its release. The song had a revival during the nation's bicentennial celebration in 1976 and was re-recorded by Pete King and the Dan Harrison singers along with McNeill's narration. As before, the proceeds were given to the Boy and Girl Scouts of America. In 1977 during a tribute to McNeill, the Pacific Pioneer Broadcasters played the recording just before he was invited to address a Los Angeles audience honoring him. The song was emblematic of McNeill's lifelong commitment to helping young people achieve their potential.

14

Loyal Listeners and Sponsors

Since he began doing the *Breakfast Club*, McNeill saw the value of receiving listener mail as a way to gauge elements of the show as well as to demonstrate its impact. Over the years, the audience ratings showed, as might be expected, that the program had its greatest appeal with women in middle income brackets who lived in small to mid-sized towns or rural areas.

In 1947, the Schwerin Research Corporation polled six hundred persons in the New York City area to discover what they liked and disliked about the *Breakfast Club*. Although the sample was restricted to women, it included a wide range of age, income, and education groups. Sixty-six percent of the women sampled reported "liking" the show, and a breakdown by level of education and income revealed that liking was greater for those who had less education and income.

Report Liking Show

Education:

Grade School	80%
Some High School	64%
High School Graduate	64%
Some College	66%
College Graduate	47%

Income:

Low	71%
Middle	67%
High	48%

The Schwerin sample was asked how they liked the show and some of its features. Ninety percent said they liked Prayer Time, 64 percent said they missed Aunt Fanny when she was not on the show, and 47 percent liked March Time. The average likable ratings for music was 77 percent, interviews averaged 57 percent, and commercials came in at 55 percent. Two negative aspects of the show emerged with the finding that 62 percent of the sample agreed with the statement that "things on this program appeal only to the studio audience," and 48 percent said "they had difficulty following the program because two or more people were talking at the same time."[1]

In order to better understand the size and makeup of the *Breakfast Club* audience, ABC initiated a study that surveyed over a thousand members of the studio audience who attended the show during a week in February 1949. Each day before the program began, questionnaires were distributed, yielding an average of two hundred completed surveys for each of five days. Although the sample was skewed toward people who were predisposed toward the program, it did offer a snapshot of this group. Over half the sample said they had been listening to the show for the past eight years or more; over 40 percent said they listened nearly every day. More than half the sample were from Illinois and Indiana, the rest came from forty-two other states, the District of Columbia, Canada, Argentina, Hawaii, and Mexico. About 70 percent of the questionnaires were completed by women, 20 percent by men, and the remainder by children under eighteen years. The most common ages of the women sampled were between thirty-six and forty, while most men were between twenty-six and thirty.

Several organizations were holding conventions in Chicago that week and their attendees found their way into the sample, including National Shippers, Fresh Fruit and Vegetable Dealers, American Nurses Association, and Trailer Dealers. Others in the sample were with a variety of groups and organizations: Evangelical and Reformed Church of Gary, Indiana; Cub Scouts of Evanston, Illinois; Wayne Township (Indiana) Republican Women; Bunco Club, Hammond, Indiana; and the Screwballs from Mundelein, Illinois.[2]

The *Breakfast Club*'s appeal to this cross section of America was crucial to the show in a number of ways. Having a group of self-anointed "screwballs" or fresh fruit dealers to call upon made it easy for McNeill to find bits of humor among the studio guests. The happy and sincere mood of the show was reflected largely by the laughter and enthusiasm generated by the presence of the live audience, which made the program that much more entertaining for listeners.

The home audience was the real target for the show and by documenting their presence and loyalty to the *Breakfast Club*, ABC could more effectively convince sponsors that the show was likely to produce desired sales results.

Getting conventioneers or club members out of bed in time to make the 8:00 A.M. air time was becoming increasingly difficult. One solution was to record the program at a later hour in the morning for airing the next day at its usual early time. Since few, if any, references were made about a specific day, taping would not destroy the veracity of the show. In truth, the humor and features had a fairly long shelf life.

Putting the *Breakfast Club* on a tape-delayed basis could address some of these issues, but since the show used live musicians, all recordings they made were subject to a transcription fee as determined by a contract between the network and the musicians union. In the 1940s the American Federation of Musicians had fought a long battle with the networks over recorded music being played on radio which resulted in the transcription fees. The union's president, James C. Petrillo, was a tough negotiator who won many victories for his members. In 1952 McNeill wrote Petrillo requesting he waive the transcription fee in order to ensure the show's future and that of several musicians in Chicago.

> I'll be very honest with you, Jimmy. Frankly and off the record speaking strictly for Don McNeill, I am interested only in my own show, the Breakfast Club, and its future. It's been my bread and butter for years, and I hope it will for many more to come, but with the inroads of TV on all radio and the practical annihilation of all other air shows from Chicago on the networks, now is the time to act.
>
> Outside of two dramatic kid strips in the early evening, there is only *one* other radio network commercial program except ours coming out of Chicago on *any* network, Welcome Travelers. We are the *only* network radio show originating here using an orchestra. This has held true for some time in the past, and it's a cinch to hold in the future. In other words, sponsors just aren't interested in paying that kind of freight any more on radio, especially out of Chicago. I venture to say that if Breakfast Club which has employed eighteen musicians for eighteen years were to leave here, ABC might as well fold up radio network broadcasting from Chicago, and just run a local station. There wouldn't be any more available work for your boys, and contract or no, that wouldn't be a desirable condition, I am sure you will agree.[3]

Radio network showing 352 broadcast areas in the United States and Canada

McNeill concluded his argument for the fee waiver by stressing that taping the show for airing the next day would accomplish several goals: quiet sponsors' jitters about declining studio audiences; increase the size of the audience; allow musicians and the rest of the cast to sleep two hours later and therefore put on a more wide-awake show; and make Chicago a more attractive origination point for sponsors and cast members.

Despite these arguments for taping the show, it continued to be fed live to stations in the midwest and east; west coast audiences continued to hear the show on a time delay. Simulcasting the show in 1954–55 muted the next-day delay rationale, but by 1957 an

agreement was reached with the union to allow for tape delaying the show. Taping the show at nine or ten rather than eight made life easier for everyone except producer Cliff Petersen, associate producer Ray Barnes, and tape editor Joe Kuhn who were responsible for making sure the time cues were met for local cutaways and that the program conformed to the overall time limits. Making sure those spaces fit the times was an exacting process which began right after the show and typically took up to two hours to complete.[4] The time restrictions had rippling effects on the program by putting limitations on features, interviews, and songs, which were usually kept at one minute, thirty seconds. Barnes discovered ways to smooth out edits so they were invisible even to careful listeners. With help from sound mixer, Ralph Davis, Barnes would trim seconds out of the middle of a song or interview so that the ending of one segment flowed smoothly to the next. Sound pickup was enhanced by using twelve to fifteen mikes and baffles in the orchestra, four desk mikes for the cast, a boom mike for the singers, plus two others over the audience. On the days when the studio audience was sparse, Davis would sweeten the sound mix with a recording of applause from a previous show. On special occasions, such as a remote broadcast or when the day of the show had an important meaning, the *Breakfast Club* was still fed live, but otherwise the one-day delay became a standard practice.

In the 1950s sponsors began changing the way they bought radio time. The concept of a sponsor owning a segment of a show was purposeful in the early days of radio in that it built a connection in the listeners' minds between the product/service and the program. Back then, advertising campaigns were designed to build a client's image, in addition to selling its product. By the mid-1950s, advertisers determined that the rates for full program sponsorship were prohibitively high and they began buying time as participating sponsors of a show or ran their messages as buyers of spot time on a station's or network's schedule.[5] As part of this trend away from advertiser ownership of programs, Swift relinquished its long-held sponsorship of the middle two quarters of the *Breakfast Club* in 1955. Swift's executive vice president broke the news to McNeill that his company was ending its relationship with the *Breakfast Club* in a way that should make advertising history for its humanness:

> You have risen to a high position in the entertainment field and you have done it on a level unsurpassed by others. This has brought you the respect and admiration of millions and that position is yours to cherish.
>
> You have been engaged this past sixteen years in literally eliminating many of our trials, our troubles and our tribulations. You have been a great leader and a good one, exceedingly wise, fair spoken and persuading—yes, and more than that—
>
> A friend of truth,
> Of soul sincere,
> In action faithful
> And in honor clear.

You broke no promise,
Served no selfish end,
And you lost no friend.

But the culminating pleasure that we treasure beyond measure is the gratifying feeling that your duty was well done.

Don, at this time I presume it becomes the privilege of both of us to say farewell—a word that has been and must be, a word that makes us linger longer, and I hope our paths will cross quite often in the days ahead.[6]

In August 1955, Philco dropped its sponsorship of the show's fourth quarter, ending an association that had lasted ten years. ABC was eager to find replacements, but advertisers were not interested in buying the quarter-hour time blocks. As an alternative, McNeill and the network sales staff decided to sell five-minute participating slots. Glamorine, Postum, and Mum were the first participating sponsors heard on the show in October 1955.

Eager to entice other sponsors to sign up, ABC mounted an aggressive campaign which reminded sponsors about the need to reach younger housewives who make 66 percent of the all household purchases. At the same time, they demonstrated that 68 percent of the housewives listening to the *Breakfast Club* were under fifty years old, according to a Nielsen survey in 1956. Since the program was heard before 9:00 A.M., they argued it was the ideal vehicle for selling just before trips to the store. Prospective sponsors were sold on the ability of the show to reach over 16 percent of the nation's radios or 7.8 million homes, according to Nielsen data collected in 1957. Finally, the ABC sales effort included merchandising and promotional campaigns to augment the on-air selling, which typically included photos or recordings of McNeill to be used as in-store or local media tie-ins.

Finding new sponsors was a challenge in the mid-1950s, since the economy was sliding toward what was to be known as the recession of 1957. Sellers were looking hard for potential buyers. After the *Breakfast Club* lost three-fourths of its sponsors, the network felt the loss of income and so did McNeill. He felt obligated to gather his family in 1957 to discuss their finances and tell them that their lifestyle might have to change dramatically if new sponsors did not fill the void created when the original advertisers left.[7] As he did twenty years earlier, McNeill worked closely with his network to devise a selling strategy to find new sponsors for the show.

The power of a personality sell by McNeill was promoted heavily in ABC's sales packets which stressed his sincerity, warmth, and credibility. According to program director William MacCallum, it was not unusual for McNeill to reject prospective clients whose products he regarded as "in bad taste or embarrassing to promote on our type of show. Underarm deodorants, for instance . . . or any sponsor who insists on the hard sell approach. Our program is soft sell—and that's that."[8] Ads for underarm deodorants were heard on the show, but they were not given by McNeill. What he did offer advertisers was a straightforward, friendly, and even humorous sales effort. For example, when Country Time Cheese signed on as a sponsor, McNeill often enjoyed mentioning the name of the town where Fisher made the product, Wapakoneta, Ohio. He had fun saying the name and did it in a way that created a friendly entree to the commercial that followed.

A rationale for McNeill's brand of selling can be found in a study that explored the relationship between viewers and programs they watched. The research was conducted by the Menninger Foundation of Topeka, Kansas, for advertising agencies in Chicago. A team of social scientists was asked to look at television, examining both the advertising and the programs. The study examined several programs but its conclusions about the *Arthur Godfrey Show* are clearly relevant to the *Breakfast Club*.

> Psychologically, Mr. Godfrey's morning program creates the illusion of the family structure. All the conflicts and complex situations of family life are taken out and what is left is an amiable, comfortable family scene—with one important omission: there is no mother in the Godfrey family. That gives the housewife-viewer the opportunity to fill that role. In her fantasy Godfrey comes into her home as an extra member of her family; and she fancies herself as a specially invited member of his family.[9]

Aunt Fanny was clearly not in the role of surrogate wife, and Kay McNeill's visits to the *Breakfast Club* were so rare that the female listener could easily fit herself into the make-believe family. McNeill's style on the air projected the manner of an ideal husband with many desirable qualities: in interactions with Sam Cowling he showed his sense of humor, with Aunt Fanny he was understanding, Prayer Time revealed his respect for God, Memory Time offered a primer on his positive values, and the Sunshine Shower showcased his humanity.

Every day during his interactions with women guests he could be, at the same time, both reserved and inviting as the exchange he had with a woman in the audience in the late 1950s indicates:

> McNEILL: A woman from Cincinnati writes, "Glad to come to the Breakfast Club. No shouting or top-10 songs." Do you listen?
> WOMAN: Occasionally.
> McNEILL: What do you do in Cincinnati?
> WOMAN: Homemaker.
> McNEILL: You strike me as a typical homemaker, attractive, wearing a red sweater.
> WOMAN: You're handsome.
> McNEILL: Yes, I am—Just kidding.

Throughout their exchange, McNeill's voice conveyed a great deal of warmth which communicated to the audience that they were let in on an intimate chance meeting of two people. Then McNeill returned to his desk where singer Dick Noel broke some of the tension by asking:

> NOEL: Didn't one woman call you dreamy recently?
> McNEILL: What did one woman call you?
> NOEL: I couldn't say it on the air.

Godfrey and McNeill had vastly different personalities and it showed on the air, but their psychological approach to their audience were perhaps more similar than might be expected. Both were champs at selling—Godfrey by being a rebel and rake; McNeill by being respectful and suave.

An example of McNeill's care and respect for all was demonstrated in a most concrete way. For twenty-five years, McNeill signed off his show with the slogan "So long and be good to yourself." Whenever he was asked about the admonition, he explained that in 1933 when he was looking for a distinctive phrase for closing the show he thought of the Shakespearean phrase, "to thine own self be true; and it must follow, as the night the day, thou canst not then be false to any man." Therefore, McNeill reasoned that the only way one could be good to oneself and true to others is to be honest with oneself, but on January 24, 1958, he announced he was changing his slogan to "Be good to your neighbor," with the explanation that the revision was prompted by his listeners. McNeill reasoned that his audience "seemed to feel that consideration of others is far more important in living in today's world. With consideration of others, being 'good' to oneself will take care of itself, they say. And we agree."[10]

The new slogan lacked the spunk of the old one and most likely reflected a mellowing of both McNeill and his listeners. He had turned fifty the year before and he was preparing to celebrate a quarter century of doing the *Breakfast Club* with a cast that included members who had been with him for most of that time. Years later, writing one of his features for ABC's *Flair* reports, McNeill pondered the change in his sign-off, concluding that people do need reminders to be good to themselves. Furthermore, he wrote, helping one's self often means being of help to others, such as the man who needs a vacation. If he takes one, he benefits and so does everyone around him.

Through his many years on the air, McNeill wore well with his audience, primarily because he came across as someone they already knew. The *Breakfast Club* tradition of celebrating McNeill family events on the air helped to foster a close connection with listeners. McNeill's fiftieth birthday party in December 1957 had all the elements that anyone might expect from a typical family. The program began with Agnes Donohue giving a testimonial about her brother's early years. McNeill often quipped that his sister had all the brains in the family since she was the chair of the English Department at Barat College in Lake Forest and also served on the Graduate Faculty at the University of Illinois' Chicago campus. Son Don, then a senior at Notre Dame, praised his dad for hitting baskets 50 percent of the time in their backyard. Tom, who was completing his last year at Notre Dame Law School, expressed his appreciation for his father's ability to be a "teacher by happy example and ready consideration for those less fortunate. The best father that three sons could have." McNeill replied that "ten years ago I was seven times as old as my youngest son, Bob, and today I'm only three times as old as he is, which means I'm holding my age a lot better than he is." Memory Time that morning was devoted to McNeill's parents who were in the audience and celebrating their fiftieth anniversary. McNeill mentioned that his father was seventy-nine years old and his mother eighty, but she did not look it. She chided him by saying "You keep telling them how old I am."

The McNeills may have been an ideal family, but the basic structure was not unlike what many Americans could identify with in 1957. Ideal, yes, but with plenty of reality which they successfully projected on the air.

The show and its toastmaster continued to score where it counted, with the audience. The show's monthly mail offered evidence that the *Breakfast Club* was still very popular with listeners. Tallies of incoming mail kept by ABC for all its programs during January 1961 indicated the *Breakfast Club* had received nearly six thousand cards and letters, beating out its closest rivals, Lawrence Welk, Paul Harvey, *Queen for a Day, Ozzie & Harriet,* and *77 Sunset Strip*.

More importantly, the network was able to show sponsors ratings data that put the *Breakfast Club* ahead of its competition, particularly Arthur Godfrey on CBS Radio. The June 1961 report from Nielsen had more homes listening to McNeill than the personalities on the other major networks. The Nielsen data revealed that McNeill's audience was up 18 percent, while Godfrey's had dropped 28 percent from the year before. In addition, coverage was at its highest level, with over four hundred stations carrying the show in 1962. Finally, advertisers continued to buy up most all of the available time on the *Breakfast Club*, assuring ABC Radio of a reliable revenue stream. To be sure, the show had relatively high expenses, not the least of which was the orchestra, but an agreement with the musicians' union allowed ABC gradually to reduce the number of musicians on staff during the 1960s.

15

Memorializing
the Silent Prayer

Variety's Chicago correspondent, Les Brown, made some astute observations about the *Breakfast Club's* looming twenty-fifth anniversary and why the program was so resilient. Brown noted that the show took many years to establish itself with sponsors, and even when it did, it was never spectacularly in vogue. According to Brown, it was a show people didn't talk about much, but they listened to it. Turning his sights on McNeill, Brown found a surprisingly low-key celebrity who was "seldom seen publicly, rarely makes the gossip columns, and has never been involved in anything scandalous or exciting . . . he is not unsung but practically is anonymous."[1] According to Brown:

> "Breakfast Club" has bucked the trends, weathered the frightened years of radio and survived all the pogroms of programming the medium has been heir to in the past two decades. Today, it has the distinction of a rock foundation on which the ABC nabobs hope to rebuild their somewhat weather-beaten network.

Had McNeill been under contract with NBC or CBS, those networks might have been more committed to using him on television than had ABC, and his being involved with television most likely would have drained his time and energy for radio and made him less dependent on income generated by the *Breakfast Club*. If McNeill had left Chicago for New York or Hollywood, his connection with, and support from, the mid-section of the nation might have been diluted. He must have struggled with these realities, debating the rewards and risks of staying put with ABC and his morning show. He stayed the course in Chicago and the *Breakfast Club* kept chugging along with several of the same folks behind the mikes.

On June 23, 1958, the show would be on the air a quarter of a century and McNeill wanted to dramatize the anniversary with something tangible. He decided to memorialize one of its most characteristic aspects, Prayer Time, in a painting, and wrote Norman Rockwell to see if the illustrator would accept a commission to create a painting with the prayer-for-peace theme. In 1943 Rockwell had painted, as one of his Four Freedoms, an illustration titled *Freedom of Worship*, which showed a montage of hands and faces in reverent contemplation. McNeill conceptualized how this image might be used to capture the Silent Prayer on canvas. Rockwell wrote back saying that he was "excited about your idea for a painting" but, unfortunately, his schedule made it impossible to accept the offer.

A search for another artist produced an award-winning illustrator, Ben Stahl, whose work had appeared for several years in the *Saturday Evening Post* and in promotional material for motion pictures such as *Ben Hur*. Stahl's most notable achievement was a set of paintings depicting the fourteen Stations of the Cross, which were subsequently printed in a special edition of the Bible.

In January 1958, Stahl was commissioned to paint the *Moment of Silent Prayer*, which he promised to complete in time for the twenty-fifth anniversary of the *Breakfast Club* that June. The central feature of the work was to be a mother in prayer, prompting a national search to find a suitable subject for the painting. The wife of a University of Michigan professor and mother of three children, Merle Lawrence, was selected to sit for Stahl in his studio in Sarasota, Florida. The *Breakfast Club* made plans to originate from Sarasota while Lawrence was sitting for Stahl, and she regularly visited the show to update McNeill on the progress of the work and her experiences with the artist.

The six-foot painting depicting the praying mother with her children was completed in time for the June 23 anniversary and became the focal point of the broadcast that day. The painting then toured several cities before being put on display at Chicago's new convention center, McCormick Place, in 1960. It was hanging in the center on January 16, 1967, when the huge structure erupted in flames and burned to the ground, but miraculously, the painting was discovered still standing on its pedestal unharmed by either the raging fire or water. Two years later it survived another threat when it was loaned by McNeill to Stahl for display in his Museum of the Cross in Sarasota. The museum's main attraction was Stahl's Stations of the Cross paintings, which were attracting a large number of visitors. The museum was called "The Jewel of Florida" because it drew tourists from all over the world to the Gulf Coast city. Early on April 16, 1969, fifteen Stations of the Cross" (Stahl added *The Resurrection* to his original fourteen), plus forty smaller paintings, were stolen, but the *Moment of Silent Prayer* and three others were left hanging. The news media called it the second largest art theft of the decade with an estimated loss of $1.5 million.[2]

The painting was seen on national television in November 1958 during Edward R. Murrow's visit with the McNeills on *Person to Person*, over CBS-TV. The live telecast began with an exterior shot of the McNeill's large yard and substantial home in Winnetka. Murrow observed how good radio had been to McNeill judging from the size and nature of his home. Inside the house, McNeill was shown standing at the top of a curving stairway next to the *Moment of Silent Prayer*, which afforded him the opportunity to tell Murrow what the work represented and why it was important to him.

Down in the living room Kay McNeill told Murrow how she placed alarm clocks under sofas so guests would realize when it was 10:30 P.M. and bedtime for the head Breakfast Clubber. McNeill took Murrow to his library-game room where he displayed his hunting rifle and shotgun collection, a prize-winning trout caught by his father, and the family's miniature schnauzer, Happy. Bob McNeill, who at six foot, four inches towered above his dad, greeted Murrow and told him he was playing football his senior year at New Trier High School. His brothers Tom and Don had finished at Notre Dame and were abroad studying at the University of Vienna before doing their ROTC military service.

Murrow inquired if McNeill had any insights into why he had been so successful with his program over the years. One explanation McNeill offered was his decision to keep the show in Chicago, which provided him with great studio audiences over the years. McNeill added that he personally gained strength to continue with his work from Reinhold Niebuhr's Serenity Prayer, which he quoted: "Lord give me the serenity to accept the things I cannot change; the courage to change things I can and the good sense to know the difference."

The strongest image conveyed during Murrow's visit was that of McNeill standing alone beside the *Silent Prayer* painting. During those few minutes he communicated to millions of viewers his sincerity, his compassion, and his reliance on prayer—qualities which made him unique among entertainers both then and now.

Stahl made another contribution to the *Breakfast Club*, but not as a painter. In February 1959, the artist was in Hong Kong researching a commission he had received to create murals for the Air Force Academy in Colorado. He wrote McNeill that soon after he had checked into the Ye Olde Barrel Hotel, he heard Mozart being played on a piano outside his room. He went to the lobby and discovered a "30-pound, five year old girl whose versatility ranged from playing Beethoven to the '12th Street Rag.'" Stahl learned that the pianist was Ginny Tiu, the daughter of the hotel's owner, William Tiu-Kao, a Filipino-born Chinese businessman who also played piano and had been teaching her for the past year. Stahl's letter to McNeill suggested that Ginny be given her first U.S. performance on the *Breakfast Club*, and afterward McNeill could advise her parents on the best path for their daughter's career. McNeill sent a telegram to Stahl saying that the pianist "sounds intriguing" and, as luck would have it, the older McNeill sons, Tom and Don, were sightseeing in Bangkok as part of their trip back home from Vienna, and he would arrange for them to contact her father. The boys went to Hong Kong next and met with Ginny and her parents and while there made a tape recording of her piano playing to send to their father.

The McNeill sons gave a full report on Ginny, writing that she was "cute, shy, seldom smiles, but when asked to bow for us after playing, she did a quarter bow and shyly grinned and hid behind a curtain." Regarding her playing ability, they wrote that "she can whip off the tunes like mad, just tell her the name of one she knows (or, maybe, hum a tune and let her pick it out—she and dad play 'by ear'). Makes a few mistakes, but pretty darn good on the whole." They speculated that with a few weeks' instruction to improve her timing she could sound professional. They also suggested a few ideas to their father as to how she might be introduced on the *Breakfast Club*.

> Have Bill Krenz get on one piano and tell the listening audience that since the young Chinese girl can't speak English—the communication must be by piano. . . . Bill Krenz could begin by playing the first few bars of "I'm In The Mood for Love" and then she could finish with "Easter Parade" on another piano.

Another thing—if she was given a tune—foreign to her by the audience, at the beginning of your show—I wouldn't be surprised if she could play it back by the end of the show—she has a great memory.

They reported that the Tiu-Kao family had planned a three-month visit to the U.S. followed by another three months' tour of Europe in an effort to get Ginny's musical career off the ground.

McNeill's response to Tiu-Kao was that he would serve as mentor to Ginny and proposed that she make her debut on the *Breakfast Club* as soon as they arrived in Chicago. Tiu-Kao agreed, and when the family reached San Francisco they were met by Tom and Don, who joined them on a flight to Chicago the next day. McNeill brought his sons to the *Breakfast Club* on March 20 where they updated their father on their round-the-world trip plus their immediate plans to begin military service. Tom was on his way to a three-year air force commitment as a legal officer at Carswell Air Force Base near Fort Worth, Texas. Don was heading for a six-month officer training program in the army at Fort Lee, Virginia. They shared some of their travel experiences and presented their mother with a sari they had purchased in India. McNeill asked the band to play "Who's Sorry Now?" with the reminder to his sons that his corn paid for their travels. The pair also took questions from the studio audience, which asked them about world events such as tensions between the East and West over Berlin. Before leaving, the sons also talked about their experiences escorting Ginny to America.

The following Monday Ginny made her U.S. debut on the *Breakfast Club*. Wearing her hair in pig-tails, dressed in a bright red and gold Chinese gown, and carrying a doll, she was an instant success with the audience and returned to the show the following week. Her repertoire included selections from Mozart, Beethoven, jazz, and traditional Chinese melodies.

McNeill realized that much of Ginny's charm was visual, which would make her a sensation on television, so he immediately began scouting for the right venue. He helped persuade Perry Como's producers that she would be right for their show, and when they agreed, April 18 was set, when she along with McNeill would be on the NBC-TV program from New York. That date was subsequently postponed a week, and then unexpectedly canceled when Mayor Robert Wagner's Office refused to issue a permit allowing Ginny to appear on the show. A New York law forbade children under seven from working and an exception was not granted, despite pleas from the Chinese Consuls General in Chicago and New York.

McNeill had been promoting the upcoming Como show visit during the preceding weeks, but now told Breakfast Clubbers the decision was a loss for American viewers:

> We don't quarrel with the law: It's probably a good law to protect children from being exploited, but it seems to us that exceptions should be possible where it can clearly be shown that the intent of the law is being fulfilled. I can testify that never has a child's welfare been so carefully protected. Little Ginny's mother and father are fine people who are making every effort to keep this wonderful little girl happy and normal. Playing the piano is fun for Ginny—she plays the piano as a fun thing like most children play with other toys, but Ginny also plays with dolls and all kinds of games, too. Her eating and sleeping habits are carefully supervised and you only have to spend a little time with her to see how delightfully happy and unspoiled she is.[3]

McNeill concluded the saga by acknowledging that he and Ginny finally were able to make their network appearance the previous night on the Ed Sullivan's show over CBS-TV. Sullivan had been on vacation and was not approached until after the other plan fell through, but when he learned the plight the little girl was having getting shown on television, he took it as a challenge to bring her to his show. New York's law was skirted by having Ginny's portion of the show originate from the CBS's Chicago station, WBBM-TV. McNeill informed his listeners that in case they missed the telecast, he and Ginny were going to make an encore appearance on Sullivan's show the following Sunday. By mid-week, however, another cancellation was announced. This time, an Illinois child-labor statute prohibiting minors under fourteen from working in "any TV or radio studio" prevented the repeat performance when the state's Department of Labor issued a restraining order three days before the broadcast. Since other underage actors had been working on television for several years, the action seemed capricious to some critics. Janet Kern of the *Chicago American* reported that Ed Sullivan suspected NBC of having encouraged Illinois authorities to apply the dormant statute after it had been outsmarted by Sullivan.[4] McNeill and his attorney went into high gear and obtained a temporary restraining order from a Superior Court judge, which stopped Illinois authorities from preventing Ginny's performing in a Chicago television studio. The injunction worked, and McNeill and Ginny kept their date to be on Sullivan's show thanks to McNeill's perseverance and some quick-acting lawyers.

The next time the two appeared on television together came as a surprise to McNeill. In January 1960 the *Breakfast Club* was winding up a trip west that included stops in Phoenix and Los Angeles. One afternoon, McNeill, two of his former buddies from Milwaukee, actors Jack Carson and Dennis Morgan, and the *Breakfast Club*'s manager Ralph Bergsten were playing golf at Lakeside Golf Club in Burbank. McNeill was having one of his better games with "long straight drives and crisp, accurate approach shots." Meanwhile, his partners were busy trying to slow the progress of the game by deliberately hitting into the rough and looking for "lost" balls. They didn't want to reach the tenth tee too soon, because they knew who planned to meet them there. Just as the foursome started putting, Ralph Edwards jumped out from some shrubbery holding a microphone and announced "This Is Your Life, Don McNeill" while an engineer was surreptitiously videotaping the ambush from a van parked nearby. That ended the golf game, because McNeill was expected to shower quickly, change, and be at the Pantages Theater for the story of his life.

Edwards and his crew invited some of the key people in McNeill's past to help chronicle his progress from being a sickly boy in Galena, Illinois, to that of a well-known celebrity. Among the guests were Marquette University's former journalism dean, Jerry O'Sullivan, who told how McNeill confided in him that since his father's furniture business failed he could not afford the course work to complete his degree. Fran Allison reminisced about their leaner days in show business in the 1930s when she and McNeill had accepted a job performing in New Orleans. The pay was lower than either of them expected, and they barely had train fare for the trip back to Chicago. McNeill's mother recalled that her son was selected as the most beautiful baby in Sheboygan. Edwards reviewed the failures and disappointments McNeill had in the early stages of his career, but emphasized that with success came an eagerness to give his time and money to others. As recognition for the Boys Clubs' camp he held every summer, Edwards gave McNeill a boat with an outboard motor for use on the lake at Himself's Hideaway. Edwards concluded his tribute to the efforts McNeill had made to help others by introducing Ginny, who jumped into her mentor's arms for a kiss.

Since getting the start on the *Breakfast Club*, Ginny had been busy making television appearances on the Danny Thomas Show,

Art Linkletter's *House Party*, Ken Murray's *All Star Review*, and with Jimmy Durante with whom she could play and sing a delightful duet of "Ink-A-Ding-Ka-Doo." *Life* magazine profiled her with a two-page spread and ERA records released an album which showcased her varied repertoire titled "All This And Ginny Tiu." She spent a portion of her first summer in the U.S. as one of the headliners at the Riviera Hotel in Las Vegas where, according the *Hollywood Reporter*, she was the "real star of the show." She was still seven years old when she landed parts in two Elvis Presley films, *Girls! Girls! Girls!* in 1962 and *It Happened at the World's Fair* in 1963.

The novelty of such a young pianist died down as Ginny grew up, but not her ability to play piano. As an adult, she made Honolulu her home, where she earned the reputation of being "Hawaii's Best Piano Player" based on her many night club and concert performances in the U.S. and Tokyo.

Tom and Don helped discover Ginny, after Ben Stahl's suggestion, at the end of a globe-circling adventure they shared. What began as four months of classes at the Institute of European Studies in Vienna became an odyssey across Europe into the Middle East, Southeastern Asia, and the Far East. McNeill offered to pay their expenses as long as the boys provided him with written accounts of what they saw along the way, which he could share with his *Breakfast Club* audience. The sons agreed and began filing their reports in late September 1958. From Belgium they reported seeing varying levels of post-war economic growth, and Tom predicted the formation of the European Community when he observed that six Western European nations saw the need to unite so as to compete with Communist countries and the United States. Their sightseeing included a major tourist attraction that year, the World's Fair in Brussels.

They found adventures to report in Germany, including some war stories. In Cologne, which Tom described a "still a largely ruined city," he recounted a strange conversation they had with an acquaintance who said he was a crew-member of a German U-boat during the war. The German said that during that time he had been to America five times. Tom wrote that "if true, his U-boat had sailed into Long Island Sound and within two kilometers of the coast. . . . He said that one night they swam around the Statue of Liberty! We didn't know what to think."

In Munich, Don wrote that he attracted a small crowd while visiting the OktoberFest. The locals were surprised by his six foot, six inch height—

This went on until along came a guy 7' 2"—taller than "Wilt the Stilt." He was walking through town with a pack on his back, levis, beard and banjo in hand. He had a following like the Pied Piper. He was from Colorado and he had been to Geology School in Germany. He'd been traveling for 8 months walking everywhere. When he gets to town—an American hotel—he explains that he has no money but plays banjo and will entertain the guests if he will be given a bed. . . . He plans on hitting Russia soon.[5]

Vienna was where they got down to being students, taking courses in international relations, the history of law, clinical psychology, and German. They found time for traveling during the semester and on one excursion they went to Yugoslavia. Tom reported that the streets of Zagreb, the country's second largest city, were nearly empty. "I see more people milling around in Winnetka on a weekday forenoon than I saw in a couple of hours of walking through Zagreb! They don't have anywhere in particular to go, that may be why they are not walking around! There are very few stores." He concluded his summary of the visit with a prediction about Yugoslavia's future:

The unfortunate thing, perhaps, is that Tito has inspired such a confidence in the people, has created such a realistic independence for Yugoslavia and has found himself geographically, economically and politically . . . able to play both ends, East and West, against the middle—that the whole idea . . . *works!* and will continue to work well in the foreseeable future.[6]

Don was recruited to join a Vienna basketball team and this involvement led to his being in a tournament in Bologna, Italy. The Austrians got trounced by the Italians. Even though the team lost, Don had the best game of his life—scoring thirty-five points. In their final match against Munich, the Viennese team won with Don's help. He was the game's high scorer with twenty-one points.

By February their classes were over, and they began a most interesting trip that took them around the world. In Egypt, they toured the Valley of the Kings in Luxor, which they described as "fascinating." They rented bicycles to see how people lived beyond the usual tourist sites. What they saw was rather bleak: "thousands of people living in dirt and seemingly liking it because they have never known otherwise." Boarding a plane, they headed for Jerusalem where they found that the "refugee camps at either end of the city gave a sobering over-tone to the whole area."

After a one night's stay in Beirut, which they described as both beautiful and modern, they flew into Tehran. *Breakfast Club* listeners who heard Tom's assessment of the Iran he saw were given a glimpse of the troubles that would engulf that country fifteen years later:

> It seems as if the Shah has a pretty good grip on the country, and the backing of the Moslems, whose Iranian style religion (different than orthodox Moslems) is fairly settled in his favor. Liberty is not a hallmark, as outspoken opponents to the government or Communist organizers will be jailed when called to the government's attention. They consider themselves as not being Arabs, but are a rather proud strain of Persian. But the educated people are not happy with the overall lack of prosperity and negligible chance to get ahead and would like to come to America.[7]

At the American embassy, they spent time talking with U.S. officials about Iranian politics and the attitude its government had toward the Communists across the border. Their next destination was another country with border problems, Pakistan, and its largest city, Karachi. Don was taken by the way life flowed through the teeming port city:

> The traffic in Karachi gives it a charm that no city can ever compete with. . . . There are no horns allowed. It was a miracle how all the elements of transportation passed on the crowded streets. Camels, donkeys and horses, oxen, water buffalo and bulls—slowly plodding along. Big cars, little cars, bicycles (with or without rickshaw attached) and motorcycles. . . . The rhythm of the bells attached to the camels' knees was melodic. Flowers were attached to the working animals to add an extra touch of grandeur. Beside this rhythmatic [*sic*] commotion on the streets slept a minimum of ten men (wrapped in dirty blankets) per block . . . not starving men, but homeless tired men.[8]

As they departed for India, Don expressed his "sorrow for their homeless and hope for their tomorrows." Bombay had even more homelessness with nearly 30 percent of its inhabitants without shelter. In Delhi they saw an Indian Ballet Drama which they found "superb" and rode an elephant in Agra not far from the Taj Mahal.

They reported on their adventures with snake charmers in Benares and touring some of Hinduism's most holy sites, including the Ganges River, before leaving for their final stop in India, Calcutta. Their story from that city was laden with sights of widespread poverty, disease, and an unbending social system that made progress difficult.

Burma was their next destination, and their arrival coincided with the latest governmental reorganization as described in Don's report back home:

> After the Japanese occupation, Burma never could get its feet politically within the democratic framework it was given. Also, there is within the Buddhist religion . . . a code of "non-killing." Therefore, thousands of grubby dogs were allowed to roam the streets along with ever more huge rats. Then three months ago, the army took control of the government. Since then, the homes have been ripped off the sidewalks . . . and all the slum areas are slowly being cleared with the thousands of people headed to a new city—outside of Rangoon. At 5:00 A.M., soldiers throw poison hamburgers to the dogs and rats . . . and then clear up the dead.[9]

After a stop in Hong Kong, where they met Ginny Tiu, their journey came to end in Japan where Don chronicled the hospitality shown them by the wife of a man they had met in Austria. She had them to her home for tea, which he described as "so small that when we were sitting in chairs in one corner, our feet touched the middle of the room when stretched out. Nevertheless, there was a great over-all beauty and warmth in this tiny home." Back at their hotel in Tokyo, while packing for home, Don wrote his father that it was a pleasant surprise to turn on the radio at 8:30 A.M. and "there was the Breakfast Club [delayed broadcast on the U.S. Armed Forces Network] and you were mentioning us and our stay in Vienna."

McNeill relished his own European travels and took vicarious pleasure in recounting his sons' experiences around the world. The detailed and sometimes pithy stories from two recent college grads struck the right chord for *Breakfast Club* listeners.

The trip had a lasting impact on the brothers, but in different ways. Being in Vienna, they did not get a chance to see their parents live on CBS-TV's *Person to Person*. Therefore, McNeill sent them a film of the show. Tom went to borrow a projector from a film agency where he had noticed an attractive employee, Ingrid. Five years later they were married.

Don, who had been searching for the best direction for his future, had two experiences that pointed the way. One was a course taught by the noted Viennese psychiatrist, Viktor Frankl. The other was his participation in a series of religious retreats set up by a Jesuit in Vienna. Later, when he and Tom toured Calcutta and witnessed the extreme poverty in that city, it became clear to Don that helping those in need would be central to his life's work.

16

Breakfast Clubbing
from Europe

Chicago became an international port in 1959 when the St. Lawrence Seaway opened, which enabled cargo ships to enter the Great Lakes from the Atlantic Ocean. One of the first ships to use the new waterway was the British royal yacht, *Britannia*, carrying Queen Elizabeth and Prince Philip. Their visit to Chicago was the first ever for a reigning British monarch and began along the city's lake front at Buckingham Fountain, where they were met by Mayor Richard J. Daley and Governor William Stratton. Later, the royal couple was taken to Navy Pier where the opening of the Seaway was being celebrated with an International Trade Fair designed to showcase the wares coming to Chicago from over forty nations. During that week, the *Breakfast Club* originated from the Fair, beginning a tradition that would continue for several years.

The *Breakfast Club* kept making annual trips around the country, often by train, since McNeill had an aversion to flying, which aggravated an inner ear problem. The cast would make the most of the long train rides, breaking the monotony by playing penny ante poker with rules made up on the spot by Fran Allison.

The trips crisscrossed America. In 1955, the cast spent a day in Canton, Ohio, helping the city celebrate its 150th anniversary. Shortly after that jaunt, they boarded a houseboat and spent a week drifting down the Mississippi, broadcasting every morning from a different location. The cruise ended in

Davenport, Iowa, where the cast disembarked and did their broadcast in front of a big crowd at the town's outdoor stadium. In the spring of 1956, the *Breakfast Club* answered a call from Mobile, Alabama, to join the festivities during its annual Azalea Festival. The cast broadcast for a week from the Gulf city. Then in the summer of 1956, the show went to San Francisco at the same time the Republicans were in town having their convention. A final trip that year took the show to the nation's population center, which in 1956 was at Olney, Illinois. They broadcast from a bandshell in the city park where the audience kept looking for the town's famous white squirrels.

Saranac Lake, New York, held a winter carnival every February and in 1957 invited McNeill to be king and Aunt Fanny to be queen of the icy affair. The cast joined him on the train trip, but a missed connection in Syracuse caused the *Breakfast Club* special to arrive much later than expected. When the single engine pulled the lone car into the station, the townsfolk were still waiting, along with singer Dick Noel who had decided to fly his own plane to New York rather than ride the rails. The week's events included ice-skating lessons at an outdoor rink for everyone who needed them. McNeill took a few spills while waiting for his. Noel headed for the ski slopes and Eddie Ballantine spent the week doing some serious bobsledding at the Mt. Van Hovenburg Bobsled Run.

In 1958, Cecil B. DeMille made what was to be the last film of his career, *The Buccaneer*, which was really a remake of his 1938 film about a pirate who controls an island strategically located off-shore from New Orleans. It was set during the War of 1812 and the buccaneer enraged both the Americans and the attacking British. The *Breakfast Club* joined DeMille in staging *The Buccaneer*'s world premier along with the stars of the film, Yul Brynner, Charlton Heston, Lorne Green, and E. G. Marshall.

In 1959, Aunt Fanny led her radio friends on a tour of her alma mater, Coe College, during a one-day *Breakfast Club* broadcast in Cedar Rapids, Iowa. The next year, the March of Dimes persuaded the *Breakfast Club* to go on tour for that organization, and the stops included Phoenix, where former singer Jack Owens showed his old friends around the city where he had become successful in real estate. Then the tour moved on to Los Angeles and the Ambassador Hotel, where a week of broadcasts originated from the famous Coconut Grove.

A closer-to-home journey occurred in 1961 when the *Breakfast Club* pitched a tent and did the program from the Farm Progress Show underway in Indianapolis. The cast took turns milking cows and, before the week was over, everyone had to wade through thick Indiana mud churned up with plenty of September rain.

During a visit to the *Breakfast Club* in 1962, Minnesota Governor Elmer Anderson invited the cast to make a return visit to his state's Aquatennial, a mid-summer festival, which they had first attended in 1946. Soon they were packed and heading for a week's worth of broadcasts from the Apache Center in Minneapolis.

One of the show's more unusual trips occurred on May 31, 1963, when, after doing the normal Friday morning show, the cast drove en masse across the Wisconsin state line to the small town of Burlington. There, on the front porch of "Stormy" Matilda Bobula's home, they set up to tape a special edition of the show for broadcast the following week. The trip was McNeill's way of repaying Bobula for all the times she had come to his show during the preceding twenty-six years. Hundreds of her neighbors joined the fun and the chance to see the radio stars. Bobula's relationship with the *Breakfast Club* began in 1937, when a customer of her husband's sewage business came by her home and borrowed a pen so he could write down an address. The pen she gave him had Tommy Barlett's ABC radio show *Welcome, Travelers* written on it. The man suggested that the next time she went to Chicago she visit the *Breakfast Club* and, as an incentive, told her she didn't need tickets if she mentioned his name. From then on she began making trips from Wisconsin to Chicago to see the *Breakfast Club* and she became somewhat of a celebrity on the show. Soon the cast began sending her anniversary and birthday cards and visiting her when they were in southern Wisconsin.[1] All of her thirteen children were given *Breakfast Club* christenings. They yielded Stormy a brood of twenty-nine grandchildren, twenty-seven great grandchildren, and three great, great grandchildren, which became a family the *Breakfast Club* was proud to celebrate. At eighty-three in 2000, she was living in Kenosha, Wisconsin.

In 1963, Alfred Hitchcock paid a visit to the *Breakfast Club* and casually remarked to McNeill he ought to take his program to England because, as he declared, "they wouldn't believe it." That started everyone thinking about the possibilities of an overseas journey, including the Armed Forces Radio and Television Services, which began planning a *Breakfast Club* tour of U.S. bases in Europe. Arrangements were made for the show to originate from a Royal Air Force base not far from London at Lakenheath, where about 450 people attended a Saturday taping on June 29, 1963. The cast was billeted in one of the base's dormitories. From there the entourage flew to France and stayed at Evreux-Fauville Air Base about sixty miles from Paris. After the broadcast, they tried to board their chartered plane for Italy but were kept on the ground by a national crew strike. In order to keep on schedule, they were switched from their C-54 (which had been used by General Douglas MacArthur during World War II) to a C-130 Flying Boxcar, which safely carried them to Genoa, Italy. The U.S.S. *Enterprise* was anchored in Genoa Bay and became their stage for a broadcast show for the 3,500 sailors on board. When the Chicagoans stepped on board they found themselves literally walking on a red carpet to the beat of a brass band. The *Enterprise* crew was expecting the arrival of a contingent from the Italian navy and, by mistake, the *Breakfast Club* cast received the military welcome prepared for the visiting sailors.

Next, they flew to Germany and went behind the Iron Curtain to stage a broadcast from West Berlin, where President John Kennedy had given his famous "Ich bin ein Berliner" speech the week before. During the broadcast, McNeill interviewed an Army sergeant from Chattanooga who told him about being captured by Russian troops during the Berlin Airlift in 1948. A private from Schererville, Indiana, described his job of raising the Russian flag everyday at the point in the city where the four military zones converged. McNeill talked with a young woman who, a few years earlier, had written to the *Breakfast Club* from Germany asking for help with her English and some information about America. She was subsequently swamped with cards and photos which she put in a scrapbook that she brought to show McNeill. A serviceman's wife, originally from Lake City, Minnesota, told McNeill that he was responsible for her getting married twenty-five years earlier. She used to listen to the *Breakfast Club* every morning at 7:00 A.M. before going to work. When daylight saving ended she would have to miss the show, as she needed to be at her job by 8:00 A.M. Therefore, she decided to marry her boyfriend, quit work, and spend her mornings listening to the *Breakfast Club*. McNeill concluded the interviews by reading a poem written by a Walnut Creek, California, woman in the audience.

> For 20 years the Army has moved us all around,
> I keep listening to Don McNeill wherever the program found.
> With every move we tried to see him in Chi,
> we hoped with our retirement to again try.
> This has been a pleasant surprise to be certain,
> here he comes to see us behind the Iron Curtain.[2]

Cartoon in Don McNeill's travel journal on a trip to Europe

During her segment of the show, Aunt Fanny tried to teach Mc-
Neill some German, but even without her coaching, he demonstrated agility with the language. Aunt Fanny declared the divided
city was "one place where you better know where you're going or you
better pack your bags for a long stay."

Hymn Time featured the tune associated with the United Nations' efforts around the world, "Let There Be Peace on Earth."
Berlin, which the Russians sliced into two cities two years earlier
with a crude wall of wire and cinder blocks, was a poignant setting for
the morning hymn. During Memory Time, McNeill shared his
thoughts on seeing the Berlin Wall for the first time that morning:

> It's ugly, it's forbidding, made of concrete blocks hastily piled to-
> gether some ten feet high with hardened mortar oozing from in
> between, topped with barbed wire and broken glass. The wall is
> not to keep the West Berliners from entering but the East
> Berliners from escaping. It's the most gigantic concentration

camp of all time. Here and there you will see pitiful sidewalk shrines for loved ones shot down trying to flee. It's like a poisonous snake winding its way through a lovely city.[3]

McNeill concluded his tribute to West Berlin by acknowledging the residents' gaiety and sense of humor as evidenced by their nicknaming the city's new and stylishly designed Kongress Halle the "pregnant oyster."

Munich came next, where everyone in the cast was given specially made beer steins. They then went to Frankfurt where an audience of more than six hundred, made up mostly of women, came to see the show and be interviewed by McNeill. That night McNeill and his on-air talent appeared on the Armed Forces Radio and Television Service's twentieth anniversary show, while the band and crew bounced for two hundred miles in an all-night bus ride to Bitberg Fighter Base near Luxembourg. When everyone finally arrived and got their bearings, they put on a July 4th show that helped American servicemen and women celebrate Independence Day. The four-nation trip with appearances at seven bases gave army and navy personnel and their families a chance to connect with something from home and also symbolized the close ties the *Breakfast Club* had had with the military service since it was first carried by military radio in 1938.

Civilians also enjoyed the Armed Forces broadcasts and for many years Dutch radio carried its own "Breakfast Club." On June 23, 1993, Dutch listeners could hear a tribute to the sixtieth anniversary of their "Breakfast Club's" namesake, which had left the air in the U.S. in 1968. McNeill's grandson, Thomas, who had taken up residence in the Netherlands two years earlier, joined the on-air celebration and sang the *Breakfast Club* theme, having introduced it in his best Dutch.[4]

McNeill's compensation made him one of the highest paid performers on radio, but, since he was the major attraction for the audience and sponsors, the network did not want to risk losing his connection with the show. An item appeared in *Variety* in 1962 indicating that Jack Linkletter was being considered as a replacement for McNeill. ABC Radio vice-president Robert Pauley denied the rumor and indicated his hope that McNeill would continue as *Breakfast Club* host through the next decade.[5] Pauley's job was to revitalize ABC Radio and his strategy was to modernize programs like the *Breakfast Club* to appeal to the younger audiences that sponsors wanted to reach. The hiring of two new singers helped give the show the fresh sound which the network sought.

The new female singer was Mary Anne Luckett, who had been singing on the radio in Louisville. She was encouraged to audition for the *Breakfast Club* after Sam Cowling heard her sing on the air during a visit he made to his hometown, Jefferson, Indiana. In reflecting on why she was hired, she believed that her experience singing religious songs on programs like the *Kentucky Barn Dance* gave her more versatility and strengthened her presentation for the job. Luckett's entry to Chicago was made easier since everyone on the show helped make her feel comfortable. During the program she often mentioned some of the challenges she faced in moving to the city and living in a high-rise building. When she complained about not knowing how to shake the dust mop out the window at such a height, listeners wrote in with suggestions like "shake it into a bag." Luckett stayed with the show for five years, then she married, had children, and became a student again while still accepting occasional singing jobs.[6] Her replacement was Cathie Taylor, whose voice and manner were similarly bright and enthusiastic.

The other new vocalist was John Gary, who had been singing professionally since he was an eleven-year-old star on KNX Radio's morning show in Los Angeles. After a tour of duty with the Marine Corps, he moved to New Orleans where he performed on WDSU-TV and in his spare time took up scuba diving. His interest in the sport was more than casual—he set a world record for underwater endurance, forty-one hours and one minute. His career with the *Breakfast Club* was cut short by an unusual incident that almost disrupted the show one morning in the Sherman House. Two police detectives and a woman told the page who met them at the entrance to the College Inn that they wanted to question Gary, who happened to be singing at that moment. ABC page, Ray Barnes, asked them to wait until Gary finished his song and suggested they sit down. Barnes said the look on the singer's face when he saw the officers with the woman was "incredible."[7] The situation involved accusations by the woman that Gary had sexually approached her daughter, who was a minor at the time. Nothing concerning the incident appeared in the newspapers, but since McNeill did not want a hint of scandal to be associated with his show, he let Gary go. It was a big loss because Gary had a fabulous voice and he proved it with a successful singing career that flourished until his death from cancer in 1998.

Pauley's efforts to modernize the *Breakfast Club* may have attracted a greater number of younger listeners—the ratings were strong, which pleased both affiliate stations and sponsors. A major strength of the show was the name recognition and continuity Don McNeill provided. In June 1963, McNeill had reached a milestone in his career, having been on network radio and television for thirty years. He received honors from several broadcast trade organizations, which recognized his long and successful career. Most likely the honor the University of Notre Dame bestowed on McNeill that June had the most meaning, because of who was also on the stage that Sunday. McNeill's honorary degree was in recognition of his having "survived the almost frenzied competition of his profession for more than half the years of this advancing century to bring joy, charity, and bright edification to multitudes by way of radio and television." He became an honorary alumnus, joining his three sons with degrees from Notre Dame. The valedictory address was given by Bob Mc-Neill, who was graduating from the College of Arts and Letters and planning to study at Oxford on a Rhodes Scholarship that he had been awarded earlier in the school year.

In 1961, Marquette University had given McNeill an honorary Doctor of Letters degree during a ceremony for its College of Journalism. The citation on the award praised him

> for the good he has achieved in his promotion of homey virtues of friendliness and charity, for the happiness and joy he has brought into the lives of millions of people each morning . . . [t]hrough his summer camps for underprivileged boys . . . his sponsorship of worthy national projects and special religious observances. . . . This is especially true of his Moment of Silent Prayer, a daily reminder, wherever the program is heard, of man's dependence upon the Mercy and Goodness of Almighty God.[8]

Marquette focused on McNeill's benevolent spirit and the resolve he showed toward keeping the Silent Prayer a part of his program in its salute to him for being more than just a successful entertainer. When public prayers became a heated constitutional issue in the early 1960s, McNeill broke from his typical posture of staying clear of controversy on the *Breakfast Club*. On June 25, 1962, the U.S. Supreme Court ruled against organized prayer in public schools in a case growing out of a dispute on Long Island, New York, over the recitation of a non-denominational prayer drafted by the state Board of Regents. The Court's decision revolved around the Separation of Church and State clause of the Constitution. Reaction to the ruling was strong and immediate. President John Kennedy had a solution for how to deal

A whistlestop on Don's tour as a presidential candidate, 1948

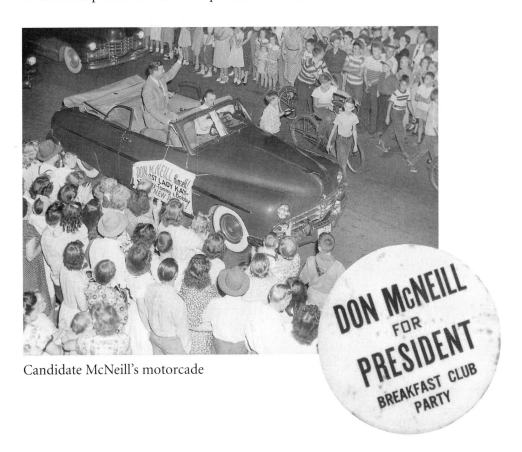

Candidate McNeill's motorcade

The Great Mouse Hunt with Singer Patsy Lee, Don, big game hunter Frank Buck, and Sam Cowling

Don with six-year-old Butch Akom, a guest from the audience

Don with the children of his cast and staff at a backyard broadcast in 1948

Don and ABC's vice chairman Mark Woods at the signing of the twenty-year contract, 1950

Celebrity guests on the Breakfast Club included Bob Hope, Jerry Lewis, and Jimmy Stewart

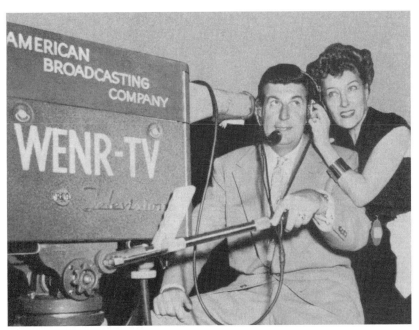

Don and Gloria Swanson, the featured guest on the premiere of the
TV Club, 1950

Don and Aunt Fanny
on the set of the
TV Club

Johnny Lujack, Chicago Bears All-Pro and former Notre Dame All-American, during a 1950 TV Club broadcast

Former heavyweight champs Jack Dempsy and Joe Lewis in the TV Club in 1951

Elmer Feagins after hitch-hiking to Chicago from Texarkana to pay a bet to his wife, 1951

Breakfast Club broadcast with the McNeill boys from New Trier High School, 1951

Cast and staff ready to travel on *Breakfast Club* road trip to the southeast in 1952

Bill Krenz, Betty Johnson, Don McNeill, Fran Allison, Dick Noel, and Sam Cowling on a riverboat cruise in Davenport, Iowa, 1955

A view of the audience during the twentieth anniversary show, 1953

An example of the popular Breakfast Club yearbooks

Breakfast Club baby Ben Round and his mother on the stage during the twentieth anniversary show

Don and Bob Hope at the Brookfield Zoo for Sidelight Reports during the 1952 political conventions in Chicago

Fishing, Don's favorite pastime

Boys Club campers show their frog harvest at Himself's Hideaway

A television close-up of Don and Aunt Fanny during a simulcast

An interview with lawyer Raymond Jenkins on the Breakfast Club set used in the simulcast

Sheet music to "Make America Proud of You"

Don holding a replica of the Moment of Silent Prayer with model Marle Lawrence and artist Ben Stahl

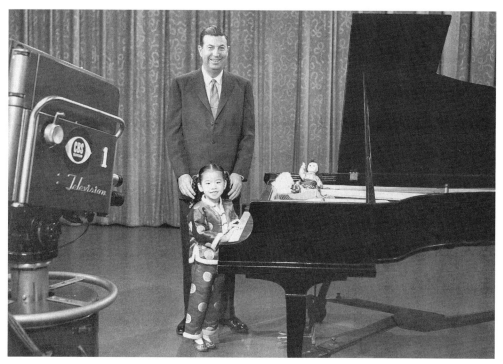

Ginny Tiu on the Ed Sullivan Show in 1959

The Breakfast Club cast and staff, including the orchestra

Don with son Don McNeill, C.S.C., following his ordination in Rome in 1965

Kay McNeill, a favorite guest of Breakfast Club fans

Don and Kay on the golf course

Don with his first grandchild, Christine, at Himself's Hideaway

with the ruling: "We have in this case a very easy remedy, and that is to pray ourselves." He urged Americans to use this ruling as an incentive to make prayer more meaningful to their children and to pray more at home.

Eight days after the decision was announced, McNeill was uncustomarily outspoken about the issue and ventured into the fray by taking a stand squarely against the banning of school prayer. He acknowledged that his speaking out would invite a lot of mail from "atheists" and "well-meaning people who do not believe in God." The negative letters arrived, but supporters of school prayer wrote in, too. A woman from Long Island, near where the court case arose, wrote that she was relieved that people in this country are "free to speak our minds, pray or not pray." A man in Rural Retreat, Virginia, was angry with what he called "Atheist-baiting" and condemned radio as being "a curse to this country for the reason that it has, since its inception, been used as an instrument of religious and anti-atheist propaganda." A Wichita listener objected to McNeill's attitude that "if you disagree with me you are either 'Atheist or Misinformed.'" He ended with a postscript, "I enjoy your program and hope you continue with it for many years to come."

Much of the mail following the July 3 broadcast praised McNeill for speaking out. From Grand Junction, Colorado, a woman wrote, "Dear Don, you, Paul Harvey and Billy Graham help restore my faith in Americans." A retired Navy chaplain wrote from Utica, Michigan, that "we have a fight on our hands—but the Lord will bless the fight with folks like you in there fighting with us." A Philadelphia woman confided that "a little prayer won't hurt anyone and I am pretty sure it will help."

Even though he took an unequivocal stand on a very controversial, public issue, he was consistent with the on-air image he had presented for nearly eighteen years. School prayer and the Silent Prayer on the *Breakfast Club* were similar in that both were attempts to provide a bridge across a religious divide. It could be argued that to the extent one fails, so does the other. Since McNeill was sincere about the Silent Prayer on radio, he had to show support for prayers in school.

Television offers brought McNeill back in front of the cameras. In 1955 and 1956 he filled in for Garry Moore on the quiz show *I've Got a Secret* over CBS-TV where the panel members, Bill Cullen, Faye Emerson, Henry Morgan, and Jayne Meadows, proved hard to stump. One night Agnes Donohue was a contestant with the secret that "Don McNeill changed my diapers." Within minutes the panel figured out this woman was the emcee's younger sister. The game-show emcee's task was to make transitions and keep up with the repartee of the panel and contestants. McNeill excelled at both those qualities and was clearly in his element. Therefore, when Don Mc-Neill Enterprises was in the process of creating a television vehicle for the star in the early 1960s, a quiz program format was eventually selected. The program they came up with was called *Take Two*, which required contestants to select two out of four images that go together with a particular theme. The program ran as a summer replacement Sunday afternoons on ABC-TV in 1963 with McNeill as host. During one of the June tapings, the producers surprised McNeill by bringing together "contestants" who were from the host's past thirty years on network radio and television. Jim Jordan, Joe E. Brown, Johnny Desmond, Ed Sullivan, Garry Moore, and Durward Kirby all paid honor to McNeill's longevity on the air.

As 1963 came to an end, McNeill vacationed in Florida during the final weeks of November and his son Tom sat in as toastmaster of the *Breakfast Club*. On Friday, November 22, President Kennedy was assassinated and commercial broadcast programming was suspended while the nation mourned and adjusted to the shock. The presidential funeral was held Monday, November 25. The following day, when the *Breakfast Club* returned to the air, Don and Kay McNeill offered their reflections on John Kennedy during a special Prayer Time.

> DON MCNEILL: Kay and I were motoring peacefully and happily through the Florida sunshine en route from Deltona to Miami, when we decided to stop for gas and an ice cream by the roadside. We hadn't turned on the radio in the car, so it was from the gas station attendant, near Orlando, that we first heard the unbelievable news—inside the little refreshment parlor, everyone was clustered around a small radio, shock and disbelief on their faces—this was a scene repeated, with but small variations, everywhere.
>
> People down here in Florida felt a special closeness to the late president—he'd just completed a tour here as you know, before going to Texas. We were in many of the spots here which he visited last week, and I'm glad to be able to be down here where he spent so many happy hours to pay my small tribute to this great man.
>
> I don't think any of us should make the mistake of labeling the assassination of our president as the work of

this or that group—or this or that factor, or this or that race, or country, or certainly state or city. The fact that this horrible deed took place in Dallas should have absolutely no bearing on the matter—this crazed fanatic could have done the same in any number of cities in any number of states.

Tom and I have frequently discussed President Kennedy and his policies. To say we always agreed with him would be untruthful. But we never quarreled with his objectives, which were the preservation of freedom in this country and the entire world, the respect for the dignity of man—regardless of race, creed, or color—a compassion for the older persons among us, and the handicapped. I say we never quarreled with his obvious sincerity in these matters—to differ with him on methods is the American way of life, a right no one recognized more than he.

I greatly admired his sense of humor, his sense of fairness, the manner in which he typified young, vigorous America on the move.

Isn't it a tragedy that with all the progress we have made in space—the fact that we have been able to project men safely around the earth time and again—and still some maniac with a cheap rifle is able to strike down the highest official in our land, in the primitive fashion in which leaders have been cruelly slain for generations.

[Hymn played—same as before President Kennedy's funeral.]

Instead of our moment of silent prayer, may I make a humble effort to voice your sentiments and mine in a prayer for our late president.

O Lord, to whom all men owe existence, we beg you to receive with loving compassion, one, who in his own way did much to serve you through his efforts to help all mankind. Never had a man more power than he on earth— we know that is as nothing compared to your power and glory over all—and that this country he died for may be the continued beneficiaries of that for which he labored—a leader, an example for the whole world to follow, to uphold the dignity of man in a free world united in Peace—under you, our God and Savior. Amen.

O Lord, to whom all men owe existence, we beg you to guide the hand of one so suddenly thrust into the highest office on earth. History notes that others before him, in similar roles, grew in stature overnight to bring to this responsibility a nobility greater than their nature seemed capable of before. May he constantly seek your guidance, O Lord, so that such may come to him, and that men of both parties may help him guide us through these troubled times, relying on your infinite goodness, justice, and mercy to bring us ever closer to the goal for which we daily pray—a free world united in peace. Amen.

KAY MCNEILL: I'm sure the hearts of all mothers around the world go out to Mrs. Kennedy and the children. We mothers want to compliment Jackie for her greatness, majesty, and magnificence during these horrible four days that shook the world. Let us remember Jackie Kennedy and the families on both sides in our daily prayers and ask God to send her extra strength and courage to carry on for her adorable children. We must also pray for President Johnson.[9]

17

Breakfast in the Clouds

During an interview in 1984 with John Callaway on Chicago's PBS station, WTTW-TV, McNeill joked that he had closed a lot of hotels with his show. The Morrison Hotel was demolished in 1965 to make way for the First National Bank Building, and in 1980 the Hotel Sherman was torn down and replaced by the State of Illinois Center (renamed the Thompson Center). The two other earlier sites of the *Breakfast Club* were "closed" as well. The radio and television studios on the nineteenth and twentieth floors of the Merchandise Mart were refitted as offices after NBC moved into its own building in 1989. In 1993 the Lyric Opera purchased the stage, seating house, and backstage areas from the owners of the Civic Building. Included in the deal was the Little Theater, which the Lyric gutted and made into a scene storage and rehearsal area.

Early in 1963, the show was looking for a new location after learning of plans to clear the block the Sherman occupied for the Illinois Center. ABC began contacting various hotels to see if they were interested in becoming the *Breakfast Club's* new home. The advantage for any hostelry was that its name would be mentioned several times during the broadcast to a reputed ten million listeners every weekday. Several landmark hotels were under consideration, including the Palmer House and the Conrad Hilton, but scheduling conflicts and other considerations ruled them out.

The Allerton Hotel had been completed in 1924 as one of a national chain of club hotels designed to offer young professionals the combined appeal of hotel services and private club sociability. It sat along a portion of Michigan Avenue that had been redeveloped with upscale shops, offices, and nightlife. Its roof line was considered to be an example of Northern Italian Renaissance with pronounced setbacks and towers. It advertised its Tip Top Tap to anyone who looked skyward. Also on the upper floors was a meeting room on the Michigan Avenue side of the building. The management of the Allerton was eager to have the *Breakfast Club* as one of its permanent guests. They promised to redo the meeting room so it would seat an audience of two hundred. In addition, they were prepared to provide a suite on the twenty-fourth floor, just above the meeting room, for McNeill to use as an office and reception area for prospective sponsors, as well as provide him with an indoor garage space. In exchange, the Allerton would receive plugs at the end of each quarter hour plus a ten-second mention of its three-day holiday plan (the arrangement was later modified with the stipulation that ABC would pay $600 rent per month).

An agreement was reached and construction began to transform the room into a radio studio complete with a stage and technical control room. On Monday, August 19, the *Breakfast Club* broadcast from its new studio, which had been designated the Clouds Room. The overall impression one got when visiting the show was that the chairs had rather hard bottoms and there was a long, narrowness to the room. But, just as the weather wasn't the reason people visited Chicago, the audience for the *Breakfast Club* came to see McNeill and his cast, not the Clouds Room.

The early morning troupe quickly settled into a routine at the Allerton on Chicago's Magnificent Mile along Michigan Avenue. The hotel's dining room was often where ABC would entertain clients and McNeill found his penthouse suite a handy place to practice his clarinet before or after the show. His musical talent was periodically displayed on the program, but without much fanfare, just a short rendition of some obscure tune. His contribution to the musical world lay more with his giving musicians a chance to be heard and make a living. The style of the music heard on the *Breakfast Club* was strictly middle-of-the-road and the changes over the decades were hard to discern, but the performance level of the band members and singers was always of the highest caliber. In 1963, the president of the local chapter of the American Federation of Musicians, Barney Richards, was a guest on the *Breakfast Club*. His sole purpose for being there was to announce that McNeill had been selected to receive an honorary membership in the union because of his contribution to live music. The union's award was truly an honor, because McNeill was only the seventh recipient of the special membership nationally. Others included Fritz Reiner, former conductor of the Chicago Symphony, and David Ribinoff, concert violinist.

As his "audition," McNeill played a tune he said he had been practicing called "Lost Love." After the rendition, Richards jokingly tore up the card he was preparing to sign. Eddie Ballantine then remarked how proud and grateful the band was to work for someone as committed to music as McNeill was.

Another guest that year was more receptive to McNeill's clarinet playing. Duke Ellington came up to the Clouds Room and during his conversation with McNeill agreed to play a duet. The result was a smooth and melodic version of "Mood Indigo."

The show benefited from a good-size audience. It gave McNeill some choice in selecting interviews and provided inspiration for the cast's performance. Cliff Petersen kept records on each day's audience which indicated that an average of 128 persons attended the show during April 1963. By April 1965, the average attendance dropped to 80. Holiday periods and summer months typically were not a problem, but those somewhat dreary weeks from November through March often yielded few visitors to the Allerton's twenty-third floor.

McNeill had a plan to avoid having to play to an empty house; he advertised on ABC's Chicago radio station, WLS, the availability of a special *Breakfast Club* bus service. Organizations from communities within fifty miles of Chicago would line up dates for a trip to Chicago, which would begin with a free breakfast at the Allerton, followed by the broadcast taping in the Clouds Room. After the show, the group could spend the day in the city as long as they paid the bus driver for the extra hours. Organizations had to guarantee a minimum of forty visitors, plus pay forty dollars for the round-trip bus trip. The plan encouraged a wide assortment of religious and community groups from the Chicago region to do what hundreds of thousands of people had done for the past thirty years—see McNeill and then the city. There would be days when only a few chairs would be filled, but judicious sound editing could fill the room with applause and laughter.

One January morning in 1967 the concern was not so much about an audience showing up but the cast and crew. Snow began falling in Chicago on Thursday, January 26, at 5:00 A.M. and continued for the next twenty-four hours. The city found itself stranded with six-foot drifts and a total accumulation of over twenty-three inches. The taping of the show was delayed until a quorum of bandsmen and crew showed up. McNeill had wisely spent the night at the Allerton. Others, who lived nearby, walked to the hotel and several arrived while the show was in progress. It would be another ten days before the city could declare the snow emergency over, and the *Breakfast Club* broadcasts helped listeners nationwide understand the challenges Chicagoans were facing that winter.

Although the program's format and personalities remained the same, McNeill kept looking for ways to improve the show with fresh ideas and talent. For example, he found a new writer while driving to work. Tom Fouts, known as Captain Stubby, did an early morning show called the *Farm Special* with Chuck Bill on WLS Radio. Fouts knew McNeill listened and had fun ribbing him on the air. One day, McNeill asked if he would come by his office, causing Fouts to wonder if his early morning jibes had offended McNeill. He was pleasantly surprised by an offer to begin writing jokes and one-liners for the *Breakfast Club*. Soon the part-time work expanded to include being on the air and conducting pre-interviews with the guests to provide McNeill with questions to ask during the show. At times, Fouts would plant himself in the audience and pretend to be various characters during interviews.[1]

In 1964 McNeill accepted an invitation from the governor of Maine to broadcast from several cities in the state during the summer. Governor John Reed had written McNeill three years earlier after learning that the toastmaster mentioned on the air that he had "been almost everywhere but Maine." The cast spent a week traveling from Poland Spring to Portland to Lewiston-Auburn and ended the week in Waterville. After returning to Chicago, they soon were down in Indiana at the Farm Progress Show and then went to New York City for broadcasts from the Hilton Hotel. Another trip was easy on everyone, a stay at the luxurious West Virginia resort, the Greenbrier.

The year 1965 began with the *Breakfast Club* originating for a week from Deltona, Florida. In March, the National Association of Broadcasters convention drew them to Washington, D.C. A broadcast for ABC Radio station owners and managers attending the convention originated from the Grand Ballroom of the Mayflower Hotel. McNeill used Memory Time that day as a way of telling the broadcasters that theirs was an important mission based on the power of words over pictures to influence people. It was an essay written by William Gleason of KIZL Radio in El Centro, California, which emphasized the aural medium's ability to reach individuals, regardless of what they are doing, to sell ideas and products. The political connection was provided with visits from Congresswomen Patsy Mink of Hawaii and Charlotte Reid of Illinois. Reid reminisced with McNeill about her earlier career as a singer on his show in 1937 when she went by the name Annette King. During the week, she invited the *Breakfast Club* cast to a party at her apartment overlooking the capital city. McNeill often retold how Illinois Senator Everett Dirksen bade farewell to the gathering that night. The senator and his wife had climbed the open stairway leading to the exit and turned. According to McNeill, Dirksen looked down on his hostess and, in his melodious voice, declared, "Romeo, Romeo, wherefore art thou Romeo? By rights she should be up here on the balcony and I should be down there, but in Johnson's great society, everything is all screwed up—good night!"

McNeill must have said the right things to the station owners because that fall ABC Radio announced it was signing him to a new five-year contract. In discussing the prospects for the show, Robert Pauley said so many new advertisers had signed on for 1966 the show's first-quarter billings would be 34 percent ahead of the same period in 1965.

The search for a male singer had been underway for some time when a young man who had been playing nightclubs and had done some television was brought in for an audition. Bob Newkirk was originally from Waterloo, Iowa, but had been making Los Angeles home when he tried out for the *Breakfast Club* slot. Newkirk's audition went well, but since McNeill was on vacation he was asked to return for a second week. His second round of auditioning began with his singing in the first segment of the show and soon afterward, during a station break, McNeill leaned over and asked Newkirk if he played golf and wanted to have a game that afternoon. As they drove to the course, McNeill told the singer he had been listening to the show during his vacation and liked what he heard enough to offer him the job. When they arrived at the golf course, there was a telegram waiting for Newkirk from ABC executive Bill MacCallum which simply read: "Bob, whatever you do, let the old man win." Obviously, the crew was tired of auditioning singers and supported Newkirk's getting the job, which gave him the confidence to show McNeill the telegram and win the game that afternoon. They would play many more rounds, often with two bandsmen, George Jean and Lee Knight.[2]

In addition to the new permanent singers, occasional guest appearances by such singers as Sonny and Cher in 1967 and the Cowsills in

1968 helped to give the show the modern sound ABC executives craved. These guests, plus Dick Noel's "Boris Beatnik" character, would help bring echoes of the turmoil of the 1960s to the show with a tinge of humor. Despite the social unrest which was occurring during the late 1960s, McNeill avoided controversy, confessing to a reporter he "never found that Vietnam, LSD or marijuana were good subjects for jokes" on the *Breakfast Club*. With the exception of his stand on school prayer, he adhered to a policy of sidestepping political or social controversy. He confided to a reporter that he was even hesitant to make fun of his being hit with the flu bug because of all the listeners who had influenza and might take offense.[3]

McNeill showed his ability to keep up with the younger crowd by being in fine form when the seasonal onslaught of vacationing students invaded the show. In August 1968 he had a room full of third graders from suburban Homewood, Illinois, plus undergraduates from Baylor University. The first card he read was from a Baylor student who wrote: "The joke today is that Don McNeill thinks he has a *live* audience this morning." After kidding them about their previous night's revelry, McNeill called some of the students from both age groups to answer a multiple-choice quiz. For the males, he asked, if they had a choice what would they take, "a dog, a cat, or a girl friend." The third grader chose the dog, but when the Baylor student did, too, they started kidding him about his taste in dates. Then McNeill brought up females and asked them to select from a doll, cookbook, or football player. For a finale, he asked the Baylor students, who were also members of the school's choir, to demonstrate their singing ability.

McNeill's ability to bridge more than generational divides was evident in his relationship with his son Don, who paid a visit to the *Breakfast Club* in September 1968. After joking about his son's being a perpetual student, McNeill proudly updated the audience on his career as a theologian, which included his ordination as a priest in the Congregation of the Holy Cross and plans to complete his doctorate in pastoral theology at Princeton Theological Seminary.

During what was to be his last appearance on the *Breakfast Club*, Don answered questions from his father about the definition of pastoral—"continually evaluating and responding to the needs of people"—and told about his work at the community mental health center at the Yale–New Haven Hospital. After two more years of study at Princeton, he would begin a ministry of teaching and service at the University of Notre Dame, where he, with others, founded the Center for Social Concerns in 1983. Through the Center's efforts, students were given learning and service opportunities in order to experience poverty and injustice in the U.S. and abroad. It became one of the first organizations to offer comprehensive service placements at a major research university.

Although their lifestyles became very different, McNeill was always interested in his son Don's activities and was generous with his financial support for projects initiated by the Center. He enjoyed visiting places and meeting people involved with Don's creative ministries. These included an African-American parish in Chicago and a project to assist blind Chileans who were living in poverty.

McNeill concluded the serious conversation with Don and eased his way into the next commercial in a seamless fashion. That was one of the many reasons advertisers liked the McNeill style and found his creative, humorous approach to their commercials both appealing and successful. AT&T began a feature called "Belle of the Day" in 1966 to promote its long-distance telephone service by letting a member of the studio audience call a relative or friend. Before dialing, McNeill would find out who the guest was about to call plus something about their relationship, which made it more likely that listeners at home would be interested. McNeill and the audience would eavesdrop on a portion of the call, but the guests were free to talk off-mike as long as they wished. One woman called her sister in Seattle whom she had not seen in forty-one years, which was the same number of minutes the two talked.

These and other features worked to keep audience ratings up and attract sponsors. When ABC Radio realized that the entire inventory of spots on the *Breakfast Club* was sold out for the first quarter of 1967, it bought large display ads in the trade press to proclaim that Don McNeill had become "A Legend in His Own Time." Under a bust of McNeill and the names of his current roster of sponsors was the following inscription:

> The 34th year of the longest continuous reign of any personality in broadcasting has come to an end. But only to begin the 35th. And what an auspicious beginning. Don McNeill and the Breakfast Club start 1967 completely sold out for the first quarter. A tribute to his increasing popular acclaim and to the friendly persuasion and believability he brings to a product message.

In May, the Broadcast Advertising Club of Chicago honored McNeill by naming him their "Broadcasting Man of the Year." The award was made in recognition of the business that his program gave advertising agencies over the years.

It would take more than one program or personality, however, to help ABC with the problems it was facing in the 1960s. The radio network, in particular, had an uphill battle because *local* radio station revenues were outstripping whatever profits radio *networks* could find. As always, ABC needed cash in order to stay competitive. It needed money to buy more attractive television series to boost its sagging ratings. As a result, ABC began looking for partners for a merger and in 1966 signed a deal with International Telephone and Telegraph (ITT), a holding company with communication and international investments. The agreement required government approval because licensed stations were involved. Despite concerns that ITT might attempt to influence ABC news coverage of international stories, the Federal Communications Commission voted to approve the merger, but the Justice Department stepped in and eventually decided to take the case to the U.S. Court of Appeals. On January 1, 1968, ITT and ABC canceled their agreement, leaving the network solidly in third place behind its two rivals.[4]

18

Last Call
to Breakfast

The ABC Radio Network died on New Year's Day, 1968, but not because of the Department of Justice. The single radio service was ingeniously divided into four different networks, each tailoring itself to a particular audience. The main advantage of the four-tiered arrangement was to give ABC more than one outlet in each radio market across the country. The American Personality Network (renamed Entertainment) served more traditional stations; the American Information Network was designed for stations with talk and/or all news programming; the American Contemporary Network was tailored for rock music stations; and American FM Network was created for FM stations with a progressive music format. The four services shared the broadcast day with a pre-set allocation of time during each hour. A waiver from the Federal Communications Commission allowed ABC to have more than one affiliate per market, thereby increasing the strength of the network to reach audiences. Although originally envisioned as being the centerpiece program of the Entertainment Network, the *Breakfast Club* was carried by affiliates of all the various formats and some in the same community, which required an additional waiver from the FCC. Although startup costs for the fourfold plan were high, within one year it attracted over 1,000 affiliates, making ABC the largest radio network in the nation. The revenues began increasing, too, and by 1972 ABC could report that its radio networks were profitable.[1]

It is unclear what part the four-tiered network had in the decision to close down the *Breakfast Club* by the end of 1968. The show provided the defining image for the Entertainment Network, which had the second highest number of affiliates of the four ABC services. Since the *Breakfast Club* ran nearly an hour, however, it did interrupt local stations' efforts to create a strong image in their market. For example, since it was purchased in 1960 by ABC to be its Chicago voice, WLS had built an image around its being a rock "MusicRadio" station with hip deejays and plenty of on-air promotional jingles. The *Breakfast Club* clearly did not fit into the format and caused local managers at stations like WLS some concern. WABC New York had built a similar top-forty music format and every weekday morning at 10:00 A.M. saw a large chunk of its audience switch to rival station WMCA when the *Breakfast Club* began.[2] As a result, in major cities like New York, Chicago, and Pittsburgh, the *Breakfast Club* was shifted to FM stations owned by ABC or other AM stations in the market so as not to disrupt the program flow on those local stations. Many of the affiliates with the largest audience ratings went to the Contemporary Network and opted not to carry the *Breakfast Club*, which reduced the reach of the program.[3] Another reason the show ended may have been that McNeill was ready to put down the microphone and retire.

In a "confidential" memo dated July 11, 1968, ABC's Bill MacCallum wrote his boss in New York that if cancellation of the *Breakfast Club* was being contemplated, notice dates would have to be adhered to for some of the personnel on the show. McNeill's contract required that he be given four-months' notice; the singers needed thirteen-weeks' warning. Since the musicians had an agreement between their union and ABC to keep them on staff until the end of the year, no notice was necessary. The rest of the cast was employed without contracts and thus advance notice was not required. Engineers and stagehands working with the show would be re-assigned, but producer/director Cliff Petersen would be terminated.

When he returned from vacation on August 1, 1968, McNeill surprised many in his audience when he announced that he and ABC had decided to "discontinue" the *Breakfast Club* broadcasts by the end of the year. He hastily added that "no one has had a longer or happier association with the ABC Network than I." The only reason he gave was that "even though things were never better, all good things must come to an end and why not quit while you're ahead." The cast was not totally surprised by the news, as he had been talking with them about retiring for several years.[4] McNeill's retirement affected ninety people at ABC.

Two weeks later, more people heard about the closing of the show from ABC Radio's Paul Harvey, when he began the story by decrying the bad example Manhattan sets for the rest of the nation's entertainment fare. Harvey then singled out Don McNeill's *Breakfast Club* as an exception.

For thirty-five years the Breakfast Club flushed our polluted air with a gasp of fresh air at least once each morning.

The program, originating in mid-America (usually Chicago), showcased an exemplary individual. Once-married McNeill has fathered a real family of washed and combed and behaving and accomplished sons and has fathered a professional family of single-entendre wit and happy music and, alone of all broadcasts, reserved a minute a day for silent prayer—"each in his own words, each in his own way . . ."

It was a personal loss to some of us, a professional loss to many, and a significant loss to us all when Don recently announced his retirement effective the end of this year.

In his professional lifetime this steady star of the first magnitude has seen hundreds of brighter meteors burn themselves out in a season.

Sometimes the less durable performer may have become the victim of his own excesses but often the Red Buttons or George Gobel or the Garroway or Brennan or Moore was just chewed up and spit out by the insatiable public appetite for something different. Don, bringing his mostly midwestern audiences on stage, stayed "different."

Don McNeill came to the top during the depths of a depression and helped Americans keep faith. Through the Lindbergh kidnapping and the Dillinger escapades, from the charleston through the frug, from earliest radio's crackly headphones through living color TV, the Breakfast Club gave continuity and credulity to a sometimes incredible industry.

Two generations marched away to war and came home to pick up where they'd left off—marching around Don McNeill's breakfast table.

He'll not be reduced to ignominy or to knocking on any doors. Don has provided for his family and for his future. He will be comfortable fishing, golfing. If he allows himself occasional "appearing," it will be only because he wants to, not because he has to.

One can never truly see the size of a tree until it is felled; until it lies there stretched out on the ground leaving such a vast, empty place against the sky. He was a big one.[5]

As the very Last Call to Breakfast approached, the cast started preparing for their final morning in the Clouds Room. The name *Breakfast Club* was dropped in favor of the *Don McNeill Show* because many stations were running the program outside the morning time slot. On November 1, Memory Time inaugurated a daily reminiscence which traced the highlights for each year in the life of the *Breakfast Club* since it began in 1933. Guests kept coming by: Al Hirt, Ted Mack, and, in the last week of the broadcast, Colonel Shorty Powers, the voice of the Astronauts, to brief everyone on the *Apollo* 8 moonshot which was to begin the next day on December 21. By Christmas Eve, the *Apollo* craft began circling the moon while sending pictures back to earth. The voyage was a successful precursor to *Apollo* 11's moon landing the following July. The *Apollo* 8 crew splashdown occurred just before 11:00 A.M., December 27, which was about the same time many Americans were listening to the end of the final *Breakfast Club* broadcast on a network of 224 stations across the country.[6]

The last show had been taped the week before in front of an audience which included friends and family members of the cast. It was a very special occasion, and everyone on the show had a chance to say good bye. Sam Cowling said he was appreciative of the loyalty of the audience over the years. He also told everyone he was ready for the change, as he had been saving for this day for the past twenty years—string. Eddie Ballantine echoed Cowling's praise of the audience, adding that he continued to hear from former listeners like Jimmie Darou and his wife. Bob Newkirk told McNeill how his life changed after joining the *Breakfast Club* cast, he got a wife and two children. Cathie Taylor read a poem to her boss thanking him for the "joy and laughter" he gave to her in the years she was on the show.

McNeill mentioned that Taylor would be the last of the girl-singers on the *Breakfast Club* while he looked into the audience and saw one of the first female singers, Annette King—Charlotte Reid, U.S. Representative from Aurora, Illinois. Reid told McNeill that everywhere she went around the country she would meet people who remembered her years of singing on the show. Then she started snapping her fingers and reciting a poem about her platform as a member of Congress.

Next up was Bob McNeill who said he could only recall the last twenty-seven years of the program, which coincided with his age.

McNeill updated everyone on his youngest son who, in addition to being married, had two children and a career in Chicago as an investment counselor.

McNeill spotted a familiar person in the audience, Stormy Bobula, who told him that with his going off the air, she decided to sell all the radios in her house. She had them everywhere so she could hear the *Breakfast Club*—a table model in the kitchen, a transistor in the wash basket, and another in her purse when she went shopping. McNeill thanked her for being such a loyal listener.

A studio guest from Chicago asked McNeill if he would recall one of the funnier bloopers he made over the air. McNeill replied, "I have done it so continually and so often and they are all so hilarious that I can't separate one from another."

The music played on the final show was written by members of the cast: "Perfect Love" by McNeill and Ballantine, "Bowling Polka" by Ed McKean, "Sam's Lullaby" by Cowling, "Tomorrows Are Made for People Like You" by Taylor.

Aunt Fanny read a poem which she wrote for the occasion.

When I think of the fun, of the laughter, the action
why some people live life-times, and still know no fraction
of what we have had 'round this Breakfast Club table.

If I live to a hundred,
I'll never be able to thank you for all the great joys I have
    known.
For the friendships I've formed and for the use of your phone.
For your understanding in days not so sunny,
for your helpful suggestions, not to mention the money.

I remember so well how you never could hula,
how we've loved the goodies from Mrs. Bobula.
How you dug Nettie's headaches that snapped, cracked
    and beeped
How we all made jokes about your oversized beak.
Oh, yes, all the memories sweet, even bitter
will cheer me when I am an old baby-sitter.
So from Annie and Zelia, from Myrt, Pearl and Tootie
From Beulah, Hermione, Hodie and Rudy, yes
From me and the whole bunch of loyal busy fingers
Your song may be ended but the melody lingers.

Then McNeill introduced a man who took Fran Allison—but not Aunt Fanny—away from the *Breakfast Club*, Burr Tillstrom. Tillstrom brought Kukla, Ollie, and the whole Kuklapolitan crew to wish McNeill well in his retirement. Seated behind them was Dick Noel who told McNeill how much he enjoyed being part of the show and would miss hearing it.

McNeill speculated that engineer Ralph Davis would also "miss this show an awful lot because every day now he'll go directly to the racetrack."

Captain Stubby told McNeill that he enjoyed his three years with the show, adding that "one thing you and the network taught me is that money is not important." Stubby added that he hated to see the show end because "I don't think ever again we're going to see a broadcaster the caliber of Don McNeill putting shows into the homes of America."

McNeill acknowledged stage-hand Bobby Becker by saying, "I'm certainly going to miss him and I think he's going to miss me because every morning for years he's made a nice cup of coffee or tea for me. . . . He won't be able to break that habit now. He's going to have to drink it himself and he'll find out what I've been putting up with all these years."

McNeill tipped his hat to Cliff Petersen, "snapping his fingers . . . in that Swedish accent of his" in the control room, by thanking him for all the contributions he made to the show over the years. Then McNeill asked his wife to come to the mike, which she did wearing a "hot pink" dress. McNeill mentioned that their other sons couldn't make it to the last show, Don because of his completing a doctorate at Princeton and Tom busy working as a lawyer in Chicago. McNeill said Tom called to say congratulations on retiring and that he hoped his parents would have even more time to baby-sit his three children. Kay McNeill said Tuesday and Thursday were their baby-sitting days and they enjoyed every minute of it.

McNeill told his wife, "It would be as much of a pleasure being with you as it has been doing the show all these years." She said, "It's going to be funny not having you leave early in the morning because I'm flying around, . . . volunteer work . . . bowl early Monday morning." He told her, "If it will make you feel better, I'll get up and go somewhere and come back." She invited him to come along and he said he'd think about it, but did have plans to teach some seminars at a couple of universities. Kay McNeill said she wanted to tell a joke that he'd been using for as long as the show was on the air. She said McNeill would often get questions from listeners who would ask, "Do you ever wake up grouchy in the morning after all these years?" His reply, "No, I let her get up by herself."

McNeill said he had been home the last few days with the flu and had a chance to think about the best way to close his final show. He concluded that,

If I haven't said all I've got to say and said it several times in the last thirty years it's too late now. I guess everybody knows how I feel about how they kept me on the air all these years.

So, I thought I'd just say a few words from the heart. After all, if there's been any secret of success in this show it's been believability. I do stumble around and I do make mistakes, but I mean everything I say and have all these years.

Nothing I would say could mean more than having all of you, many of you, sometimes three generations of you, with me all these years. And so I hope you'll be seeing me and hearing me hither and yon someplace. I wish all of you the greatest of success and happiness.

I think perhaps the best way to leave would be with our moment of silent prayer in which I always asked each of you, in his own words, in his own way, for a free world united in peace, let us bow our heads and pray.

[Interval of silence]

Amen. And if you want peace where you are, don't ever forget Don McNeill and the gang saying so long and be good to your neighbor.

19

Don McNeill— A Super Senior

Two months after completing the last *Breakfast Club* broadcast, McNeill received his fourth honorary degree. Loyola University in Chicago awarded him its Doctor of Laws with the proclamation that he was "a man who has been able to offer laughter, wisdom, humanity, kindness, sanity, and genuine emotion to thousands each morning." That ceremony probably inspired McNeill to prepare for his latest challenge, being a college professor. In 1969 he agreed to teach a course at Marquette University titled "Broadcast News Workshop," which would draw from his well-crafted ability to present information and his deep understanding of audiences. Despite the fact that campuses were bubbling over with protests and rebellion, he approached the classroom with eagerness, telling a reporter, "I think I have something to communicate to young people who are interested in careers in radio and television. I want to share my experiences with students, translate my enthusiasm, perhaps even inspire them." At Marquette he shared an office with Professor John Grams, who remembers McNeill struggling a bit over having to grade students, but otherwise enjoying the experience. Grams noted that the twinkle never left McNeill's eyes throughout the semester and surmised that the veteran radio philosopher used some of his people-savvy skills to help students bridge the generational divide separating them from the distinguished broadcaster who faced them in class.[1]

When asked his opinions about how well the media were doing their job, McNeill had no reluctance expressing them. Regarding violence, he said, "There has been too much . . ." As to the criticism of television being a cultural wasteland, McNeill said, "It's unfair. TV is primarily an entertainment medium, not a cultural medium. People are expecting too much of television, trying to make something out of it that it wasn't intended to be." Concerning program censorship, he declared that "good taste should be the ruling factor," adding, "I was my own censor on the Breakfast Club. I'd cut out things if I thought they were in bad taste—or if they were dull."[2] In class sessions he used his professional experiences as the basis for his teaching. His trove of anecdotes combined with his personable nature must have made him an effective mentor for the students. He was not interested in being a full-time teacher, but he did enjoy the opportunity to reflect on his career with young people who had an interest in him and in broadcasting.[3] He set standards for his own performance during the first class meeting, when he promised the students that he would "not impose my generation's philosophy on you, not try to give you any pat formulas for success, and not bathe us all in constant nostalgia." The goal, as he saw it, was for each student to become a better communicator, and he had strong ideas on how to be successful at sending messages. Predicting the revolution that would occur in the coming years, he declared that broadcasting "was one business where you can thwart the computer. You can't computerize personality, warmth, or charisma."

McNeill's relationship with Marquette extended beyond the classroom. In 1971 he established the Don McNeill Collection at the university's library, which consisted of tapes, kinescopes, papers, and memorabilia associated with his career and especially the *Breakfast Club*. Included in the collection was the *Moment of Silent Prayer* painting by Ben Stahl, which was put on permanent display in the corridor leading to the campus chapels in the University Union building. In addition, the Kay and Don McNeill Communication Fund was established at Marquette to provide scholarships for students interested in careers in radio and television. The school has also used the fund to upgrade its broadcast news lab.[4]

The other university in McNeill's life, Notre Dame, was eager to have him share his professional experience with its students in South Bend. In 1971 he taught a course that was similar to his Marquette offering. In addition to helping students understand issues confronting the broadcast industry, the class was designed to examine specific communication situations. In one exercise, students made presentations to several married couples who were later debriefed about the effectiveness of the message.

McNeill's professorial duties at both universities were fairly limited and involved only part of one day a week during a term. Full-time faculty members were prepared to fill in for McNeill in the event he could not make it to campus on the day of class. Part of the reason for this arrangement was that he continued his career as a professional broadcaster. He was still heard regularly on ABC Radio's *Flair Reports*, which offered him an outlet for humor and self-expression.

Don McNeill at Himself's Hideaway—a wooded retreat not too far from Chicago—where I now have time to relax and share my thoughts with you.

Someone asked me if I didn't fear retirement. I said, "Look, I've lived through two world wars, the great depression, bell-bottom trousers, the Charleston, college kids swallowing gold fish, Maresy Dotes, Art Linkletter, the Beatles, the Monkees, and Mini-skirts. What makes you think I'd be afraid of retirement?"

Dr. Joseph Peck, in his book *Life with Women and How to Survive It!* says, "The day a man retires, he lays away the masculine horns which indicated that he was the bread-winner and protector of the home. Unfortunately, too often his wife grabs them up . . . and nothing is quite so sad as a lady deer wearing antlers!" He says to any male retiree, "Never leave your pants around where your wife can slip into them."

How can you tell when you are ready to retire? Well, as Cory Ford said, "You can look at yourself in the mirror and be amazed that the glass they use in mirrors isn't nearly as good as it use to be."

I suppose you're ready to retire when you wink at a girl and hope she won't wink back—or when the gleam in your eye turns out to be the sun hitting your bifocals!

It was no surprise that one of the nation's best known family men would comment on the goings-on of his grandchildren.

Don McNeill from Himself's Hideaway. And you know, sitting here admiring this lake and the weeping willows, and the stately oaks, and the gnarled hickories, and the gentle pines, and the contrasting birches—wups! A big bass just broke water right in front of me. Sitting here, I think, gee, how peaceful. Isn't it great to have a sense of security. Maybe not tomorrow, but right now. Right from the time we're infants we start searching for security. That bit about the security blanket for kids is real—you parents know—and as you grandparents should remember. I'll never forget a few weeks ago when one of our grandchildren spent the day at our house. Because she may be listening to this, I won't say which of the [eight] it was, but it could be any of them. We had a great day together, Kay and I and our little granddaughter. We find it's the most fun to have them one at a time, and truthfully, it gets to be a bit much to handle at that. When you reach a certain age—well, you know what I mean. Well, this day went along wonderfully well, and it came time to bring the little gal home, which we did. She was good as gold. Her mother thanked us profoundly for taking her off her hands for the day, and Kay and I left for home, happy as larks. But, just as we got in the door the phone was ringing and a little voice I recognized at once as belonging to the little granddaughter we'd just delivered home, said, tearfully, "Papa." (They all call me that—I guess grandpa's too long a word) "Papa, I left my blankie." Well, to the uninformed, blankie means blanket—and not just any old blanket— *her* special old beat-up security blanket. I could see in an instant—this was a crisis! I said, "Have no fear. Papa's here, and I'll bring your blankie right away." So back in the car I dashed— blankie in hand—and her wonderful smile when she saw me coming up the walk with her treasure . . . Well, I'll treasure it always. So, all was secure again, and blankie in hand, she hightailed it for bed. I hope she always feels as secure as she did right then. This is Papa. Don McNeill to you.

Tom and his wife Ingrid gave the McNeills their first grandchildren, Christine and Thomas, later adding Stephanie to their family. Bob and his wife Martha began contributing to the roster with Jennifer, Don, Vicky, and twins Steve and Elizabeth. These eight grandchildren fall short of the eighteen that the boys threatened to sire when they visited the *Breakfast Club* in 1954. However, adding the family's thirteen great-grand children, including triplets, to the count, the total in 2000 was twenty-one.

The McNeills enjoyed being with their grandchildren, often taking them to their lake property for a weekend of swimming or fishing. They made time for these new McNeills the same way they did for their own sons—only it was easier once McNeill gave up the demands of a daily broadcast. In their home, one bedroom was set aside for the grandchildren and contained displays of their artwork.

It was not that McNeill did not have opportunities for work; he did. Many organizations were eager to build a partnership with him to sell a product or further a cause. In 1975 Bell Savings in Chicago was one of the few he accepted. The following year, McDonald's restaurants and McNeill teamed up to bring about a revival of some *Breakfast Club* routines to listeners and viewers in parts of Illinois and Wisconsin. The spots began with the familiar *Breakfast Club* theme followed by McNeill's suggestion to join McDonald's Breakfast Club and receive coupons for meals at a reduced cost. The ads worked, because after six days of running them, breakfast sales in the target stores increased 22 percent above the figures reported before the campaign began.[5]

Florida developers, the Mackle brothers, approached McNeill to become the principal spokesman for a community they built near Daytona called Deltona. Beginning in 1963 and for the next twenty-five years, McNeill extolled the virtues of living in Mackle developments including Marco Island. In 1964 and 1965, the *Breakfast Club* originated from Deltona, and in the 1970s former cast members would periodically re-create the show at the community. McNeill and members of his family would spend time on Marco Island during the winter, taking advantage of the opportunities for fishing and golf. One year, McNeill left with more than a suntan. Here's how he described his most thrilling afternoon of golf:

> I've . . . played what I laughingly call "golf" for 50 years, give or take a few. I played in all 14 of the Tony Lema Tournaments at the beautiful Marco Island Country Club, with such super golfers as . . . Gene Sarazen, Tom Kite, Mark Hayes, J. C. Snead, Ken Venturi, and many others, but the one I want to brag about, was in 1980. In all the tournaments, no one, pro or amateur, had made a hole-in-one. Now, I'd never had one on any regulation golf course anywhere. I have watched my handicap advance with age. . . . So talk about a thrill! To hit your career shot on #15, playing with pro, Don Pooley, son Bob, with my wife, Kay, Bob's wife, Martha, and a huge gallery around the tee, and behind the green—the cheering—the back slapping—the "how does it feel?"—the numbness of having done something that's one in how many million! . . . I was presented with the

keys to the beautiful Toyota Celica Supra car that I'd won, by Gene Sarazen, before a cheering and incredulous crowd. From a dub to a hero in one lucky shot! So, I'd like to congratulate myself . . . once more. Not for making a great shot, not for making a lucky shot, but for not having a heart attack . . . immediately thereafter.[6]

In 1977, McNeill took advantage of an opportunity to complete the golf game he began but couldn't finish seventeen years earlier at the Lakeside Country Club in Burbank, California. In 1960, he was rushed from the tenth green to NBC's studios for his appearance on *This Is Your Life.* The return visit was prompted by his being honored at a luncheon by the Pacific Pioneer Broadcasters. The affair was a chance for McNeill to reminisce with some of his original radio colleagues such as Van Fleming, who was living in Capistrano, California. Fleming had fun reminding McNeill that, despite press releases to the contrary, the *Two Professors* was really called the *Van and Don Show,* not "Don and Van." Jim Jordan had everyone howling over a mistake he made in 1934 on the *Breakfast Club* when he mispronounced his wife's radio name as "Tits" rather than Toots. Fran Allison served as emcee and introduced a roster of *Breakfast Club* singers who paid tribute to their former boss, including Clark Dennis, Pasty Lee, Evelyn Lynne, Nancy Martin, Peggy Taylor, and Jack Owens.

When McNeill got his opportunity to speak to the Pacific Broadcasters, he thanked everyone for recognizing him and gave regrets from his wife, who he said was not up to coming to the affair. He joked about being at the age when he has a wife and a set of golf clubs, but couldn't swing with either one. Then he acknowledged that many in the audience were getting along in years and he asked rhetorically, "What's wrong with being a super senior?" He added that the dirtiest words in America were not related to sex but those that describe someone as being "too old." For what, he asked rhetorically, "work, recreation, creativity, sex?" concluding that he knew plenty of seniors who were more interested in "passion than pension."

McNeill told about the sense of satisfaction he got from doing the *Breakfast Club,* such as the morning over 17,000 New Yorkers jammed into Madison Square Garden to see a radio show, which prompted *New Yorker* magazine to label it a "traveling Lourdes." He recalled the many fine singers they were smart enough to hire and then jokingly listed some of those who did not pass the *Breakfast Club* audition, including Doris Day, Eydie Gorme, Peggy Lee, Ann Margaret, and Patti

Page. He concluded by admitting his minor annoyance at seeing parts of his broadcast routine while watching Johnny Carson, Mike Douglas, or Merv Griffin on television, but then acknowledged also having swiped from others a good deal of the material that he had used.

The reason Kay McNeill did not join him in Los Angeles was related to the fact that she had been diagnosed as having Alzheimer's Disease. She had symptoms typically associated with the disease, including not remembering things that had been part of her life. The change was notable from her lifelong habit of never forgetting a birthday or anniversary and the careful organization she had fostered at home. She began to have trouble performing routine tasks and speaking her mind. What made these occurrences all the more poignant was the fact she often acknowledged her difficulty by saying, "That's not what I meant."

She had been a loving and unselfish mother and grandmother who enjoyed being with children and was a devoted volunteer in the children's ward at Evanston Hospital where she provided comfort to homesick infants. She also was committed to helping children with developmental disabilities, in those years called "retarded," by building an awareness of the programs available to provide assistance to these needy youngsters. In recognition of her efforts, in 1961, the McNeills were named co-chairs of National Retarded Children's week in Illinois.

Kay McNeill's love of children was expressed in many ways. McNeill's secretary, Mary Canny, recalled the time her brother-in-law suddenly died of polio, leaving his wife and three children grief-stricken. The youngest, a two year old, would not leave her crib. Kay McNeill learned of the tragedy and went to their home the day of their father's funeral. She headed for the crib, murmuring "the little darlin'," and engulfed the girl in her arms. She bundled all the kids and their grandmother into her car and took them home where she had plenty of games and little gifts. That evening when they returned, the children were quiet and the grandmother looked rested, according to Canny.[7]

McNeill frequently credited his wife as the helpmate who got him up and out the door every morning. She was the ideal wife for the emcee of a morning show, as she arose everyday at 4:30 A.M. to begin her own busy day, which usually involved going to Mass and then writing lots of letters and cards to family, friends, and shut-ins, followed by volunteer work, bowling, or a round of golf. When McNeill wanted to escape to his hideaway, she would join him, where she, too, found pleasure in fishing. She was the perfect hostess for the retiring

McNeill and exuded friendly energy in everything she did, including *Breakfast Club*–related events. She also accompanied the cast on their road trips across the country, infusing them with her special brand of friendliness. Her high energy and humor were reflected in the quaint phrases that she often used on the spur of the moment. McNeill prepared a list of her expressions which he annotated with definitions.

> "Cripes Mahoney"—[to exclaim for] any reason, good or bad
> "I'll say nothing"— while talking incessantly
> "Full as a tick"—[after a] satisfactory meal
> "I was bent in two"—[while] carrying something heavy
> "Bad cess to him/her"—the Irish curse
> "Like a moving mountain"—awkward [describing one's movement]

After attending their son Don's ordination in Rome, the McNeills were driving along Italy's southern coast on the Amalfi Drive. She called it "Minestrone Drive" until McNeill corrected her, whereupon she labeled it "Mafia Drive."

The changes caused by Alzheimer's became more noticeable. Friend and neighbor, Dorothy Mulroy, could observe the progression the disease took in Kay McNeill since they often saw one another socially. After one of their frequent dinner parties, McNeill thanked Dorothy for behaving as though nothing was wrong with his wife, adding that he wished everyone would treat her that way.[8]

McNeill's interest in helping seniors adapt to changes in their life circumstances must have been fueled, in part, by his wife's condition. As a member of the board of directors of the Sears Roebuck Foundation, he supported the organization's plan to produce a television series on aging designed to improve the image most people had of senior citizens. *Prime Time: Positive Portraits of Aging in America* was produced by the Los Angeles public station KCET-TV with the Ethel Percy Andrus Gerontology Center at the University of Southern California. McNeill served as host for the series and also became actively involved in the many aspects of the production. He would introduce each episode with comments on the realities of getting older, which led into the story of the senior being profiled. Their life stories dealt with how they faced the challenges of being retired, getting older, and having less energy. McNeill concluded each episode with the admonition that, although "no universal formulas for survival" exist, "feeling sorry for oneself is outlawed." That advice must have spoken to the experience he was facing at home.

Retirement afforded McNeill the time to become involved in other projects. In January 1977 he wrote Jimmy Carter about an idea to help the newly elected president achieve his goal to regularly meet the people. McNeill's suggestion was built around a talk show titled, "The People Talk with Jimmy," which, he was confident, could be designed to serve the new administration well. McNeill told of his experience in making "a neighborhood of the nation" with his morning show and the periodic trips he made to various cities for *Breakfast Club* broadcasts and special shows. He argued that going to the people in their own locale will produce many pluses for the president.

> Unlike the "big debates," informality replaces stiffness, and the audience is not only seen, it *is* the show. Besides talking to a cross section from each state, local pride is enhanced. . . . I feel this format might serve your avowed concern finally to bring people close to their President, to have an interest in what they have to say, and yet focus on your image as the man who is in control, and not swayed by everyone's complaints or concerns unless it's for the common good of all.[9]

He suggested Carter travel to a state every month and moderate an hour-long program in which he would take questions and talk with residents of that region. At each location, he visualized an audience of about five hundred. In eight years, McNeill speculated Carter could cover every state twice.

McNeill concluded with a confession that he thought "Ford (who was my choice for the 'safe' candidate) was a decent man who did a worthwhile job, but I became disillusioned with his Vice-Presidential choice [Senator Robert Dole], and other things. Gradually your sincerity, family-orientation, respect for values and the kindling of a spirit of hope won me over."

Within a month, President Carter wrote back thanking McNeill for his suggestions and promising to give them "careful consideration." The next correspondence from the White House came in April when McNeill was informed that the television program would require more time than the president would be willing to commit considering his tight schedule. During his presidency, Carter did attempt to reach people in a less formal fashion when he initiated Saturday morning radio talks to the nation.

The program scenarios McNeill drafted reflected a penchant for telling real-life stories. During World War II, he had proposed a radio series in which he would interview the families of servicemen overseas in a series entitled, "The Home Front." Another series he created called for him to spend a week with a person who was getting ready for a big challenge, such as "adopting a baby from the cradle," "marriage," and "airport—first flight." Even though these series never reached the airwaves, McNeill's brand of story-telling was infused into every interview he conducted on the *Breakfast Club*.

The human interest story unfolding in his own household undoubtedly led him to become more active in the effort to increase awareness about Alzheimer's disease. In 1983, *Newsweek* magazine, in its "Update" column, carried a brief story about McNeill, which mentioned his making filmstrips about Alzheimer's disease and the fact that his wife had the disorder. About this same time, he joined the board of directors of the National Alzheimer's Disease and Related Disorders Association (ADRDA) and began helping to plan a national public awareness campaign. In 1984, McNeill participated in a video interview about the effects of the disease on his family. Asked how his wife was doing, he answered, "I'd like to lie and say 'just fine', you know, but as of yet there is no cure of it—there's no known cause—so she's just progressively worse, worse, worse."

In the interview he also mentioned the creation of regional Breakfast Clubs to tell the Alzheimer's story. McNeill had said he was "hesitant to resurrect the 'Breakfast Club'" because of the difficulty in living up to the memories people had of the show, but he was aware that the program had "blessed my family and me for many years and I couldn't turn down the opportunity to return some of this goodwill." McNeill brought Fran Allison back to Chicago to join him in doing the show at the ADRDA national convention in 1984 where they kicked off their part of the national effort with a bit of nostalgia. While 250 people crowded into the ballroom of the Hotel Continental, an orchestra played tunes that were popular thirty to forty years earlier. During the program McNeill discussed how the disease affected his household. "With Kay, it started slowly—she'd forget small things—her keys, recipes—then it got worse. She couldn't recognize old friends—our kids—or even me." During one of the lighter moments, a member of the audience told how McNeill had pinned a tie on her husband. He had just returned home from serving in World War II in 1947 and was wearing civilian clothes for the first time to the show and McNeill helped by providing a necktie. The ADRDA convention program was shown on local Chicago television and McNeill's fears of not living up to the memories listeners had of his show were dispelled when one reporter wrote that it was a "sophisticated and clever re-enactment" of the original *Breakfast Club*. Spin-offs of this program were held in many of the 118 chapters of ADRDA around the country. Regional versions of the *Breakfast Club* were presented with local television personalities joining the cast, which often included someone who played an Aunt Fanny character and area folks with musical talent.

In 1983, McNeill joined others in lobbying President Reagan to proclaim November National Alzheimer's Disease Awareness Month, which he did. In fact, the following year, the president met with the association's board at the White House to make the proclamation again as well as announce that federal funds would provide for a comprehensive research effort to discover the cause of the disease. The meeting gave McNeill an opportunity to remind Reagan that he was a guest on the *Breakfast Club* several times during his visits to Chicago as a spokesman for General Electric. Later, McNeill wrote a note to the president thanking him for his support of the Alzheimer's efforts and noting that his wife was one of its victims. He also mentioned that as he left the office he overheard someone say: "Well, he certainly seemed happier to see Don McNeill than he would Tip O'Neill" (the Democratic House Speaker).

McNeill had joined the Alzheimer's Disease education effort as a way of soothing his own pain, but seeing his wife slowly deteriorate had become an increasingly difficult turnabout in his family. It took an enormous toll on McNeill's spirit and energy. Those close to the family often had joked that he spoke one hour a day on the radio and she spoke the other twenty-three. For fifty-three years he had depended on her for his grounding in life—she was cheerful, energetic, loving, empathetic, and attended to his every need at home, providing him with a security zone where he would feel comfortable after being the public personality his job demanded. According to son Don, his mother had been a paragon of strength for everyone, but especially his father.[10] McNeill's nature was not to speak about his deeply held feelings and, with his wife's condition worsening, his silent pain was noticeable. During his frequent visits from the University of Notre Dame, Don and his father would converse and pray together. With his son's encouragement, McNeill was able to overcome a surprising modesty about speaking about and to God. Gradually, he was able to evoke prayers which revealed the depth of his faith and relationship with God. Don felt that these visits and the support of family and friends provided his father with emotional relief and strength to face the reality when Kay needed to leave their home and receive full-time, professional nursing care at a nearby "villa."

Kay McNeill died in November 1985 but, in reality, her vitality and relational ability had left several years before. Fran Allison notified many of McNeill's friends and former associates about his loss, which prompted several to write and express their support of him and appreciation of her. Nancy Martin remembered "when we were all vigorous and full of joy—and Kay was the most joyous of all." Gertrude Darou wrote to say how sorry she was for both McNeill and his sons. She told him that Jimmie had died ten years earlier and how her thirty-one-year-old son was doing. Close friend Jen Haider-O'Brien reminded McNeill about the time when he hurt his back and Kay McNeill tried to get an ambulance, but could only manage to have a hearse take him to the hospital. Her letter also recalled a cold and windy golf game when, after nine holes, one of the players in their party was shivering pretty badly and asked Kay McNeill to get him a shot of Jack Daniels at the course bar. With exuberance, Kay, who often mixed up names in a funny way, asked the bartender for a shot of "Benjamin Franklin!" Sister Cyrille Gill, O.P., of Dominican University, wrote that when, by chance, Kay McNeill discovered her secular name, Lumina, and began calling her that

> in her pixyish manner, eyes dancing with a mischievous gleam . . . pronouncing the unusual name again and again. What a lovely combination she was of happiness, fun, dedication, love and interest in others. She always reminded me of the lines written by Wordsworth:

> A perfect woman, nobly planned,
> To warn, to comfort, and command;
> And yet a Spirit still, and bright
> With something of angelic light.

The loss of his wife was eased somewhat by McNeill's strong faith and ability to find enjoyment in being with people and sharing ideas. He was blessed with family and friends who were present to help ease some of the sadness. His sister, Agnes, or "Sis" as she was called, was a constant companion as she was during Kay's illness. Tom, Don, and Bob adhered to the McNeill tradition of always having time for one another and spent time with their father. A frequent visitor to McNeill's home was spiritual writer and theologian, Henri Nouwen, a priest from the Netherlands, who first became acquainted with the family when he was a visiting professor at the University of Notre Dame in the mid-1960s. Nouwen, son Don, and another priest, Douglas Morrison, wrote *Compassion: Reflections on a Christian Life*, that was published in 1982 and had been well received. Nouwen's visits were energizing affairs during which he would describe in passionate and dramatic ways his ideas or latest project, such as the development of a spiritual center, L'Arche Daybreak, near Toronto. These encounters, and other occasions with family members, provided McNeill with the comfort and support that he had given to others for so many years.

McNeill continued the tradition of hosting family gatherings— summers at Himself's Hideaway, and on Thanksgiving, Christmas, and Easter at his Winnetka home. At these affairs, "Papa," as he was called by the grandchildren and great-grandchildren, "rose to the oc-casion." The eight grandchildren, whose ages ranged from nineteen to thirty-one at his death, all remember affectionately what a special man Papa was in their lives. He wanted to know what they were doing, their accomplishments, set-backs, and plans for the future. He was excited about their marriages and the eventual great-grandchildren those unions produced. They were moved by his expressions of love for his family, and were tickled by his jokes.[11] At these gatherings, son Don would celebrate the Eucharist with the family and sometimes friends, during which McNeill could always be counted on to con-tribute a reminiscence, funny story, and a poignant prayer, as only he could do.

20

A Radio Pioneer

Today, radio is undergoing a resurgence due to the large amount of time so many commuters spend in cars, the ease and speed with which radio delivers information to specific audiences, and the potential to combine audio signals with the Internet. In some ways, the older medium is becoming new as it competes with new forms of electronic communication.

For any radio program to succeed, it must reach through the maze of stations and make a connection with the listener. Once the broadcaster has the attention of listeners, the rest is simple, as long as the relationship is maintained. That sounds almost like a friendship or marriage, which is the way McNeill approached his audience. Over the years, McNeill was asked why his show lasted so long and his answers ranged from the fact he was on the air before listeners were fully awake to his good fortune to have come along when he did. In a slightly more serious vein he wrote:

> "How has it been being in radio these [35] years?"
> My usual answer is . . . "Well, it hasn't been easy."
> And then if I had memorized [the whys], I'd like to add this . . .
>> But there's no thrill in easy sailing
>> When the sky is clear and blue,
>> There's no joy in merely doing
>> Things which anyone can do.
>> But there is some satisfaction

That is mighty sweet to take,
When you reach a destination,
That you thought you couldn't make.

McNeill knew his limits and abilities, as was evidenced by his determination to rid himself of the script requirement, but that was only half the battle. From that day on, he not only had to be consistently friendly and entertaining, but, at the same time, had to have the mental agility to avoid disasters. Right up to the final broadcast he was conscious of his role as an audience filter when Kay McNeill said she wanted to tell a joke. McNeill momentarily reared back and Sam Cowling laughed knowingly, aware that McNeill wanted to be sure the story would not offend. The boss's wife wasn't immune to being checked at the gate to the network. She did get to tell the joke about "getting up grouchy," but the interchange served as a reminder to everyone in the cast that McNeill was very much in charge of what went into the program.

McNeill was no singer or dancer, but simply someone who communicated with such simple ease that it looked like he was not working. However, tapes of guest toastmasters who falter and stumble as they attempt to coordinate the elements of a *Breakfast Club* broadcast say a lot about how disciplined, hard-working, and able McNeill was.

He developed and executed pioneering features that would engage the audience like the March around the Breakfast Table, Memory Time, Sunshine Shower, and the Moment of Silent Prayer. These elements invited listeners to become participants in a morning ritual that would become a routine in their daily lives.

Inviting an audience into the studio and then making it part of the show was innovative, brave, and sensitive to the interests of listeners. McNeill's personality also played a part in the audience's participation, in that he worked better when responding to situations and people than when performing alone. He was capable of doing a monologue, but his real talent lay in facilitating others to open up.

His vision of building a "neighborhood of the nation," conforms with the personality he projected over the air—that of a strongly committed family man. Stormy Bobula's assessment of McNeill, that he was "an honest person," is indicative of how *Breakfast Club* listeners would describe him. Any celebrity who emphasized and lived family values and prayer the way McNeill did engendered trust.

McNeill was also corny, which helped him avoid being self-righteous or seemingly judgmental. Anyone who was so unabashedly self-effacing and unsophisticated would not come across as the keeper of the national morals. In truth, he was well read and intelligent, but those traits never got in the way of his openness and good nature on the air.

On commercial radio, sponsors determine which program will survive. McNeill understood advertising from the viewpoint of both the sponsor and the listener. His approach was to work hard for both sides of the relationship. He took the initiative to approach sponsors with his ideas for selling their products. At the same time, he made sure his program was an appropriate vehicle for almost any ad campaign. The effort worked and everyone associated with the *Breakfast Club* prospered, especially McNeill.

As is the case with many successful people, he realized that he needed others to contribute to whatever accomplishment he might achieve alone. He was successful at building one of the largest and most long-lasting staffs ever assembled on radio. No on-air relationship matched the care, respect, and energy evidenced between McNeill and Fran Allison. Any observer could see that they were a team that worked. When Allison died in 1989 McNeill was the first of those offering "reflections" at a memorial service at the Museum of Broadcast Communications in Chicago. His commentary reflected the affection both shared for one another.

I have only one sister except for Fran Allison who was like a second sister to me. She was on the Breakfast Club almost from the beginning. We were about the same age. She was a wonderful human being and we got a big kick out of each other. Fran used to read letters on the air from her friend Nettie who always started every letter the same way. I knew it so well that I'd say it right along with Fran, "I've had a siege of my old headaches, they have just snapped and cracked, throbbed and beat, front and back."

I think it was Nettie who had a plastic surgeon tighten her skin up. He overdid it and every time she sat down her mouth flew open.

Fran and I had wonderful chats together off the air too. I remember she said one time "I guess the three things we crave most in life are happiness, freedom, and peace of mind and that they are usually attained by giving them to someone else."

Bless you Aunt Fanny, and treat her well in heaven, God. You've got another beautiful person with you.[1]

Radio treated McNeill well and he returned the favor by being respectful of the network and the industry that had been so good to him and his family. ABC, for all its growing pains during its lean, early years, was loyal to McNeill and he returned the same, but he did have opinions about the way radio programming was changing and shared them with his audience.

> We are hurtling, on the wings of broadcast frequencies, toward the age of the *ultimate hum*. The end result of all conformity, all compromise, all pandering to the great and revered middle of the road, which will send each inhabitant of the United States within earshot of a radio into the same interchangeable permanent drooling stupor. Then, and only then, will we see true rapture: the apotheosis of the American Research Bureau rating, with listeners divided equally among all the stations, because there is no reason—and nowhere—to turn. Someday we will have *all* rock/contemporary stations. And then, some other day, the station owners will figure out which sounds within those formats have the least general acceptance, and they will be pruned out. And then the next-least will go. And all such lesser sounds will wither and die, until we are left with the primal drone that bores every sheep in the flock with beatific equality. And the Ultimate Hum will reign forever and ever and ever. Ah, Man.[2]

McNeill, the masterful radio personality, had some strong views on new-age airmen and the culture they inhabit.

> Disc jockeying is crowded with throbbing egos, neurotic overachievers, dunderheads of all descriptions and strange flowershirted creatures who believe themselves to be in touch with the Ultimate Intelligence. A plain old everyday garden variety *male*, f'gawdsake, would have trouble keeping his sanity in that zoo. But a woman, in the flood tide of the Movement, has to fight a rear-guard action in the broadcasting milieu as well: against the strident ones who expect her to behave not only as a female but as a *symbol* besides.[3]

Contrasting radio with television gave McNeill an opportunity to reflect on possible reasons why he was so successful on radio and faced repeated disappointment on television.

> No program on television has commanded the long-term loyalty of dozens of old radio shows, when a whole nation paused to listen. Television doesn't give shows enough time to win a loyal audience: the "numbers game" is so ruthless and competitive that a show that doesn't make it in a few weeks is marked for the ax. But, more importantly in my belief, the very visual aspect of TV overexposes the characters and leaves no room for fantasizing on the part of the audience. As Arch Obler put it so beautifully, "radio is the theatre of the mind." I know that you people out there listening visualize us perhaps seated around a huge Breakfast Table. Well, that's strictly up to you. You design our sets for us. If you don't like the color of our drapes, in your own mind's eye, you can change them to a color of your choice. You can't do this in movies or television. In your mind's eye, you can make me look like Rock Hudson, or like I really am. You can visualize the band sitting here in clean, white freshly laundered shirts, or like they really are. Perhaps you imagine me pulling up in front of the Allerton in a chauffeur driven limousine, or like it really is—our orchestra leader and I went together in a Honda. We don't care how you picture us, just as long as you continue to listen "To the Theater of the Mind."[4]

McNeill, by nature, was more comfortable ignoring these philosophical differences and living in the moment. That's the way Christine Flaherty remembers her grandfather. She experienced him as having a "cozy" quality even though he was not that expressive verbally. Instead, when they were together, there was a "unspoken closeness," which they shared many times. He taught her how to fish at his Hideaway where the two spent hours together fishing for bass. She remembered his quiet, observing nature, which was broken by occasional bursts of humor and playfulness. As he became less active and getting to the lake became a chore, she would visit him at his home and they would play lots of double solitaire.

Christine recalled seeing her grandfather for the last time in the hospital not long before his death. As she was leaving, she looked back and saw him cock his head while pointing his finger at her, as if it were a gun, and wink at her. He was not well, but she could see a spirit in his rosy cheeks and happy smile at that moment.[5]

McNeill died on May 7, 1996, in Evanston Hospital where he was being treated for heart and respiratory problems. Up until then he had been living in his Winnetka home with his sister and a housekeeper. The news of his death was reported on National Public Radio's *All Things Considered* by host Noah Adams, who talked with Sterling Quinlan about McNeill's career.

> ADAMS: I heard this program from a small town in Kentucky, and I think there was something to it, that you got some excitement being out in the country, listening to a very sophisticated—it seemed—radio program coming from a great big city like Chicago.
>
> QUINLAN: —the energy came through and it was—you could talk to people in Kentucky or Iowa or Indiana or Washington, D.C., or Seattle, Washington. It had a great hold because—I think one of the reasons [was] because you didn't have to hear it every day. Most people did, but it wasn't something that, you know, was absolutely essential but it was a common chord through our lives at that time—
>
> ADAMS: You know, when you listen to these old programs, you notice that a lot of what's going on with television seems derivative of what may have happened on radio before— and I'm thinking of the David Letterman Show.[6]

Testimonials to McNeill typically emphasized his longevity on the air and the homespun nature of the *Breakfast Club*. The *New York Times* obituary repeated the observation that Fred Allen made of McNeill: "He's a big, friendly fellow whose good nature pours through the microphone, and listeners react in the same way anyone reacts meeting him in person."[7] A columnist at the Nashville *Tennessean*, Jerry Thompson, took a different approach and told about his being a guest on the *Breakfast Club* and how the experience touched him.

> When I heard the news last week of the death of Don McNeill, host of the popular radio show, Don McNeill's Breakfast Club, it evoked a special twinge of sadness.
>
> I'm sure Don McNeill never remembered me, but I never forgot him. We met one morning in the mid-1950s. I was a guest on his long-running radio show. I had listened numerous times

back home in Tennessee, but it couldn't compare to sitting in the same room and hearing his voice boom out over the airwaves.

I was in Chicago on a 4-H Club trip with a number of other kids from Rochester County. . . . One morning during our stay we visited the Breakfast Club. Each of us were given a card on which we filled in our names, our address, our occupation and a short story if we had one. . . . I listed my occupation as "farmer." I briefly related a story that involved milking the family cow "Lucy." McNeill liked the story and called me to the microphone to relate it to his millions of listeners. He was a little taken back at my youth but seemed to thoroughly enjoy the interview and my story.

The story was about the morning Lucy dragged me all over the stable. I momentarily forgot that the cold weather had caused Lucy's udder to dry out and crack which obviously made it sore. When I touched that area, she instinctively kicked . . . her kicking hoof somehow wound up in my jacket pocket.

McNeill and his audience seemed to enjoy that story and I was invited to join him and his staff in their daily march around the Breakfast Table. I remember McNeill as a big, friendly man who was just as friendly to a teen-age "farmer" from Tennessee as he was to his celebrity guests. That memory has always held a special place in my mind.[8]

A Mass of the Resurrection for McNeill was held at Saints Faith, Hope, and Charity Church in Winnetka during which family members participated along with many friends and colleagues, including former Notre Dame President, Father Theodore M. Hesburgh, C.S.C. There were several priests who participated in the service. Son Don presided and in his homily stressed his dad's special gifts as a "host [who] nourished—on the air and in his life," recalling a line from John's gospel when Jesus said to his disciples "come and have breakfast." In his reflection before the final blessings and burial, Tom recalled that his father "had an unusual word for someone who was superlative, extraordinary. He'd call that person a Darb. . . . Dad was a Darb!" Tom said how he had experienced the various sides of his father by observing that the man the public often saw was similar to the one he experienced at home. Both, he said, had an "unsophisticated, easy humor . . . put a positive spin on things . . . [and had a] consistently cheery welcomingness." Tom thanked his dad for "being so interested in what I was doing and planning that made him such a good friend in addition to being a good father. The friendly tutor provided constant encouragement and . . . a sense of the importance of accomplishment" within a spiritual context. Bob's remarks highlighted his father's generosity, integrity, and his life as a peacemaker. Bob repeated the call for a Moment of Silent Prayer as his dad's final call to peace.

Several children of *Breakfast Club* cast members attended the service, including Barbara Ballantine, Don Dowd, Jr., Pat Murphy, and Terry Petersen. The occasion provided them with an opportunity to come together and, following the service, these "Breakfast Club Kids," as they described themselves, gathered to reminisce on how the program influenced their lives and those of their parents, many of whom had passed away. Pat Murphy recalled how the cast enjoyed being with one another and regularly got together socially. According to Murphy, doing the *Breakfast Club* was not a job for these radio men and women as much as a chance to have fun together.[9]

McNeill's strengths were apparent that day. He had provided the vehicle which brought many talented entertainers together and then rewarded their achievements. He used the same approach at home where his good parenting was repaid in triplicate. Tom has recently retired from a successful career as a commercial trial lawyer with one of Chicago's leading firms, Mayer, Brown, and Platt. For several years when his father vacationed, Tom filled in as the head of the radio breakfast table. He is an honorary trustee of Lawrence Hall Youth Services, which serves needy Chicago boys and girls, and is a long-time member and past president of Lyric Opera of Chicago's Guild Board. Tom and his wife, Ingrid, raised three children, who have married and started their own families: Christine and Tom Flaherty and Stephanie and Jamie Fargo in the Chicago area and Thomas and Amarens near Utrecht in the Netherlands.

In his cross-cultural experiences, Don continually experienced extreme poverty and injustice which challenged and inspired him to use his vocation as a priest and educator to respond to those in need. With his leadership, Notre Dame brought together its student volunteer effort with the programs in experiential and justice education to create the Center for Social Concerns in 1983. Due to the fact that Don has viewed the Center's mission in such broad terms, it has become a major contributor to the University of Notre Dame's achieving its mission to "bring about a more just and humane world." His efforts were formally recognized in 1999 when his administrative position was given endowment status as the Leo and Arlene Hawk Director of the Center for Social Concerns.

When he finished his Rhodes experience at Oxford, Bob began working his way up the ranks of one of the nation's leading investment firms, Stein Roe & Farnham, to become its executive vice president and a senior managing partner. He helped the firm realize its global potential by establishing international partnerships in various world capitals. Conscious of the benefits he gained from studying abroad, Bob has served for over twenty-five years on the board of the Institute of European and Asian Studies as well as the U.S. Rhodes Scholarship Selection Committee. He has been actively involved in helping organizations which help those in need by serving on the boards of the Hadley School for the Blind, the Chicago Center for Peace Studies, the Joseph P. Kennedy School for Retarded Children, Catholic Charities, Big Shoulders Fund, United Way, Bonaventure House for Homeless AIDS Victims, Adler Planetarium, and the Rush Alzheimer's Disease Center. Bob and his wife Martha have five children. Jennifer and Andy Heck and Don and Mary live with their families in the Chicago area, as does Vicky. Their twins, Elizabeth and Steve, graduated from college in 1999.

The McNeill legacy is both simple and clear. At its foundation is a commitment to family and spiritual values, which provide sustenance for being a public personality. Next comes a striving for accomplishment, but tempered with a sensitivity to others, especially those in need and the disadvantaged. Finally, there is an expectation to be of good humor. In essence, the standards are to be good to one's self and others.

What is remarkable is how closely McNeill was able to follow these values in his life. In 1931 when he was packing for California and his first network radio job, McNeill's grandmother sent him off with the admonishment: "Don't go Hollywood, Don."[10] She really didn't have to say it because it was not in his makeup to become a star in the traditional sense of the word. McNeill, by nature, was not a flashy performer, if what he did was performing at all. The unsophisticated fun with the audience, corny jokes, homespun poems, silent prayers, and familiar music extended McNeill's legacy beyond his intimates to the nation and many parts of the world. What everyone heard was a friendly voice with a message that complemented whatever the listener was doing and could be welcomed back. These are goals which broadcasters should strive to accomplish every day.

McNeill personified the *Breakfast Club* both on and off the air for well over three decades. How did he do it? One answer can be found in the description Elizabeth McNeill has for her grandfather, with whom she spent time in the last few years of his life. She found him to be someone who knew who he was and, in addition, was at peace with himself.[11] His easy manner, self-assurance, and determination helped him overcome the challenges of the Depression and getting his career started on network radio. He skillfully managed to figure out ways of improving the *Pepper Pot*, and then worked to make its sleepy time slot come alive as the *Breakfast Club* every morning. His consistently polished performance on the show combined with his tentativeness about being on television and a determination to remain in Chicago indicate that he knew his strong qualities and his weaker ones. It is extraordinary that even in the raucous 1960s McNeill stayed on the course he had set for himself during the fast-changing period after World War II and into the 1950s. With hindsight, it is easy to see how right he was for radio and the *Breakfast Club*. McNeill marshaled his energy and talent and created a remarkable radio legend.

Epilogue

Eddie Ballantine found a new career after the *Breakfast Club* went off the air. He became co-anchor on the *Stock Market Report* on Chicago station WCIU-TV. He lived in Skokie, Illinois, where he died in 1995.

Sam Cowling did not stop commuting to North Michigan Avenue when the Breakfast Club ended its lease on the Clouds Room. Since he was an avid fisherman, he joined the sales staff at Abercrombie and Fitch where he helped customers find the right rod and reel at the firm's store two blocks from the Allerton Hotel. Later, Cowling and his wife moved to southern California to be closer to one of their sons. He died there in 1984.

Cliff Petersen joined his friend Cowling at Abercrombie and Fitch, when he appropriately sold men's furnishings, as he was a walking haberdashery ad. Petersen and his family lived in Wilmette, where he died in 1985.

Don Dowd left the *Breakfast Club* cast when Swift departed the show in 1955, but was soon heard over ABC Television as one of its staff announcers based in New York. He retired to Florida in 1965 where he lived until his death in 1972.

Bob Murphy died unexpectedly at the age of forty-two in 1959 leaving a large family grief-stricken. He had been a major Chicago television personality up to the time of his death.

The Breakfast Club was the title of a popular film produced in 1985 about five high school students assigned to a Saturday of detention. There was no connection with the radio show.

Tom resurrected his father's weekend summer camp in 1998 when he invited Lawrence Hall School in Chicago to send groups of boys to take advantage of the outdoor recreation available at Himself's Hideaway.

Chicago's Museum of Broadcast Communications' Radio Hall of Fame contains an interactive kiosk which features excerpts from *Breakfast Club* broadcasts. McNeill was inducted into the Radio Hall of Fame in 1989. The Museum's collection contains several audio and videotapes of broadcasts featuring Don McNeill and the *Breakfast Club*, which are readily available to the public.

In Milwaukee, Marquette University's Memorial Library Archives houses an extensive collection of print and electronic material, which document the development of Don McNeill's career with the *Breakfast Club*. Gaining access to these materials requires advance arrangements with the archive staff.

Bob's son Don and his wife Mary named their firstborn Don, ensuring that there will be a Don McNeill well into the twenty-first century.

Chronology

1933   NBC Blue's *Pepper Pot* becomes *Breakfast Club* with Don McNeill.

1934   Tom McNeill is born.

1936   Stanley McAllister begins the tradition of a studio audience during *Breakfast Club*.

       Second son Don McNeill is born.

1937   Sam Cowling joins *Breakfast Club* cast as guitarist with Three Romeos.

1938   First *Breakfast Club* book is offered.

1941   Swift is the first *Breakfast Club* network sponsor.

       Bob McNeill is born.

1942   St. Bonaventure awards McNeill an honorary degree.

1944   Prayer Time begins as a regular *Breakfast Club* feature.

       Fran Allison rejoins *Breakfast Club* as Aunt Fanny.

       Walter Blaufuss dies; Eddie Ballantine is named director of the *Breakfast Club* orchestra.

       NBC Blue becomes ABC.

       Swift inaugurates and then stops offering Charter Memberships of *Breakfast Club*.

1945   Cliff Petersen is named producer for *Breakfast Club*.

       Breakfast Club drops its Saturday morning show.

1946   *Breakfast Club* attracts 17,000 to watch the show in Madison Square Garden.

       Don McNeill Dinner Club for Marshall Field's airs on WBKB-TV, Chicago.

       Ole Olsen's suggestion for a Sunshine Shower begins a new *Breakfast Club* tradition.

1947 McNeill makes a guest appearance on Fred Allen's radio show.

1948 Laugh Party nominates Don McNeill for president.

Breakfast Club moves from the Merchandise Mart to the Civic Theater in the Opera Building.

Frank Buck joins the great mouse hunt in the Civic Theater.

1950 ABC signs McNeill to a twenty-year contract.

Don McNeill Club begins airing Wednesday nights on ABC-TV.

1951 Don McNeill Dinner Club ends its run on ABC-TV.

1952 McNeill does Convention Sidelights for Philco on NBC-TV.

1953 Breakfast Club moves to the Terrace Casino in the Morrison Hotel.

Twenty Breakfast Club babies help celebrate show's twentieth anniversary.

McNeill makes Himself's Hideaway available as summer camp for Chicago Boys' Clubs.

1954 Simulcast of Breakfast Club begins over ABC Radio and TV for one year.

1955 Swift concludes sponsorship of Breakfast Club after fourteen years.

Breakfast Club moves into the College Inn at the Sherman House.

1957 Breakfast Club begins the policy of taping the show for the next day's airing.

1958 Ben Stahl completes painting Moment of Silent Prayer.

McNeill fills in for vacationing host Garry Moore on CBS-TV's What's My Secret?

McNeill family is interviewed by Edward R. Murrow on CBS-TV's Person to Person.

1959 McNeill gives Ginny Tiu her U.S. premiere on Breakfast Club.

1960 McNeill is featured on NBC-TV's This is Your Life.

1961 Marquette University awards McNeill an honorary degree.

1963 Breakfast Club tours U.S. and European military bases in Europe.

University of Notre Dame awards McNeill an honorary degree.

McNeill hosts a summer replacement series, Take Two on ABC-TV.

Breakfast Club moves to the Clouds Room in the Allerton Hotel.

McNeill becomes the spokesman for the Mackle Brothers and the Deltona Corporation.

1967 Chicago Broadcast Advertising Club selects McNeill as its Man of the Year.

1968 The final Breakfast Club show is aired December 27.

1969   Chicago's Loyola University awards McNeill an honorary degree.

McNeill teaches a broadcast news seminar at Marquette University.

1971   The Don McNeill Collection including *Moment of Silent Prayer* is given to Marquette University.

McNeill teaches a communication seminar at University of Notre Dame.

1976   Kay McNeill is diagnosed as having Alzheimer's Disease.

1977   McNeill is honored by Pacific Pioneer Broadcasters of California.

McNeill hosts *Prime Time* series over WTTW-TV, Chicago, and other PBS television stations.

1979   McNeill is inducted into the National Broadcasters Hall of Fame.

1983   McNeill joins the board of directors of National Alzheimer's Disease and Related Disorders Association.

1985   Kay McNeill dies.

1989   Fran Allison dies.

McNeill is inducted into the Museum of Broadcast Communications' Radio Hall of Fame.

1996   Don McNeill dies.

Notes

INTRODUCTION

1. *Paul Harvey News* (ABC Radio), August 15, 1968.

CHAPTER 1

1. Rich Samuels has traced the development of early Chicago broadcasting; see www.mcs.net/~richsam (July 1998).

2. Gerald Nachman, *Raised on Radio* (New York: Pantheon, 1998), 18.

3. Joseph Kaye, "Don McNeill Tells His Own Story," *True Story*, November 1949, 91.

4. Joseph Kaye, "The True Story of the McNeills," *True Story*, June 1947, 156.

5. NBC formed the country's first radio network from a station it bought from AT&T in New York City, WEAF, in 1926. The following year it created a second network fed from a station RCA owned in Newark, New Jersey, WJZ. The colored lines on maps indicating the routing of the two networks were red and blue, hence the names NBC Red and NBC Blue.

CHAPTER 2

1. Kay McNeill recalled hearing the first broadcast of the Breakfast Club during an interview; R. Froman, "The Man Who Came to Breakfast," *Collier's*, May 13, 1950, 28.

2. Don McNeill, *Breakfast Club* script, June 30, 1933 (punctuation amended). Typed scripts from the first months of the Breakfast Club were among the mementos in the McNeill family's personal collection.

3. Don McNeill, *Breakfast Club* script, July 3, 1933, McNeill family collection.

4. Don McNeill, *Breakfast Club* script, September 6, 1933 (punctuation amended), McNeill family collection.

5. Ray Barfield, *Listening to Radio, 1920–1950* (Westport, Conn.: Praeger, 1996), 19.

6. Kaye, "Don McNeill Tells His Own Story," 157.

7. Don McNeill, letter to Mrs Harry McNeill, May 24, 1929, McNeill family collection.

8. Kaye, "Don McNeill Tells His Own Story."

9. Philip G. Zimbardo and Shirley L. Radl, *The Shy Child* (Garden City, N.Y.: Doubleday, 1982), 15.

10. McNeill family collection.

11. Ibid.

12. Anton Remenih, "McNeill's Club Has Its 5,000th Air Breakfast," *Chicago Tribune*, April 22, 1950.

CHAPTER 3

1. Stanley McAllister's letter is in the Don McNeill Collection, Department of Special Collections, Memorial Library, Marquette University, Milwaukee, Wisconsin. The holdings include scripts, memoranda, and correspondence from the *Breakfast Club*'s beginning on NBC-Blue to its sign-off in 1968 over ABC Radio. The collection also contains audio and video tapes of the *Breakfast Club* and McNeill's early television series *Don McNeill's TV Club*, 1950–1952.

2. Fred F. Montiegel, *Walgreen Pepper Pod*, 1945. This was a newsletter prepared by ABC publicist Fred Montiegel for radio editors. Montiegel also edited and wrote material for many of the *Breakfast Club Yearbooks*.

3. Barfield, *Listening to Radio*, 99.

4. Ibid.

5. Kaye, "The True Story of the McNeills," 159.

6. Gregory Merwin, "Chicago's Clan McNeill," *Radio-TV Mirror*, September 1958, 76.

7. Mrs. Don McNeill and Isabella Taves, "10 Million Women Are in Love with My Husband," *McCall's*, December 1951, 52.

8. Montiegel, *Walgreen Pepper Pod*, 1945.

CHAPTER 4

1. E. R. Borroff, Vice President, Blue Network, memorandum to McNeill, December 15, 1942.

2. Christopher Sterling and John Kittross, *Stay Tuned* (Belmont, Calif.: Wadsworth, 1978), 533.

3. Foster Rhea Dulles, *History of Recreation: America Learns to Play* (New York: Appleton, 1965), 329.

4. Annual summary of network revenues, *Broadcasting Year Book*, 1947, 38.

5. Don McNeill, letter to Frank Cooper, April 16, 1938, McNeill family collection.

6. Donald McNeill, "Radio in Newspaper Promotion," senior thesis, Marquette University, May 1929, McNeill family collection.

7. Bill Thompson, "Swift Success," *Broadcasting-Telecasting*, July 12, 1948, 23.

8. Ibid.

9. S. R. Bernstein, "Swift and 'Breakfast Club' Start 10th Year," *Advertising Age*, February 6, 1950.

10. Remenih, "McNeill's Club Has Its 5,000th Air Broadcast."

11. *Breakfast Club* broadcast, June 19, 1941, Radio Archives, Recorded Sound Division, Library of Congress, Washington, D.C.

12. Thompson, "Swift Success," 66.

13. Bernstein, "Swift and 'Breakfast Club' Start 10th Year."

14. "Over 48 Tons of Food Received by Salvation Army through ABC'S 'Breakfast Club Share-A-Meal Plan,'" American Broadcasting Company press release, August 2, 1946.

15 John Feehery, "Radio Is More Relaxed Medium, Says McNeill: 'Club' Marks Its 35th Year," *Advertising Age*, March 13, 1967.

16. *Breakfast Club* broadcast, August 9, 1962, from the McNeill Collection, Marquette University.

17. "Radio's Subliminal Salesman," *Sales Management*, February 5, 1965.

18. Nathaniel Homes, "Don McNeill—Salesman," *Specialty Salesman Magazine*, March 1950, 24–25.

19. Don McNeill's remarks prepared for a gathering of ABC Radio affiliates in 1958 during the twenty-fifth anniversary of the *Breakfast Club*.

20. In a landmark decision, the Supreme Court affirmed that the Federal Communications Commission had broad powers to regulate broadcasting (*NBC v the United States*, May 10, 1943).

21. Ned Midley, *The Advertising and Business Side of Radio* (New York: Prentice-Hall, 1948), 113.

Chapter 5

1. William Irvin, "Don McNeill Wakes Up Chicago," *PIC Radio*, October 1945, 71.

2. *Breakfast Club* broadcast, July 17, 1942, Radio Archives, Recorded Sound Division, Library of Congress, Washington, D.C.

3. Kay McNeill, postcard to sons, May 14, 1945, McNeill family collection.

4. Kay McNeill wrote her recollections about D-Day in the *Breakfast Club Yearbook* for 1944, "Don's Other Life." The yearbooks were published and sold to listeners during the 1940s and 1950s. The annual publications contained photographs, poetry, and anecdotes from the show.

5. Don McNeill, "Each in His Own Way," *Breakfast Club Yearbook*, 1950, 52.

6. Ibid., 54.

7. Don McNeill, "Don McNeill: King of Corn," *Magazine Digest*, 1945, 84.

8. McNeill, "Each in His Own Way," 53.

9. Merwin, "Chicago's Clan McNeill," 77.

10. Froman, "The Man Who Comes to Breakfast," 30.

11. McNeill, "Each in His Own Way."

CHAPTER 6

1. Don McNeill, "20 Years of Corn," *Breakfast Club Yearbook*, 1956, 26.

2. Kaye, "The True Story of the McNeills," 16.

3. Don McNeill, "Chicago Voices, Reminiscing with Chicago's Favorite Breakfast Companion," *Chicago Tribune Magazine*, December 6, 1992, 10.

4. Froman, "The Man Who Comes to Breakfast," 34.

5. ABC Press Office, profile of Sam Cowling, "Fiction and Fact from Sam's Almanac," January 11, 1950, McNeill Collection, Marquette University.

6. ABC Press Office, profile of Aunt Fanny, "Aunt Fanny and the People Who Inhabit Her World," December 23, 1947, McNeill Collection, Marquette University.

7. Bill Fay, "Allison in Wonderland," *Colliers*, March 4, 1950, 52.

8. Gloria Vann, interview with author, November 11, 1998.

9. "Breakfast Club's Music Arranger and Conductor with McNeill for 14 Years," *Daily Times*, New Philadelphia, Ohio, August 10, 1948.

CHAPTER 7

1. McNeill family collection.

2. Irvin, "Don McNeill Wakes Up Chicago," 71.

3. Evan M. Wylie, "Breakfast Every Day with 2,000,000 Women," *Cosmopolitan*, September 1953, 76.

4. McNeill, "Don McNeill: King of Corn," 83.

5. John Kuenster, "Thirty Years before the Breakfast Table," *St. Jude*, December 1962, 19.

6. Fred Allen, letter to Don McNeill, April 8, 1947, McNeill family collection.

7. Fred Allen, *Treadmill to Oblivion* (New York: Atlantic-Little Brown, 1954), 217–18.

8. Ibid., 216.

9. John Dunning, *Tune in Yesterday* (Englewood Cliffs, N.J.: Prentice-Hall, 1976), 573–74.

10. *Breakfast Club Yearbook*, 1948, 18.

11. A kinescope machine produced film images on a television picture tube. The resulting film provided a poor quality reproduction of the original program which enabled programs to be rebroadcast at more convenient times. The kinescope of the 1948 *Breakfast Club* telecast is part of the McNeill Collection, Marquette University.

12. Fred Allen, letter to Don McNeill, June 5, 1948, McNeill family collection.

13. Robert E. Kintner, letter to Don McNeill, May 17, 1948, McNeill family collection.

14. Don McNeill, letter to Fred Allen, April 26, 1948, McNeill family collection.

15. *Fred Allen Show* broadcast, May 9, 1948, McNeill Collection, Marquette University.

16. "Onward and Upward with the Arts: The All-American Breakfast," *New Yorker*, August 10, 1946, 40.

17. Irv Kupcinet, "Kup's Column," *Chicago Times*, June 25, 1947.

18. "Broken Dish Incident Upset Don," *Daily Times*, New Philadelphia, Ohio, August 10, 1948.

19. *Breakfast Club Yearbook*, 1948, 55.

CHAPTER 8

1. *Breakfast Club Yearbook*, 1949, 23.

2. Patsy Lee, interview with author, August 4, 1998.

3. *Breakfast Club Yearbook*, 1948, 17.

4. *Breakfast Club Yearbook*, 1947, 31.

5. "ABC Balks at 94G to Give McNeill Chance at Long-Sought Pic Break," *Variety*, December 3, 1947.

6. Walter O'Keefe, speech given at Pacific Pioneer luncheon honoring Don McNeill, May 20, 1977.

7. Durward Kirby, *My Life, Those Wonderful Years* (Charlotte Harbor, Fla.: Tabby, 1992), 96.

8. McNeill family collection.

CHAPTER 9

1. Merlin H. Aylesworth, "Radio Is Doomed," *Look*, April 26, 1949, 66.

2. "Don McNeill's Dinner Club," *Billboard*, October 5, 1946.

3. The number of television sets in New York in 1946 was estimated at 2,500 according to Allan Carpenter, "Where Is Television?" *Science Digest*, December 1946, 54.

4. Jack Mabley, "Outshine Big Names on Video," *Chicago Daily News*, September 18, 1948.

5. Sterling Quinlan, *Inside ABC* (New York: Hastings, 1979), 22.

6. ABC Press Release, June 19, 1950, "Don McNeill Signs Unprecedented Twenty-Year Contract," McNeill Collection, Marquette University.

7. Val Adams, "He Gets Paid To Be Neighborly," *New York Times*, June 13, 1950, II 7.

8. Dwight Newton, "Day and Night," *San Francisco Examiner*, April 20, 1950, 18.

9. Ralph Bergsten became general manager of the *Breakfast Club* and vice president of Don McNeill Enterprises in the fall of 1950 and kept those positions until 1961.

10. ABC's Press Office prepared profiles of the cast and information concerning the production of the *TV Club* series, "1951 Press Book, *Don McNeill's TV CLUB*," 6.

11. "The Chicago School," *Time*, September 11, 1950, 73.

12. "Don McNeill's TV Club," *Variety*, September 20, 1950, 30.

13. Larry Wolters, "Breakfast Club Verdict on TV; Simple, Folksy," *Chicago Daily Tribune*, September 15, 1950, II 4.

14. Val Adams, "'Breakfast Club' Has Dinner on TV," *New York Times*, September 14, 1950, 62.

15. Jack Mabley, "McNeill's New Show Good TV," *Chicago Daily News*, September 16, 1950, 21.

16. McNeill and Taves, "10 Million Women Are in Love with My Husband," 55.

17. Larry Wolters, "'Easy Does It' Is Formula for Garroway Show," *Chicago Daily Tribune*, September 25, 1950, III 12.

18. Janet Kern, "An Open Letter to Don McNeill," *Chicago Herald-American*, November 5, 1950, 39.

19. "1951 Press Book—*Don McNeill's TV CLUB*," 9.

20. "Television Follow-Up Comment," *Variety*, December 13, 1950, 38.

21. "McNeill TV'er Loses Half of Philco Coin," *Variety*, February 21, 1951, 34.

22. "Philco's '51 Dip," *Variety*, November 20, 1951, 36.

23. Edmund Leamy, "'Breakfast Club'—Has TV Offspring," *New York World-Telegram & Sun*, June 2, 1951, 9.

24. "Please Come Back Don McNeill," *TV Forecast*, September 9, 1951, 31.

25. "Don McNeill's TV Club," *Variety*, September 19, 1951.

26. "McNeill Exits TV as Philco Cancels," *Variety*, November 21, 1951, 26.

27. Patsy Lee, interview with author, August 4, 1998.

28. Leonard Will, "Tower Ticker," *Chicago Daily Tribune*, December 14, 1951, III 13.

29. Farrell Davisson, "Chicago Laments Orphan Status," *Variety*, September 19, 1951, 31.

30. Ibid.

31. Jack Gould, "TV Makes Inroads on Big Radio Chains," *New York Times*, June 27, 1951, 20.

32. Larry Wolters, "There's Money in TV But It's Not Easy Money," *Chicago Daily Tribune*, January 31, 1951, I 11.

33. Quinlan, *Inside ABC*, 37.

CHAPTER 10

1. Don McNeill, letter to Larry Wolters, *Chicago Daily Tribune*, April 30, 1948.

2. Froman, "The Man Who Comes to Breakfast," 34.

3. "United Press Hollywood Correspondent," United Press International, February 28, 1951.

4. Evelyn Bigsby, *TV-Radio Life*, March 2, 1951.

5. Charles Hirshberg, "How Good Are Our Schools?" *Life*, September, 1999, 40; "New Trier, A Good High School," *Life*, October 16, 1950, 44.

6. Bob McNeill, interview with author, June 5, 1998.

CHAPTER 11

1. Janet Kern, "Don McNeill Sidelight Shows Impressive," *Chicago Herald American*, July 14, 1952, 24.

2. Mary Canny, "My Boss, Don McNeill," *Radio-TV Mirror*, February 1951, 53.

3. Ibid., 85.

4. Ibid., 61.

CHAPTER 12

1. Max Wilk, *The Golden Age of Television* (New York: Dell, 1976), 199.

2. Janet Kern, "TV Doldrums End as Godfrey Returns," *Herald American*, September 4, 1952.

3. Harry Harris, "Don McNeill's Breakfast Club Goes on Television Tomorrow," *Philadelphia Inquirer*, February 21, 1954, 10.

4. John Crosby, "Et Tu, Julius! No One's Safe," *Chicago Sun Times*, October 26, 1953.

5. Harris, "Don McNeill's Breakfast Club Goes on Television Tomorrow," 10.

6. Lynwood King, interview with author, July 17, 1998.

7. Betty Johnson, interview with author, July 7 1998.

8. Leonard Goldenson and Marvin J. Wolf, *Beating the Odds* (New York: Scribner, 1991), 116.

9. Ratings data provided by the Research Department, A. C. Nielsen Company, New York, July 19, 1999.

10. Don McNeill, letter to Robert Kintner, December 16, 1954, McNeill family collection.

11. Robert E. Kintner, letter to Ralph Bergsten, January 12, 1955, McNeill family collection.

12. Quinlan, *Inside ABC*, 62.

13. Sterling Quinlan, interview with author, August 3, 1998.

14. Del Cowling, interview with author, March 15, 1999.

15. Dick Noel, interview with author, August 17, 1999.

CHAPTER 13

1. Don McNeill, memos, December 2, 1955, McNeill Collection, Marquette University.

2. "Secretary Hobby: Youth Is Your Business," *Newsweek*, November 9, 1955, 35.

3. "The Kids Grow Worse," *Newsweek*, December 6, 1954, 26.

CHAPTER 14

1. Audience survey of *Breakfast Club* listeners in the New York City area during the first quarter hour of the program on October 17, 1947, conducted by Schwerin Research Corporation for Toni Company.

2. Questionnaires were distributed to *Breakfast Club* audiences the week of February 14, 1949 and summarized in a report (April 1949) by J. Walter Thompson Company for ABC.

3. Don McNeill, letter to James C. Petrillo, American Federation of Musicians, March 10, 1952, McNeill family collection.

4. Ray Barnes, interview with author, February 18, 1999.

5. Sterling and Kittross, *Stay Tuned*, 335.

6. Ollie E. Jones, letter to Don McNeill, June 27, 1955, McNeill family collection.

7. Bob McNeill, interview with author, June 5, 1998.

8. Feehery, "Radio Is More Relaxed Medium, Says McNeill." McNeill's contract with ABC gave him the right to refuse products.

9. David Halberstam, *The Fifties* (New York: Fawcett Columbine, 1993), 196.

10. McNeill's changing his on-air signature prompted ABC's press office to prepare a news release explaining the decision, "After 25 Years, Don McNeill Changes Sign-Off Slogan of 'Breakfast Club' from 'Be Good to Yourself' to 'Be Good to Your Neighbor'," ABC Press Release, January 24, 1958.

CHAPTER 15

1. Les Brown, "Like the River of the Same Name, Don Goes On & On," *Variety*, June 18, 1958.

2. History of The Museum of the Cross, www.mcs.net/~richsam and Leonard Maltin, *Great American Broadcast* (New York: Dutton, 1997), 167.

3. *Breakfast Club* broadcast, April 13, 1959, McNeill Collection, Marquette University.

4. Janet Kern, "Ed Sullivan Blames NBC for Barring of Ginny Tiu," *Chicago American*, April 17, 1959.

5. *Breakfast Club* broadcast, November 19, 1958, McNeill Collection, Marquette University.

6. *Breakfast Club* broadcast, January 7, 1959, McNeill Collection, Marquette University.

7. *Breakfast Club* broadcast, March 4, 1959, McNeill Collection, Marquette University.

8. *Breakfast Club* broadcast, March 6, 1959, McNeill Collection, Marquette University.

9. *Breakfast Club* broadcast, March 16, 1959, McNeill Collection, Marquette University.

CHAPTER 16

1. Matilda Bobula, interview with author, July 21, 1998.
2. *Breakfast Club* broadcast, July 3, 1963, McNeill Collection, Marquette University.
3. Ibid.
4. Thomas McNeill, interview with author, November 23, 1999.
5. *Variety*, October 20, 1962.
6. Mary Anne Luckett, interview with author, July 21, 1998.
7. Ray Barnes, interview with author, February 18, 1999.
8. Anniversary Convocation, Marquette University, College of Journalism, April 15, 1961, McNeill family collection.
9. *Breakfast Club* broadcast, November 26, 1963, McNeill Collection, Marquette University.

CHAPTER 17

1. Tom Fouts, interview with author, April 1, 1998.
2. Robert Newkirk, interview with author, September 11, 1999.
3. Dean Gysel, "The Last Breakfast," *Chicago Daily News*, December 28, 1968, 23.
4. Quinlan, *Inside ABC*, 107.

CHAPTER 18

1. Quinlan, *Inside ABC*, 131.
2. David Hickey, "Don McNeill's *Breakfast Club* Was a Wholesome Start to the Day," New York *Daily News*, May 9, 1996.
3. Edward McLaughlin (ABC executive who implemented the four-network structure), interview with author, September 1, 1998.
4. Dick Noel, interview with author, March 15, 1999.
5. *Paul Harvey News* (ABC Radio), August 15, 1968.
6. "'Breakfast Club' Ending Its 35-Year Stay on Radio," *New York Times*, December 27, 1968.

CHAPTER 19

1. John Grams, interview with author, October 8, 1999.
2. Katie Murphy, "After 35 Years at Breakfast Club, McNeill Trades 'Mike' for Classroom," *Catholic Herald Citizen*, September 27, 1969.
3. A. L. Lorenz, interview with author, October 4, 1999.

4. William Elliott (Dean, College of Communication, Marquette University), interview with author, November 16, 1999.

5. "Don McNeill Back on Air," SAM [Society for the Advancement of Management journal], May 21, 1976.

6. Don McNeill, "From the Breakfast Club to the Country Club," *Marco Island Eagle*, 1982, 51.

7. Canny, "My Boss, Don McNeill," 85.

8. Dorothy Mulroy, interview with author, May 27, 1998.

9. Don McNeill, letter to Carter-Mondale Transition, January 24, 1977, McNeill family collection.

10. Don McNeill, C.S.C., interview with author, January 31, 1998.

11. Author interviews with family members: Elizabeth McNeill, July 8, 1998; Christine Flaherty, December 21, 1998; Vicky McNeill, November 6, 1999; Stephanie Fargo, November 22, 1999; Thomas McNeill, November 23, 1999; Don McNeill, November 24, 1999; Jennifer Heck, December 6, 1999; Steve McNeill, December 9, 1999.

CHAPTER 20

1. McNeill family collection.

2. McNeill family collection.

3. McNeill family collection.

4. McNeill family collection.

5. Christine Flaherty, interview with author, December 21, 1998.

6. "Host of Chicago Radio Show Breakfast Club Remembered," *All Things Considered* (NPR), May 8, 1996.

7. Lawrence Van Gelder, "Don McNeill, 'Breakfast Club' Host, Dies at 88," *New York Times*, May 8, 1996, 21D.

8. Jerry Thompson, "Memories of McNeill Very Special," *Tennessean*, May 13, 1996, 1B.

9. Pat Murphy, interview with author, September 15, 1998.

10. Agnes Donohue, interview with author, June 28, 1997.

11. Elizabeth McNeill, interview with author, June 8, 1998.

Index